W9-BKQ-371

Information Structures

A UNIFORM APPROACH USING PASCAL

DISCARDED
JENKS LRC
GORDON COLLEGE

Information Structures

A UNIFORM APPROACH USING PASCAL

B. J. Lings
Department of Computer Science
University of Exeter

LONDON NEW YORK
Chapman and Hall

JENKS L.R.C.
GORDON COLLEGE
255 GRAPEVINE RD.
WENHAM, MA 01984-1895

First published in 1986 by
Chapman and Hall Ltd
11 New Fetter Lane, London EC4P 4EE
Published in the USA by
Chapman and Hall
29 West 35th Street, New York, NY 10001

© *1986 B. J. Lings*

Printed in Great Britain at the
University Press, Cambridge
ISBN 0 412 26490 0 (hardback)
ISBN 0 412 26500 1 (paperback)

QA
76.9
.D35
L56
1986

This title is available in both hardbound and paperback editions. The paperback edition is sold subject to the condition that it shall not, by way of trade or otherwise, be lent, resold, hired out, or otherwise circulated without the publisher's prior consent in any form of binding or cover other than that in which it is published and without a similar condition including this condition being imposed on the subsequent purchaser.

All rights reserved. No part of this book may be reprinted, or reproduced or utilized in any form or by any electronic, mechanical or other means, now known or hereafter invented, including photo-copying and recording, or in any information storage and retrieval system, without permission in writing from the publisher.

British Library Cataloguing in Publication Data

Lings, B. J.
   Information structures: a uniform approach
   using Pascal.—(Chapman and Hall computing)
   1. Data structures (Computer science)
   I. Title
   001.64'42   QA76.9.D35

   ISBN 0-412-26490-0
   ISBN 0-412-26500-1 (Pbk.)

Library of Congress Cataloging in Publication Data

Lings, B. J., 1950–
   Information structures.

   Bibliography: p.
   Includes index.
   1. Data structures (Computer science) 2. PASCAL
(Computer program language) I. Title.
QA76.9.D35L56 1986   001.64'2   85–4209

ISBN 0-412-26490-0
ISBN 0-412-26500-1 (Pbk.)

Contents

Preface

The study of computer science has become well-enough established for there to be a certain uniformity across the basic course offerings of a wide range of universities and colleges. This book covers those aspects of a computer science course normally referred to as 'Information Structures' or 'Data Structures'.

The book is aimed at students, typically in their first and second years of study, who need a clear presentation of course material in a cohesive framework, which puts the wealth of information about data structures into context. The emphasis is placed on demonstrating the development of ideas and techniques, rather than simply on presenting results.

The approach taken is that of data abstraction, with emphasis on the practical aspects but including discussion, where appropriate, of the underlying theory. The vehicle used for developing examples, of which there is a wealth, is the language Pascal. Although Pascal does not explicitly support data abstraction, it is still the best language readily available for teaching purposes.

The techniques of information hiding, specification, data type realizations and tuning are all covered in a homogeneous structure. The book explores these techniques as well as the construction and analysis of the major data structures. In this way, new material can be quickly fitted into its appropriate place in the materials available to system developers.

The book is divided into three parts. Part One is suitable for students entering an introductory course in information structures after already being exposed to the language Pascal. As an informal approach to data-abstraction theory and practice, it is intended to be self-contained. Part Two introduces the idea of parametrized data types and looks at three which are fundamental in computer science: set, tree and graph. The material is conventional, but the presentation once again stresses the disciplined approach of abstraction techniques. Part Three covers material often placed under the subheading 'Sorting and Searching'. It is a study of a simple associative data type.

My thanks are due to my wife, Pam, who has proof-read the whole typescript in its earliest stages, and to Marlene Teague, whose major efforts transformed my manuscript into machine-readable text.

PART ONE

The concept of type

1

The Pascal type concept

1.1 INTRODUCTION

This book is all about data types. It is assumed that you have already
had an exposure to the language Pascal and that the basic notion of a
type is therefore not new to you. What will probably be new is the
approach taken to studying such types: we shall be looking at the
fundamental concepts involved and learning how we can use this
understanding in structuring our programs.

Programs are composed, as far as we are concerned here, of two major
components:

(i) An algorithm.
(ii) A set of data items, each item being associated with a data type.
These represent the 'state of play' at any given moment during the
execution of the algorithm. Only 'appropriate' operations may be
performed on these data objects by the algorithm. As an example,
addition is an appropriate operation on two objects each associated
with type integer.

You should already have some exposure to algorithms and you may
even have studied the theory of algorithms to some extent. Only the
notion of an algorithm is assumed as a prerequisite to reading this book:
the Bibliography lists some suggested texts for this purpose.

Our intention is to study practical aspects of component (ii) above and
to present material on data items in a manner consistent with
approaches suggested by current research and (to a lesser extent at the
present time) current practice.

The scope of the book is that portion of a computer science
undergraduate course normally entitled 'Data Structures' or 'Information Structures'. It is suitable as a text for such courses. The approach
taken is that of data abstraction, emphasizing the advantages and
techniques embodied in the principles of data independence and
information hiding. The book is split into three parts.

Part One is suitable for students entering an introductory course in information structures after already being exposed to the language Pascal. It covers the major concepts of data-abstraction techniques, and discusses basic data types (integer, boolean, char), simple user-defined data types and the 'structured' types related to those provided by Pascal. As an informal introduction to data-abstraction theory and practice it is intended to be self-contained.

Part Two introduces the idea of parametrized data types and looks at four such information structures which are fundamental in computer science: set, tree, graph and list. Once again the basic material is conventional: a study of these data types and a comparison of the various implementations (we will use the term realizations for reasons that will become clear) open to us. The presentation, however, will once again stress the approach of data abstraction. As an example, the tenth chapter of the book uses type graph in order to demonstrate how to develop programs from abstract algorithms, in such a way as to improve their longevity and reliability.

Part Three covers material often placed under the subheading 'Sorting and Searching'. It is a study of a simple associative data type. Associative (or key) retrieval is a simple abstract notion. Its realizations can be complex and are very varied.

One aspect of this study which will pervade all sections is the effect usage has on choosing an optimum realization for a data type. Each different realization will, in general, favour a different subset of its defined operations. It is important to bear this in mind when reading the book, and to consciously assess each suggested realization by determining its behaviour with each operation.

1.2 WHAT IS A TYPE?

1.2.1 A type as operations + domain

You will have come across the notion of a data type in Pascal. Pascal is a strongly typed language, by which we mean a language in which every defined data item is associated with a specified data type. For example, in introducing two variables **SUBTOTAL** and **TOTAL** we may have a definition of the form

var SUBTOTAL, TOTAL : INTEGER

at the head of a Pascal program block. Let us recap on the implications such a statement has in a Pascal program.

(i) It identifies those values which **SUBTOTAL** and **TOTAL** may take. For example

TOTAL : = 6

is perfectly legal, whereas

SUBTOTAL : = TRUE

is not. The set of legal values associated with a type is called its *domain.* The number of elements in a domain is called the cardinality of the domain. The cardinality of the boolean domain is 2, that of the Pascal character domain 128 and so on.

(ii) It is a message to the compiler concerning the way in which **SUBTOTAL** and **TOTAL** are to be represented. In this case the compiler may, perhaps, deduce that one word of memory should be allocated to each data item, and that values will be stored in twos-complement binary representation. We will see later that this 'implication' is in fact of a different nature to (i) and (iii).

(iii) It is a message to the compiler concerning the way in which **SUBTOTAL** and **TOTAL** are to be used. Each of the pre-defined object types has associated with it a set of operations. In the case of integer these will include $+$, $-$, **MOD**. All manipulations of integers must (ultimately) be specified in terms of these operations.

Therefore we have as a fact in Pascal that

SUBTOTAL + TOTAL

is a meaningful expression whose value is obtained by adding together the current values of **SUBTOTAL** and **TOTAL**, whereas

SUBTOTAL AND TOTAL

is not a meaningful expression (it is in some weakly typed languages) and is therefore defined to be 'illegal'. Such a statement will be identified as erroneous by the compiler.

We note three things about the legal expression

SUBTOTAL + TOTAL   (∗)

(i) It has a parallel in mathematical integers. By looking at the mathematics of the expression and the values of the two variables we can deduce the value that the expression should have (and will normally have – see (ii)). In mathematics type integer can be specified starting from Peano's axioms. Later we will attempt to specify all types that we use in a program, many of them informally at this stage. To specify a type is to give a method, independent of the given system, by which we can establish the expected result of each operation performed. Normally we try to be formal in our specifications (mathematical) because the more rigorous we are the more confident we can be of our pronouncements.

(ii) The parallel with mathematical integers is not complete. Peano's axioms are for integers with an infinite domain. On the other hand, computers are finite. The immediate impact of this is that (∗) may yield a perfectly 'normal' value when calculated using our specification, but may cause *overflow* on a typical machine when, for example, **SUBTOTAL** and **TOTAL** are both very large integers. We note the problem here, but shall not attempt to develop these thoughts at this stage.

(iii) Becoming less esoteric, expression (∗) tells the compiler what code to generate. The compiler knows that **SUBTOTAL** and **TOTAL** are both integers, so that + refers to integer arithmetic. The 'integer addition' instruction from the machine instruction set may therefore be called for. This instruction is an *implementation* of the integer ' + ' operation. Each of the defined operations for a type must have such an implementation defined.

None of this is new: it is merely documenting what we already know about types from our Pascal experience. Much of it we may never have consciously formulated: it will have remained implicit in our own model of what our programs are actually about.

Let us summarize, then, what we mean by a (Pascal) type:

- A type *specifies* a domain: a set of legal values.
- A type *specifies* a set of legal operations on those values and the results of applying these operations (the semantics).
- A type *prescribes* a representation for values from its domain: this representation is chosen by the compiler writer. An example would be the representation of integer values by twos-complement binary values.
- A type *prescribes* an implementation for each operation from its operation set: these implementations are also chosen by the compiler writer, who in turn is constrained by the architecture of his machine.

We chose our words carefully above, because whereas the domain and operation set for, say, an integer are fixed for all Pascal implementations (and for those of most other languages) the representation of integers and the implementation of integer operations varies widely and is particularly dependent on the hardware of a system. Obviously the implementation of an operation is intimately bound up with the representation of its values; change this representation and you must change the implementation.

Before we leave this section, note the correspondence which will form the basis of an approach to building our own data types. If we look at the summary it is not hard to see that, for each data type

- Operations are *specified* on values from the domain.

- Values from the domain are given a *representation* which associates each value from the domain with a value in a different domain (for example, that of twos-complement binary values in the case of integer).
- Operations are *implemented* by defining which operations are to be performed on values from the representation domain in order to achieve the desired (specified) result (for example, Logical Shift to achieve multiplication by 2).

In other words, there is an isomorphism defined between a type and its realization (the representation and implementation combined).

1.2.2 A type as operations only

It is a fact that the concept of a data item (a *variable* in Pascal) to denote a data value is not strictly necessary, and we could concern ourselves solely with operations. A variable is only 'visible' because operations are available which make it so, for example

WRITE(J)

In this case J is simply a shorthand notation for the expression from which its 'value' was constructed: say

MULTIPLY (2,2)

But 2 is itself only the shorthand (denotation) for another expression:

SUCCESSOR (SUCCESSOR (ZERO))

(see Peano's axioms). In this *applicative* notation we can see that data items are indeed unnecessary and can always be replaced by functional expressions. In particular, our **WRITE(J)** can be replaced by

WRITE (MULTIPLY (SUCCESSOR (SUCCESSOR (ZERO)), SUCCESSOR (SUCCESSOR (ZERO))))

As we are dealing with a Pascal environment, presenting practical as well as theoretical aspects in that environment, we will retain the notion of a data item. If you are interested in the 'pure' approach you will find references in the Bibliography.

1.2.3 Defining type INTEGER

For us, then, type integer is realized by choosing a more basic type to represent it and by defining a correspondence (Fig. 1.1).

(i) Between integers and values from the representation domain.

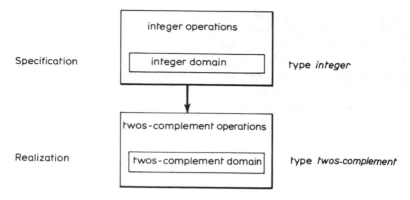

Specification   type *integer*

Realization   type *twos-complement*

Figure 1.1 Type **INTEGER**.

(ii) Between integer operations and operations on the representation domain.

Examples

INTEGER		TWOS-COMPLEMENT (16 bit)
Value:	− 32768	1000000000000000
Value:	0	0000000000000000
Operation:	+	IADD (integer add)
Operation:	**DIV**	IDIV: return quotient
Operation:	**MOD**	IDIV: return remainder

We now introduce a notation for explicitly expressing all the facts contained in this correspondence. Such a definition is implicit in every Pascal program using integers: it will become more useful as and when we introduce our own data types. For simplicity the specification given as Fig. 1.2 is not complete.

We make the following observations about it:

(i) Under *operations* we give the *form* of each operation: + acts on two integers to give a result which is an integer.

(ii) The only operations allowed on the right of '→' in an implementation are those defined for the type in the *representation* or the type in question. Here, we are at the level of the Assembly language. If we were not, then a specification and realization for *binary twos-complement* would have to appear as well.

That concludes our section on 'What is a type?'. If you are more confused than when you started it is because we are having to force many issues into the consciousness which have hitherto, quite rightly,

---

Specification for **INTEGER**

Domain
    $-32768\ldots32767$

Operations
    $+,-,*$, **DIV, MOD** : $-$ **(INTEGER, INTEGER): INTEGER**
    $<,<=,=,>=,>$: $-$ **(INTEGER, INTEGER): BOOLEAN**
    $:=$: $-$ **(INTEGER, INTEGER)**

Semantics
    Based on Peano's axioms, suitably modified because of finite domain

Realization of **INTEGER**

Representation
    Binary twos-complement
Implementation
    $+(X, Y)$ $\rightarrow$ load X
                       iadd Y, etc.

Figure 1.2 Type **INTEGER**.

been left covered by 'black boxes'. As always, opening a black box leads to more complexity in our model of what a program actually means, and an increase in the jargon so necessary to allow brevity in future developments. As we move on you will see that the benefits of opening this box far outweigh the initial cost, so the exercise is well worth while.

It will be time well spent if you study this section until its concepts and technical terms are absorbed into your modelling kit. Once this has been done the rest of the book will make far easier reading.

Technical terms

- Strongly typed.
- Domain.
- Cardinality.
- Specification.
- Realization.
- Representation.
- Implementation.

1.3 THE BASIC PASCAL TYPES

In Pascal, as in all strongly typed languages, a number of data types are both specified and realized implicitly. These can be used by a programmer with no further definition.

On the positive side this means that the programmer is saved the problem of delving into details of the machine architecture in order to devise a realization for these very fundamental and frequently used types. Together they form the blocks from which the user's own types can be built.

On the negative side, it means that the user must accept whichever realization has been chosen by the compiler writer for these types. The chosen realization will almost certainly be a compromise which may be far from optimum for the particular circumstances which an algorithm dictates. For example, integers may be used primarily in input and output instructions; multiplication by 2 may use the general multiply instruction rather than a *shift*.

In Pascal the basic types include

> **INTEGER**
> **BOOLEAN**
> **CHAR**
> **REAL**

We say that these types are defined 'in the language prelude', that is, all programs can be written as if their specifications and realizations form a part of the code.

We have already seen what the language prelude could look like for type integer. Of course, the notation we used is not in the Pascal language and so we have to adapt it when we define our own types. We return to this issue in Chapter 2. For the moment, however, we keep the notation and look at another basic type: **CHAR**.

The first thing we notice is that **CHAR**, unlike **INTEGER**, has no universal specification. Indeed, in most languages type **CHAR** has its domain specified in the language prelude by listing all elements in the domain. The cardinality of **CHAR** in Pascal is 128. As with **INTEGER** the domain is totally ordered. Each value in the domain has a unique predecessor (except one which we call 'low') and each value in the domain has a unique successor (except one which we call 'high'). The comparison operations ($<$, $=$, $>$, etc.) are therefore applicable. Two further operations are applicable, as indeed they are for type **INTEGER** and any other ordered type. These are the successor and predecessor operations. We left them out of the discussion of type **INTEGER** purely to simplify the exposition. We introduce them shortly, but first a remark on notation.

The operations listed in Fig. 1.2 for **INTEGER** are all binary operators (that is they all operate on two **INTEGER** values). We are used to writing expressions in infix notation, so that notation is adopted by Pascal. However, there is nothing particularly special about the notation. In fact there is no reason why we should not have

PLUS(X, Y)

instead of

X + Y

other than the fact that we are more accustomed to the latter. The former is in fact used in applicative languages like LISP. The point is not to challenge infix notation, but rather to recognize that a Pascal operator is nothing more nor less than a Pascal function which has been given a special notation. Under *operations*, therefore, we list not only the operators specified for the type but also the relevant functions and procedures (a procedure can be viewed merely as a function which returns its result in its arguments). As with the operators, any function appearing in a specification must also be given a form. For the successor and predecessor operations, which are both functions, we have the form

(CHAR): CHAR

Let us return to the definition of type **CHAR**. We can now specify it in the manner of Fig. 1.3 (with an argument of a procedure underlined if it returns a result).

Specification for **CHAR**

Domain
      ASCII(the ASCII character set and ordering)

Operations

$<, <=, =, >=, >$	$:-$ **(CHAR, CHAR):BOOLEAN**
ORD	$:-$ **(CHAR):INTEGER**
:=	$:-$ **(CHAR, CHAR)**
LOW, SUCC, PRED, High	$:-$ **(CHAR): CHAR**

Semantics
      Based on mathematics of ordered sets

Figure 1.3   Specifying type **CHAR**.

To complete the definition of type **CHAR** we need a realization. We can look to the 7-bit representation, defined in the American standard (ASCII). This represents each character by a unique pattern of 7 bits. If we consider the 7-bit values for the characters we notice that, not unreasonably, the '*low*' character is given a code which, as the binary representation of an integer, could be interpreted as 0: that is

0000000

and the *'high'* value is given the code

1111111

which, if interpreted as an integer, would have the decimal value 127. This representation is useful because it allows us to use the same hardware instructions to implement the **CHAR** operations as those **INTEGER** operations with the same name.

For simplicity we assume all characters are stored, by our Pascal implementation, in 16 bits (as with **INTEGER** above) with the nine most significant bits all zero. Hence we have

'low'   →   0000000000000000
'high' →   0000000001111111

We can now present a partial realization of type *char* (Fig. 1.4). Note that low (X) is 'implemented' by replacing it with the value 0 whenever it occurs. No imperative code would be generated by the compiler.

Realization of **CHAR**
Representation
        binary twos-complement
Implementation
        succ(X) → load X
                          iadd one
                          . . .
        low(X) → 0, etc.

Figure 1.4   Realizing type **CHAR**.

1.4 THE ADVANTAGES OF TYPED LANGUAGES

You will notice that both **INTEGER** and **CHAR** are represented in our examples by *binary twos-complement*. If we were to complete the realizations it would be clear that the implementation of each **CHAR** operation is identical to that of its **INTEGER** counterpart. Is it perhaps artificial to claim that we have a different type? Indeed, in FORTRAN IV, for example, no such distinction is made – character information can be stored in variables which have been declared as integer. Why then do we distinguish between two types which have the same representation? Is it only dogma which forces us to use **ORD (CH)** to map a character onto an integer when (in this realization) no conversion is actually required?

The argument above, in fact, is placing the cart before the horse. The realization of a type is a pragmatic issue which, as we shall see later, has many and varied solutions. The developer of a program should, initially, pay heed only to the type specifications. We will go even further: during the development of a section of program code from an algorithm we should be totally unaware of the realization of any data types used. This issue will be pursued more rigorously in Chapter 5. Suffice it to say that types **CHAR** and **INTEGER** are distinct because their specifications are distinct. Although the operations for type **CHAR** superficially bear a striking resemblance to a subset of those for type **INTEGER**, this has no significance in most programming situations (see, however, Section 5.4) as the types are defined on totally different domains.

What advantages are there in taking this approach? To determine the advantages let us first look at the opposing concept: languages which do not support types. In these languages it is open to the programmer to apply any operation to any data item – as in Assembly language programming. A key fact is that no power is lost at all: all algorithms can be realized in such a language. If adding types in no way enhances the power of a language, then the type concept is *redundant* in this context – and here lies one of the secrets of its success.

In everyday speech we find that sentences can be understood even when little of them is actually heard, or they are incorrectly formulated. There is a significant amount of redundancy in most of what we say – so much so that we can detect inconsistencies and mistakes in a sentence and, perhaps, even have enough information to reconstruct what must actually have been intended. This is the advantage given by redundant information: it can be used to detect accidental mistakes. Mistakes come in the form of incorrect use of words, the inapplicable use of verbs and from many other sources. The same is true in programming languages. The use of types allows us to specify many rules of 'sentence' (statement) construction. It is then possible to detect, for example, the inapplicable use of operations or operands.

We shall see that this is not the only advantage to be derived from the use of types. Perhaps the major advantage involves the discipline which typed languages impose on their users. Enforcing the use of the type concept as envisaged in this book encourages a more structured approach to program design. As we shall see in Chapter 5, this results in longer lived and more reliable programs which are easier, and therefore cheaper, to maintain. It should be emphasized that the maintenance cost of a large program surpasses the total of its design and development costs.

2
User-defined types

2.1 WHY USER-DEFINED TYPES?

We have looked at the basic types provided by Pascal and seen how their specifications and realizations are predetermined. The specifications are determined by the definition of the language Pascal itself, whereas the realizations are determined by the given system (and in particular the given compiler) we are using. We need know nothing of a realization in order to be able to use a data type.

The types built into a language provide us with a useful starting point for building our own types. Before we look at how we will do this, let us first convince ourselves that it will be a useful exercise: why should we not be satisfied with the types provided? In a sense this question has already been answered in the first chapter. We saw there that **INTEGER** and **CHAR** could both be realized by the same type. We justified type **CHAR**, and will use the same argument here to justify user-defined types. Consider, as an example, manipulating bank accounts which hold **STERLING** balances. A typical Pascal program for this might decide to hold **STERLING** values as **INTEGER**s representing number of pence. Pascal allows us to define a type **STERLING** for the purpose:

TYPE STERLING = INTEGER   (* in new pence *)

Is this a satisfactory arrangement? Once again let us look at the implications of such a statement, this time in terms of the attributes of our newly 'specified' type.

(i) *Domain:* The domain of **STERLING** is the same as the domain for **INTEGER**. In particular, any **INTEGER** value can be assigned to a **STERLING** variable. The danger in this can be depicted best by an example. Consider yet another type, **TIME**, representing the time of day in hours and minutes on a 24-hour clock. An obvious procedure is to introduce the type as

TIME = INTEGER   (* 24 hour clock in minutes *)

where **TIME** will be stored as the number of minutes past midnight.

To finally set the scene for our (perhaps now obvious) anomaly let us define two variables

> **VAR SALARY: STERLING;**
> **LUNCHTIME: TIME**

We are now perfectly entitled to introduce such meaningless statements into our program as

> **SALARY: = LUNCHTIME**

This offends the sensibilities of the programmer and can obviously be made illegal by adhering to the principles of strong type checking. **STERLING** does not have the same domain as **INTEGER**: there is merely a trivial mapping between the two.

(ii) *Operations:* The operation set for **STERLING** is the same as that for **INTEGER**. Again it is not difficult to generate meaningless constructs, in this case in the form of expressions. It is true that most operations transfer across to our new type and have useful interpretations in the type (there is a true isomorphism). For example

> **SALARY1 < SALARY2**

and

> **SALARY1 + SALARY2**

have obvious interpretations. However, what is the meaning of

> **SALARY1 * SALARY2**

and of

> **SALARY1 DIV SALARY2**   ?

We deduce that **STERLING** is a distinct type with its own domain and own set of operations. Type **INTEGER** is an obvious possible **REALIZA-TION** for **STERLING**, not a specification for it. We see then that, just as we need distinct basic types provided in a language, we need to be able to define our own types to gain the full benefits of a strongly typed language.

A language which fully supports type definitions will have at least:

(i) A mechanism for specifying new types which is sufficient for expressing defined operations, their form (necessary for compiler checking) and their semantics.

(ii) An independent mechanism for introducing a realization for a type, which comprises its representation and implementation.

(iii) Strong type checking by the compiler, to enforce usage compatible with the specification.

As will become apparent, Pascal has the following limitations:

 (i) There is no general mechanism for specifying new types. Certain templates are provided, but these pre-determine the operations which are defined for a type. User-definition of types must therefore be simulated.
(ii) There is no independent mechanism for introducing a realization. Two mechanisms, not specifically designed for this purpose, must be utilized: the Type declaration (for the representation) and the Procedure/Function declaration (for the implementation).
(iii) Because of (i), compiler enforcement of correct usage is not possible and so data independence may be compromised.

In summary, the basic types provided in a programming language form the building blocks from which realizations of user-defined types can be constructed. The specifications of user-defined types will all be distinct.

2.2 AN EXAMPLE

For our example we shall take type **CLOCK** discussed above. You will notice that, as with most of the examples in this book, a formal specification of each type is not given: at best a reference is made to some well-known concepts which are involved. Formal specification of the semantics of types is a topic in its own right, which we do not attempt to summarize here. Instead, we use examples which are very familiar to us, or else informally specify the semantics of a type using descriptive text and illustrations. These are not intended to replace the concept of formal specification: they are merely aids to be used until formal techniques are available to us. Some simple examples of formal specification will be introduced, in particular in Chapter 5, for demonstration purposes. With this in mind we present, firstly in the notation used so far, our definition of type **CLOCK** (Fig. 2.1). Notice once again that the operations on the right-hand side of an implementation definition (i.e. to the right of →) act on the representation of a **CLOCK** item, that is, they are **INTEGER** operations. For brevity we have not expanded all the comparison operators.

Once we have a definition for type **CLOCK** we can freely introduce **CLOCK** items into our programs, for example

    VAR WATCH, GMT:CLOCK

and use these in our program code with fragments such as:

    SET (WATCH, GMT);
    ⋮

```
                      Specification for CLOCK
Domain
    (H, M)   (* an ordered pair *)
    0 < = H < 24
    0 < = M < 60
Operations
    <, < =, =, > =, >   : −  (CLOCK, CLOCK): BOOLEAN
    SET                 : −  (CLOCK, CLOCK)
    TICK                : −  (CLOCK)
    HOUR, MINUTE        : −  (CLOCK): INTEGER
Semantics
    SET allows the first clock to be synchronized with the
    second clock
    TICK increments the clock time by 1 minute

                     Realization of CLOCK
Representation
    INTEGER   (* in minutes *)
Implementation
    SET (CLOCK1, CLOCK2) → IF DEFINED (CLOCK2)
                               THEN CLOCK1 : = CLOCK2
                               ELSE REPORT__UNSET
    TICK (CLOCK)           → IF  CLOCK < (23*60 + 59)
                               THEN CLOCK : = CLOCK + 1
                               ELSE CLOCK : = 0
    HOUR (CLOCK)          → CLOCK DIV 60
    MINUTE (CLOCK)        → CLOCK MOD 60
    < (CLOCK1, CLOCK2)    → CLOCK1 < CLOCK2   etc.
```

Figure 2.1 Specifying type **CLOCK**.


```
TICK (WATCH);
 .
 .
 .
WHILE HOUR (WATCH) = 12 DO LUNCHBREAK
```

2.3 DEFINITIONS IN PASCAL

In order to give a clear separation of the important concepts of
specification and *realization* we have adopted a notation which has
nothing to do with the Pascal language. Pascal, in fact, does not support

user-defined types to anything like the degree of its basic types. There are languages which do support the constructs needed to a greater or lesser extent; these include Ada, Clu, Alphard and Pascal Plus among others. Until one of these becomes widely available (the most likely one being the Ada language) the most commonly used demonstration language will remain Pascal, so it is to this language that we turn our attention.

Pascal does not fully support the definition of new types. What does this mean to the programmer? The first and most important implication is that Pascal compilers will be less helpful in enforcing correct use of data items; we will be thrown back on our own discipline of programming, forcing ourselves to adopt rules which govern the definition of types and the use of data items. We concentrate, in this section, on type definitions. Rules for the use of data items will be described in Chapter 5.

2.3.1 Specification

The specification section is entirely missing from the Pascal language. As this is primarily what distinguishes one type from another we can see that this is the root of a major problem when programming in Pascal. The fact that it is formally absent does not imply that it should be ignored. If we are introducing a new type to a program then we must document the fact: the specification becomes a *comment* in the program code. As a comment there is no reason why it should not conform exactly to the notation so far introduced. The *semantics* section can usefully contain the comments which one methodically places at the head of every procedure to describe its effects.

2.3.2 Realization

The realization section of a type definition ties the newly defined type down to the chosen implementation. As such it obviously cannot be reduced to mere documentation. We must therefore look for Pascal features which can be used actively in this part of the definition.

The representation subsection is actually catered for by the so-called **TYPE** section of Pascal. If we once again take the **CLOCK** as our example we must declare in our program

    TYPE CLOCK = **INTEGER**   (* in minutes *)

Unfortunately this has an implication which we do not want: all the operations defined for type **INTEGER** are inherited by our new type. On the positive side this means that (in this case) operators $<$, $=$ (etc.) are implicitly specified and implemented for us. On the negative side we see that so are all the other integer operators, such as * and **DIV**. These have no obvious meaning (semantics) for our new type and it is left to us (as a discipline) not to use them. In fact, operators in Pascal are peculiar to the basic types; we cannot define our own. If the '<' operator for **CLOCK** had not had the semantics governed by its representation as an integer, we would not have been able to use it. It is often necessary to write a function or procedure to replace an operator. As we said earlier, operator notation is syntactically redundant. An example is the use of **SET** instead of ':=' in our example.

The remaining operations must now be defined as straightforward Pascal procedures and functions. Once again, documentation in the form of our current notation will help make the structure of the program clear. We therefore introduce **CLOCK** in the following way.

2.3.3 A full definition in Pascal

A full definition of type **CLOCK** is given in Listing 2.1.

```
PROGRAM CLOCK __ EXAMPLE;
   CONST CLOCKMAX = 1439  (* 23*60 + 59 *);
(* SPECIFICATION for CLOCK: a 24-hour clock
   DOMAIN
     (H,M): 0 < = H < 24, 0 < = M < 60
   OPERATIONS
     <,< =, =,> =,>  : − (CLOCK, CLOCK) : BOOLEAN
     SET            : − (CLOCK, CLOCK)
     TICK           : − (CLOCK)
     HOUR, MINUTE  : − (CLOCK) : INTEGER
   SEMANTICS
     SET(CLOCK1,         will result in CLOCK1 taking the current
        CLOCK2)          value of CLOCK2. EXCEPTION: unde-
                         fined CLOCK2.
     TICK (CLOCK)        will result in CLOCK being advanced by
                         one minute in the 24-hour cycle.
     HOUR (CLOCK)        will return the current hour on the 24-
                         hour clock.
     MINUTE (CLOCK)      will return the current minute on the clock.


 (* END of SPECIFICATION for CLOCK *)
    ⋮
       any other specifications
    ⋮
```

```
TYPE CLOCK = INTEGER;
    ⋮
    any other representations
    ⋮
(* IMPLEMENTATION of CLOCK *)
PROCEDURE SET (VAR C1: CLOCK; C2: CLOCK);
  BEGIN
    IF DEFINED (C2)
      THEN C1 := C2
      ELSE REPORT_UNSET
  END;
PROCEDURE TICK (VAR C: CLOCK);
  BEGIN
    IF C < CLOCKMAX
      THEN C := C + 1
      ELSE C := 0
  END;
FUNCTION HOUR (C : CLOCK) : INTEGER;
  BEGIN
    HOUR := C DIV 60
  END;
FUNCTION MINUTE (C : CLOCK) : INTEGER;
  BEGIN
    MINUTE := C MOD 60
  END;
(* END OF IMPLEMENTATION of CLOCK *)
    ⋮
    any other implementations
    ⋮
```

Listing 2.1 A Pascal definition of type **CLOCK**.

2.3.4 Initialization

So far we have ignored the important question of the initial value of a
data item. As we well know, every data item must be given a value
before it is manipulated. Some systems will automatically set all data
items to a default value (for example, 0 for integers). This default is
system wide and normally relates to the bits by which all data values are
ultimately represented, rather than to the semantics of each type. Each
type should, therefore, specify an **INITIALIZE** procedure which must be

invoked when a variable of the type is declared. Remember that correctness frequently depends on all items having an acceptable value all of the time.

In some languages the initialization procedure is called automatically as the first operation on a data item in a program block. In Pascal we must call the procedure ourselves: it is another part of our discipline. We should, therefore, modify the **CLOCK** definition to incorporate

$\quad$ **PROCEDURE CLOCK_INITIALIZE (VAR C: CLOCK)**

which could, for example, set its value to $(0, 0)$ meaning midnight.

To complete our Pascal implementation guidelines we therefore introduce the program block:

BEGIN
$\quad$ **CLOCK_INITIALIZE (GMT);**
$\qquad \vdots$
$\quad$ any other initializations
$\qquad \vdots$
END.

3

Data structures:
the structured types of Pascal

Up to now we have been considering simple data items. By 'simple' we mean a data item which bears no defined relationship to any other data item within the system. For example, we have introduced a **TIME** type and a **STERLING** type. This allows us to define a **TIME** item, **TRANSACTION-TIME**, and a **STERLING** item, **DEBIT**. These items are totally independent of each other: we have defined no interrelationship. Suppose, however, that we wish to associate a sterling **DEBIT** with a given value for **TRANSACTION-TIME** so that banking transactions can be accurately logged. We are logically associating two data items, one of which contains a time and the other of which contains a sterling value. Together they form a *data structure:* an item with identifiable components. This particular data structure would comprise two data *elements*.

A data structure defines a new data type in terms of existing data types. It will have (at least) the following operations defined on it:

Composition: Form an item of the new (structured) type from instances of each type which it comprises.

Selection: Select one constituent of the structured item, which will be one of the items which it comprises.

3.1 TYPE **RECORD**

If we compose two (or more) data items into a structure which allows their direct selection by name, we have what we normally refer to as a record: a set of logically related data items. By 'logically' related we mean related in the microworld (model) which we are attempting to build with our program. Data items are normally related in this way because they represent

either a (logical) object in the system (in which case each component represents an attribute of this object) or   an event in the system (in which case each component represents a facet of this event)

Generically we will say that a record represents an *entity* in the system and that entities have *attributes*.

Example 3.1
Our system may be a model of an enterprise which involves people. We can decide which attributes of people (age, sex, salary,...) are relevant in the model and form a record to represent each 'person' item in the system. In Pascal this can be performed with

```
TYPE PERSON = RECORD
                AGE:0..130;
                SEX:(MALE, FEMALE);
                SALARY:STERLING
              END;
     VAR JIM, JULIE:PERSON;
```

JIM and **JULIE** are now defined to be **PERSON** items with attributes (in Pascal records we refer to 'fields') **AGE**, **SEX** and **SALARY**. Selection and composition must be provided on these structured items.

In Pascal the selection of a field is represented by the notation

RECORD. FIELDNAME

examples of which are

JIM. AGE

and

JULIE. SALARY

A **PERSON** value can be visualized as the three values (triple)

(AGE, SEX, SALARY)

with one instance being (with *salary* in new pence)

(26, *MALE, 748000*)

The above notation in fact represents a composition of three data values into a single, structured data value. As such it would (and does) suit languages allowing record structures. Unfortunately, it is not provided in Pascal: in fact, no explicit composition function appears in the language. Instead, record values must be 'built up' one value at a time by assigning values to individual fields rather than to a whole record item. When creating a new record value, therefore, we should remember to define explicitly a value for each field of the record:

```
(* JIM: = (26, MALE, 748000) *)
  WITH JIM DO
    BEGIN
      AGE: = 26;
      SEX: = MALE;
      SALARY: = 748000
    END
```

It is, of course, possible to 'miss' one of the assignments shown. In this case we have an ill-defined value for one of the attributes of **JIM**. Once again, incomplete notation results in more potential pitfalls for the programmer.

Example 3.2
The banking transaction already introduced represents an event in a banking system. There are two facets to this event: a time and a sterling value. In this case an appropriate Pascal record would be

```
TYPE TRANSACTION = RECORD
                     WHEN: TIME;
                     AMOUNT: STERLING
                   END;
```

with examples of events being

```
VAR DEBIT, CREDIT: TRANSACTION
```

Examples of selection in this system include

```
CREDIT. AMOUNT
```

and

```
DEBIT. WHEN
```

It is even more apparent, in the banking model envisaged, that no partially completed events should be represented: both fields must be defined for a transaction to be meaningful.

Let us investigate the **TRANSACTION** type a little further. We have already developed a notation for defining types, so how is **TRANSAC-TION** to be fully defined? It must have a specification and a realization, so what do these look like? We will look at the specification first (Fig. 3.1), as we have already covered most of it informally.

Specification for **TRANSACTION**

Domain
    (TIME, STERLING)

Operations
    .WHEN   : − **(TRANSACTION): TIME**
    .AMOUNT : − **(TRANSACTION): STERLING**
    COMPOSE : − **(TIME, STERLING): TRANSACTION**
    : =   : − **(TRANSACTION, TRANSACTION)**

Semantics
    A logical event with two facets: **WHEN** and **AMOUNT**

Figure 3.1   Specifying a record type: **TRANSACTION**.

Notes

1. The selection operations are represented using the '.' notation, as it is provided in Pascal. There is no reason why they should not be normal functions (except that Pascal functions are only allowed to return values of simple type).
2. **COMPOSE** can be written by the user (see realization) to provide the 'missing' function.
3. The assignment operation (: =) is provided.
4. New transaction values must be composed from individual values of type **TIME** and type **STERLING**. A shorthand notation is provided in Pascal for statements such as

    CREDIT: = COMPOSE (1506, CREDIT. AMOUNT)

In fact, we have changed the value of only one facet of the transaction. Abstractly we have generated a completely new **TRANS-ACTION** value. In Pascal we know this as field assignment. We could introduce this into our specification, if required, by the operation definition

    .WHEN: = : − (TRANSACTION, TIME)

The realization for records in Pascal is system defined. Typically the realization will consist of juxtaposing in memory the values representing the given fields, with the fields themselves having their defined representations. We can therefore envisage an implementation in which

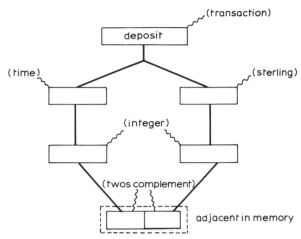

Figure 3.2 A representation of **TRANSACTION**.

each **TRANSACTION** field is ultimately represented by a single memory word holding a twos-complement value, and a **TRANSACTION** is ultimately represented by two such words which are 'adjacent' in memory. This is shown in Fig. 3.2. The transaction item **DEPOSIT** (named in the diagram) is shown as a compound object: it comprises one **TIME** item and one **STERLING** item, each of which is represented by an **INTEGER**. Of course, this diagram represents only one of the many possible for **TRANSACTION**; it is based on the representations developed earlier. In Pascal itself, as implemented on your system, this diagram is unlikely to be far from the truth.

3.2 TYPE **SET**

A loose collection of related items is referred to as a **SET**. Individual items in a set are referred to as *members* of the set. Membership is determined by a *membership property*, called a *predicate*, which defines the set.

Example 3.3
If the set **COLOURS** has the predicate 'is a colour' it will include **RED**, **BLUE** and **GREEN** amongst its members.

A set need not always contain the same members. Its predicate may result in an ever-changing membership.

Example 3.4

If the set **LICENSED** has predicate 'has a current licence to drive' then its membership will vary as new drivers pass their tests and as former members receive suspensions or lose licences.

Theoretically, there is no necessity for the members of a set to be similar items (i.e. items of the same type). There is no reason why one should not define a set **PET_HATES** with predicate 'I have a dislike for' and including **GMT** and **DEBIT** in its membership. In practice, those languages which directly provide a **SET** data type (including Pascal) insist on members being of the same type.

The first reason for this lies with one of the two basic operations so far defined on structured types: selection. It is frequently useful to be able to process the members of a set one by one, symbolized by the pseudo-program fragment

> *foreach* member *in* set *do*
> *process* (member)

The procedure *process* needs to know what type of item a member is, in order that the advantages of strong type checking are maintained. This is trivial if all members are of the same type.

The second reason lies in the simple realization made possible by such restrictions, and discussed later. We will find the restriction a common practice with all structured types, and in order to keep things simple we will adopt it as a matter of course in this book except where it is explicitly stated to the contrary.

In Pascal we are allowed to define a set with membership from any ordinal type.

Example 3.5

> **TYPE COLOUR = [RED, ORANGE, YELLOW, GREEN, BLUE, INDIGO, VIOLET];**
> **BROCHURE = SET OF COLOUR**

We will take type **BROCHURE** as that which we wish to specify. Appropriate operations on **BROCHURE** which are provided by Pascal appear in the Pascal standard. They include set union (+), set difference (−) and set inclusion ($\langle$). Apart from these, we will be interested in composition and selection also. Set composition is provided by the notation

> [$\langle$member list$\rangle$]

which allows us to create an instance of a brochure:

> **[RED, BLUE, INDIGO]**

Members can be added to, or deleted from, a set by composing a further set (as above) with the specific members to be added (deleted) and then using set union (difference) to deliver the result:

[RED, BLUE] = [RED, BLUE, INDIGO] − [INDIGO]

Member selection is not so well supported in Pascal. In fact, in order to select a current member of a set we need to cycle through all the conceivable members and for each of them ask whether they belong. To illustrate this we can declare

VAR MEMBER: COLOUR;
      CATALOGUE: BROCHURE;

and rewrite the pseude-program fragment as

FOR MEMBER: = RED TO VIOLET DO
  IF MEMBER IN CATALOGUE
    THEN PROCESS (MEMBER)

Specification for **BROCHURE**

Domain
    Set of **COLOUR**
Operations
    +,*, −   : − (BROCHURE, BROCHURE): BROCHURE
    <,<=,=,>=,>   : − (BROCHURE, BROCHURE); BOOLEAN
    IN   : − (COLOUR, BROCHURE): BOOLEAN
    [ ]   : − (COLOUR*): BROCHURE
    (* **COLOUR** represents 0 or more arguments of type **COLOUR** *)
Semantics
    As defined in set theory for finite sets

Figure 3.3 Specifying a set type: **BROCHURE**.

We are now in a position to specify type **BROCHURE** (Fig. 3.3). As Pascal provides the **SET** as a built-in structuring facility, the realization of **BROCHURE** will be determined by the system. There is a very simple mapping between the operations on sets and logical operations on memory words provided by the hardware of most machines. Instead of fully defining a realization for **BROCHURE** we will simply give examples which provide insight into it, and leave you to complete the realization as an exercise.

A **BROCHURE** item may have at most seven members. As with sets in mathematics a member is either present or absent and cannot 'appear' twice. One *bit* of memory can therefore record whether one allowable member is in fact a member or not. Seven bits will suffice to describe the status of each allowable member of the **BROCHURE** set and this in turn will fully define the set membership. As examples, we can represent

>**[RED, BLUE]**   as   1 0 0 0 1 0 0
>   (**RED** is present, **ORANGE** is not, etc.)
>**[BLUE, INDIGO]**   as   0 0 0 0 1 1 0

and

>**[BLUE]**   as   0 0 0 0 1 0 0

If we look at the operation of set intersection we can see that

>   **[RED, BLUE]**
> ***[BLUE, INDIGO]**
> = **[BLUE]**

The parallel in the representation we are investigating states

>   1 0 0 0 1 0 0
> ? 0 0 0 0 1 1 0
> = 0 0 0 0 1 0 0

From this we can derive the truth table

?	0	1
0	0	0
1	0	1

It is not hard to see that the appropriate logical operation (? above) to implement set intersection (∗) is *and*. There are similar simple implementations for the other set operations.

This simple realization of sets leads to restrictions, in many systems, on the cardinality of the member type. This is because many implementations allocate a fixed number of computer words to represent any set item.

There are, in fact, many and varied realizations of sets used in computer systems. Each will have its own advantages and disadvantages in terms of space requirements and the speed with which each operation can be performed. Several alternative realizations will be presented and analysed in later chapters.

3.3 TYPE *sequence*

A sequence is a totally ordered set of items. This means that, in a sequence, each item (except one) has a unique predecessor, and each item (except one) has a unique successor. The item with no predecessor (successor) is referred to as the *first* (*last*). A sequence may, of course, be empty.

Example 3.6
The sequence *text* is composed of a totally ordered set of *word*s.
The sequence *word* is composed of a totally ordered set of characters.

This is an example of a type which is structured from elements which are themselves structured. In theory any structured type can have structured elements, and in practice no fundamentally new concepts or complications are introduced by this.

Elements of a sequence are totally ordered. This means that there must be some ordering function defined for the sequence. Examples of functions for the sequence *text* are:

'words in dictionary order'

and

'words in chronological order of their insertion'

Unlike records and sets, items in sequence are related to each other by virtue of the ordering function. This means that it is meaningful to 'navigate' through a sequence, from one item to another, using the ordering to specify the path. We can therefore select items according to their relative positions in the sequence.

In order to support this idea, the notion of an identified element of a sequence is introduced. Different items within a sequence can be identified using the operations **FIRST**, **LAST**, **SUCCESSOR** and **PREDE-CESSOR**. If **S** is a sequence, then **FIRST(S)** will identify that element in **S** which has no predecessor. We can then select this element by

   SELECT (FIRST(S))

Other elements can be selected after identifying them by their position relative to the first or last elements, viz.

   SELECT (SUCCESSOR (FIRST(S)))

But what does **FIRST(S)** actually return as a value? Function **FIRST** does not affect the value of **S** itself, as **S** still contains the same items in the same relative order. What is changed is the item in **S** to which we wish to draw attention. The state of a sequence is therefore represented by the ordered items together with an item identifier (when we wish to draw attention to this aspect of a sequence we will refer to a sequence-pair). This should be borne in mind when sequences are realized.

The forms of the operations so far introduced are as follows:

FIRST, LAST, SUCCESSOR,
PREDECESSOR   : – (SEQUENCE): SEQUENCE
SELECT   : – (SEQUENCE): ITEM

We define three further fundamental operations. These allow elements to be added to and deleted from a sequence, and an empty sequence to be created. They are (resp.):

INSERT : – (SEQUENCE, ITEM): SEQUENCE
DELETE : – (SEQUENCE): SEQUENCE
NEW   : – (): SEQUENCE

At this point we do not fully specify type sequence: in particular we make no statement regarding the identified item after each of these operations. Sequence can usefully be specified in several different ways in this regard, some of which are explored in Chapter 4.

Note that, in Pascal, functions are not allowed to return structured items. The functions for Pascal should therefore be implemented as procedures, with their result returned in a var parameter, called an *output* parameter. This is merely a syntactic issue: the semantics remain unchanged.

As an example, suppose we wish to implement the **COMPOSE** function for type **TRANSACTION** (see Section 3.1). We cannot return a record as the result of a Pascal function, so

COMPOSE: – (TIME, STERLING): TRANSACTION

would, in practice, be implemented as a procedure with a heading of the form

PROCEDURE COMPOSE (T: TIME; S:STERLING; VAR TN: TRANSAC-TION)

All sequence values can be built up by successively inserting elements into an initially empty sequence. In pure functional notation such a sequence is typified by the expression

INSERT (INSERT (NEWSEQ, 'A'), 'B')

In the Pascal procedural form this would appear as

S: = NEWSEQ;
INSERT (S, 'A');
INSERT (S, 'B')

We are now in a position to specify type **TEXT** (Fig. 3.4).

```
                        Specification for TEXT
        Domain
            WORD*
        Operations
            NEW                         : − ():TEXT
            FIRST, LAST, PREDECESSOR,
            SUCCESSOR, DELETE           : − (TEXT):TEXT
            INSERT                      : − (TEXT, WORD): TEXT
            SELECT                      : − (TEXT): WORD
        Semantics
            As for totally ordered, finite sets
```

Figure 3.4 Specifying a sequence type: **TEXT**.

Sequences are used in many different ways in computer programs, with different ordering functions and distinct patterns of usage. Some combinations of ordering function with access pattern are so common that they have been individually specified and named: they are new types which are *restrictions* of type sequence. One of these is called type *stack*, another type *queue*. We will be looking closely at these in the next chapter.

3.3.1 Type Pascal-FILE

A common use of a sequence is to process its elements in their defined order. For a non-empty sequence such processing is of the form:

```
identify first of sequence;
while not⟨end of sequence⟩do
    begin
        Process (selected item);
        identify successor in sequence
    end
```

The *Pascal-file* is a sequence of variable length. It is a restriction on type **SEQUENCE**, designed for processing elements in the above way. If we assume a file **F** in Pascal then we note that **F** refers not only to the underlying sequence: it refers also to an associated item identifier and so is a sequence-pair. This is in keeping with our convention about sequences.

The restriction on **SEQUENCE** is that all **INSERT**s must be made at the end of the file, and **DELETE** is not available. If we translate the pseudo-program fragment above into Pascal we will be in a good

position to point out the correspondences between operations on a
Pascal file and operations as we have defined them for a **SEQUENCE**:

```
RESET (F);
WHILE NOT EOF (F) DO
  BEGIN
    PROCESS (F^);
    GET (F)
  END
```

- 'RESET' is the Pascal-file notation for **FIRST** with, of course, the added
  semantics that the *first* of an empty file leads to a specially defined
  condition (what is it?).
- *Selection* is provided explicitly by the operator ˆ.
- 'GET' is the Pascal-file notation for **SUCCESSOR**.
- '*End* of sequence' is a more interesting operation which is discussed
  below.

We have so far said nothing about the semantics of operations which
lead to problematic results. For example, what is the result of applying
the **SUCCESSOR** function to the sequence

   LAST(S)

where **S** is itself a sequence?
   There is no one correct answer to this: we must specify the semantics
and any defined result could be acceptable. Certainly some decisions
would seem more 'logical', or 'consistent' with our image of what a
sequence is – but remember that any such criteria are subjective and
biased by our knowledge of particular uses of sequences.
   The decision taken with Pascal files gives one such treatment. It states
that a sequence has a further aspect to its state, besides an item
identifier. This aspect is accessible as the result of a function called **EOF**:

   EOF: − (Pascal-FILE): BOOLEAN

Let us generalize to an equivalent function for sequences. We introduce

   EOS: − (SEQUENCE): BOOLEAN

and investigate possible semantics. In order to define the semantics we
need some formal mechanism for expressing them. We will use
algebraic methods for this purpose, in particular those developed by J. V.
Guttag. This method is a substitution method, by which complex
expressions are simplified using defined rewrite rules. 'Semantics' are
therefore defined by giving a particular expression form on the left of a
rewrite rule, and its simplified form on the right. To give our example on

the semantics of **SUCCESSOR** of a sequence **S**:

successor (last(S)) = terminal
successor (terminal) = **undefined**
eos (last(S)) = **false**
eos (terminal) = **true**

This is not intended to capture all the semantics associated with the *'end of sequence'*. It does serve, however, to illustrate a principle. In simple English we are saying

- **EOS** returns **TRUE** only when we have asked for the **SUCCESSOR** of the **LAST** of a sequence.
- Asking for the **SUCCESSOR** of the **LAST** of a sequence leads to a special sequence which we will refer to as *terminal*.
- Asking for the **SUCCESSOR** of *terminal* will lead to an undefined result.

We really need to say more to fully define the semantics in this particular specification. For example, what is the result of applying **SELECT** to *terminal*? We will come back to this form of algebraic specification later in the book.

The file as provided in Pascal is usually referred to as *sequential* for reasons that have been explained. The fact that it is referred to as a file is merely an historical issue tied to its usual *realization* with reference to secondary memory.

3.3.2 Type **ARRAY**

(a) Informal introduction

The array is the data structure which most closely models the most basic data structure we consider in this course: random access memory itself. As we shall see below, an array is technically a sequence of fixed length. Before studying it as such, we present an informal discussion of its most salient features.

Memory is composed of words, each word comprising a number of bits. Each word has a unique address. An address is nothing more than a pattern of bits, but it can be useful to view an address as an integer (which, using the integer representation given earlier, identifies the appropriate bit pattern). Hence, we can view memory itself as a data structure whose elements are identified by an integer in the range **0..MEMORYMAX**. We can then refer to memory locations by merely quoting this address.

To use memory directly in this way would be very limiting. We can identify two major drawbacks:

(i) The program will only execute correctly if it is stored at the same place in memory each time it is run.

(ii) An item must be represented ultimately by one word of memory.

Each of these could be overcome, but would require a programmer to perform calculations every time he wished to identify a specific item in memory. The array relieves the programmer of the burden of these calculations, forcing the compiler to do the work in translation.

The first drawback is overcome by never using absolute memory addresses: we always use addresses relative to some point. Hence, if we wish to identify a group of ten items as having special significance, and we wish to be able to identify them as a group, we can give them a generic name (say A) and then refer to them with subscripts as

$$A_0, A_1, A_2, \ldots, A_9$$

Subscripts are not normally provided on computer terminals, so Pascal adopts a different notation for them. In Pascal they are called *indexes* and notated:

A[0], A[1], ..., A[9]

The important thing is that we can refer to, say, **A[6]** without needing to know exactly which location it is stored in: the compiler and loader are responsible for allocating memory, hence determining the address of **A[6]**. The programmer is relieved of this chore.

The second drawback is overcome by allowing any (single) type of item to be chosen as the item type for any given array, irrespective of the size of an item. Hence, **A[1]** need not have an address in memory which is one greater than that for **A[0]**, it could be two, three,... greater, depending on the size of an item. Once again, the compiler looks after the details of these calculations, so life is much easier for the programmer.

The final point to make about the use of arrays in Pascal is that we do not have to refer to the elements via the subscripts $0, 1, \ldots$ We can choose any ordinal type for our index. This not only allows us to refer to elements starting from any integer base (for example, referring to the first element as **A[1]** instead of **A[0]**), it also allows us to index via **COLOUR**, etc. Some examples are given below.

Example 3.7
An array of integers, indexed from 1 to 50.

TYPE A = ARRAY [1..50] OF INTEGER

Elements can be accessed by referring to **A[1]**, **A[2]**, ..., **A[50]**.

Example 3.8
An array of sterling values, indexed on **COLOUR**.

   TYPE B = ARRAY[COLOUR] OF STERLING

The elements can be accessed by

   B[RED], B[ORANGE],…, B[VIOLET]

Example 3.9
An array of characters, indexed on **BOOLEAN**.

   TYPE C = ARRAY[BOOLEAN] OF CHAR

Elements can be accessed by

   C[FALSE], C[TRUE]

(b) A more formal introduction

An **ARRAY** is a sequence of fixed length. Each item in an array is identified by an *index* value taken from the domain of an *ordinal* type (the index type). The cardinality of this type dictates the number of items in the array, and hence the cardinality of the array which is

$$\text{cardinality (item type)}^{\text{cardinality (index type)}}$$

For the sake of exposition we introduce an example array which we will specify but not attempt to realize at this stage.
   We can see that the Pascal type definitions

   INDEX = 0..15;
   BITVECTOR = ARRAY[INDEX] OF BOOLEAN

define the domain of the type **BITVECTOR**. This domain has cardinality

   2^{16}

comprising, as it does, values with every combination of sixteen boolean values.
   Selection of an item from an array is performed by a special selection function, which is given its own notation in Pascal. For the array

   WORD:BITVECTOR

we may select the boolean value of the constituent item identified by index 0, with

   WORD[0]

which is shorthand for

   SELECT (FIRST (WORD))

in its full sequence clothing. For an array a sequence-pair becomes a pair with the array as its first element and an index as its second. Hence, for example, the selection function takes an array-pair as its argument and returns an item. In the case of **BITVECTOR** this particularizes to

[ ]: – ((**BITVECTOR, INDEX**)):**BOOLEAN**

The composition function is once again absent, and must be effected by identifying and assigning each individual item within an array. The notation exemplified by

WORD[0]: = **TRUE**

states that any further selection of **WORD[0]** will return **TRUE**, until its next assignment. This leads us to the operation definition for element assignment:

[ ]: = : – ((**BITVECTOR. INDEX**), **BOOLEAN**)

Arrays are considered to be random access data structures: any element can be accessed in constant time. This contrasts with its sequence nature, by which elements are accessed only by repeated applications of the successor or predecessor functions. The reason for this dichotomy lies with the nature of the item identifier, and can be expressed using algebraic methods once again.

Let I be an index. As with all ordinal types, the operations **PRED** and **SUCC** are defined. We can assert that

$$predecessor(word[I]) = word[pred(I)]$$
$$successor(word[I]) = word[succ(I)]$$

We therefore have the special situation with arrays that any element can be selected by denoting its index, either as an ordinal value or as the ordinal value represented by a variable. Hence

I: = **WORD[1]**

is actually a shorthand for, and so represents,

I: = **SELECT (SUCCESSOR (FIRST (WORD)))**

This leads to the 'direct access' notion of arrays. We will see in Chapter 6 that efficient implementations of these operations can be devised, so that the directness of access is actual rather than merely notational. We therefore specify the array **BITVECTOR** in its 'direct access' form, which is a restriction of that for a general sequence (see Fig. 3.5).

There is no reason why the elements of an array should not themselves be structured. We may, for example, have an array of **TRANSACTION**s, an array of **BROCHURE**s or even an array of **BITVEC-**

```
                        Specification for BITVECTOR
Domain
      (BOOLEAN¹⁶) (* sixteen boolean values *)
Operations
      [ ]              : − ((BITVECTOR, INDEX)): BOOLEAN
      [ ]:=            : − ((BITVECTOR, INDEX), BOOLEAN)
      :=               : − (BITVECTOR, BITVECTOR)
      INITIALIZE :− (BITVECTOR)
Semantics
      Composition by assigning each element value.
      Total assignment is provided
```

Figure 3.5 Specifying an array type: **BITVECTOR**.

TORs. Let us introduce an example of an array of **BITVECTOR**s. We may well be writing a program in which we wish to model the memory of a small machine. The machine has 1 K (1024) words, each word comprising 16 bits. As before we introduce the appropriate Pascal definitions, in this case

MEMINDEX = 0..1023;
MEMORY = ARRAY [MEMINDEX] OF BITVECTOR

We are now free to introduce an instance of such a memory, for this example a random access memory

RAM: MEMORY

and to select individual words of memory:

WORD:= RAM[5]

Remember that **RAM[5]** returns a value of type **BITVECTOR**, itself an array. Hence, the selection function can be applied to **RAM[5]**. As an example, we are entitled to test

IF RAM [5] [0] THEN..

Pascal provides special notation for arrays which have arrays as elements. For example, it is legal in Pascal to define our memory in the alternative form of the definition thus:

MEMORY = ARRAY [MEMINDEX, INDEX] OF BOOLEAN

With either definition we are also entitled to select constituent booleans with a single selector, for example,

RAM[5,0]

This is exactly equivalent to **RAM[5][0]** as used above. In many situations this new notation may be natural and therefore beneficial (see below). In the example introduced it would be, for most people, more natural to keep the definitions as they are.

We said that our program was to model the random access memory of a small machine. 'To model' is simply another way of saying 'to realize'. The array is being used to realize a new data type which, for clarity, we will refer to as a **RAMMEMORY**. This type inherits all operations from its representation type except full assignment: it is a restriction of the **MEMORY** type. Notice that if we also wanted to model a ROM we would introduce **ROMMEMORY** as a further restriction of **MEMORY**: no full assignment and no element assignment, though some form of initial 'memory load' would be required in their place.

Arrays can be used to model matrices: hence, the special Pascal notation for multidimensional arrays (arrays with array elements). In such an environment we would need to provide such operations as **MATRIX-MULTIPLY** and **TRANSPOSE**. Some languages (for example APL) support matrices rather than arrays, so matrix multiplication is provided gratis. Pascal is not one of these.

3.4 TYPE *ring*

A sequence is also referred to as a linear list. The description 'linear' refers to the total ordering of elements in the list. A related data structure is the circular list, or *ring*, which differs in only one major respect: every element has a predecessor and a successor. In sequence terminology, the predecessor of *first* is defined to be *last*, and the successor of *last* is defined to be *first*. The concepts of *first* and *last* are, of course, redundant for a *ring*.

An important aspect in the general use of *ring*s is that any element can be reached from any other element in a single scan. This feature is particularly useful when elements are constituents of several different data structures simultaneously. An element containing an item of interest can be identified using one structure, and then all associated items in the *ring* structure can be identified in one pass. Such complex data structures form the basis of many data base management systems.

3.5 TYPE *heap*

A Pascal heap comprises a set of pairs. Each pair contains an item, which may be of any defined type, together with an associated item identifier. When an item is inserted into a heap it is allocated its unique identifier, which must be used in any subsequent selection of it. The identifier is therefore returned as the result of an insert operation, and must be stored by the program using the heap: if it is not then the item will remain unselectable for the duration of the program run.

In Pascal, an identifier is called a *pointer* and can be stored in a pointer variable. Recall that with Pascal sets we always know what type of item is being selected because all member items are of the same type. This is not true for a heap, so another method of identifying type must be used.

The technique used in Pascal is to associate a type with each pointer variable: an **INTEGER** *pointer* may only identify an **INTEGER** item, a **TRANSACTION** *pointer* may only identify a **TRANSACTION** item and so on. In general, if we wish to insert an item of type **T** into the heap then we must provide a **T** *pointer* variable to receive the item identifier. When selecting the item, we use the **T** pointer and hence the system knows that an item of type **T** is being selected.

In practice, Pascal explicitly provides one heap. The defined operations for manipulating individual items need not, therefore, have a parameter specifying which heap is being used. The insertion of an item into the Pascal heap is achieved in two stages:

(i) 'Create' an item of the required type in the heap (its value will be undefined) and return its item identifier.

(ii) Assign the required value to the heap item which has been created.

The creation of an item is achieved using the operation

NEW

which returns a pointer of appropriate type. An example will clarify Pascal notation.

Example 3.10
Insert an **INTEGER** item with value 1056 into the heap:

```
VAR INT:^INTEGER;  (* An INTEGER pointer variable *)
    :
    :
    INT  := NEW;    (* i *)
    INT^ := 1056;   (* ii *)
```

The notation **INT^** refers to 'the item pointed to (identified) by **INT**'. We can use it anywhere where an **INTEGER** variable is expected. For example we can, given the above, incorporate

WRITE (INT^)

and rightly expect the value 1056 to be printed. **INT^** is, in this context, the notation for 'select the item identified by **INT**'

Pointer variables are extremely useful in practice. We can build arbitrarily complex data structures by creating records in the heap which contain:

(i) A data item.
(ii) Pointers to other data items which are related in some defined way.

We will give many examples of this technique in the following sections.
One further operation is provided for the programmer:

DISPOSE

This operation will remove an item (identified by an argument) from the heap.

Example 3.11
Remove the item identified by *int* from the heap:

DISPOSE (INT)

int can now no longer be used for selection until it has once again been set to identify an item.

When a pointer variable is not identifying an item (i.e. when its value is undefined) it should have a special value called, in Pascal, **nil**. Hence we can say,

INT: = **nil**

to initialize **INT** to this special value. Any attempt to select an item using a **nil**-valued pointer will result in a Pascal run-time error.
Finally, assignment is provided between pointers associated with the same type. For example, if **INT1** and **INT2** are both pointers to **INTEGER**s, we can write,

INT1: = **INT2**

This will result in the item identifier stored in **INT2** being copied into variable **INT1**. We now have the situation in which **INT1** and **INT2** both identify the same item. This can be represented diagrammatically as in Fig. 3.6. These pointer diagrams can be useful in visualizing what is meant by the various Pascal pointer operations. For example,

INT1ˆ

can be explained as 'the item we arrive at if we start at **INT1** and follow the arrow'.
In the case above, **INT1ˆ** and **INT2ˆ** both refer to the same item. We

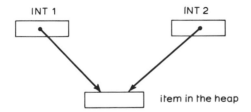

Figure 3.6   The same item identified by two pointer variables.

therefore have the unusual situation in which the same item can be selected in two different ways. This is known as 'aliasing'.

Example 3.12.
    INT2ˆ: = 2;
    INT1ˆ: = 6;   (* BEWARE! Bad practice *)
    WRITE (INT2ˆ)

will result (if *int1 = int2*) in 6 being printed.

We must obviously be very careful in the way we use pointers, so that confusions like this do not become troublesome.

The specification for type heap can now be considered. A special feature of the operations is that many take a type as an argument. This is the first occasion when it has been necessary to treat a type in this way: on all previous occasions the element type was fixed for the structured type and so was implied rather than explicitly communicated. A specification for heap is given in Fig. 3.7. Realizations of a heap are considered in Chapter 7.

Specification for *heap*

Domain
    (any*)   (* 0 or more elements of any type *)
Operations
    newheap $:-$ (): *heap*
    NEW $:-$ (*heap*, *type*$\langle T \rangle$): ˆT
    DISPOSE $:-$ (*heap*, *type*$\langle T \rangle$, ˆT)
      ˆ $:-$ (*heap*, *type*$\langle T \rangle$, ˆT): T
    ˆ: = $:-$ (*heap*, *type*$\langle T \rangle$, ˆT, T)
Semantics
    As discussed in the text
    ˆT identifies an item of type T

Figure 3.7   Specifying the Pascal **heap** data structure.

3.6 GENERAL REMARKS

We have now encountered all of the structured types of Pascal and in each case have specified an example type. We have specified only selected examples because in fact Pascal provides a generic capability: a vast number of types can actually be specified (and automatically realized by the compiler) merely by varying the base type. This generic aspect is considered in detail in Part Two of the book. For the time being, we can continue to treat each generated type as a special case.

One aspect which has emerged in manipulating objects of structured type is the necessity for an item identifier: the procedural view insists that we can represent the state of a structured item, and as selection is one important operation it follows that an item must be identified before a meaningful selection can be performed.

An item in a record can be identified directly, by name. Identifying an item in a sequence is more problematic: a sequence has the 'navigational' operations of **FIRST**, **SUCCESSOR**, etc., built in. This means that item selection is implicit (i.e. is a function of the state of the computation) rather than explicit (as with records and randomly accessed arrays). This leads to the concept of a *sequence-pair* rather than a *sequence* as the basic argument of a general sequence operation, and hence to the convention that in fact a general sequence is denoted by a sequence-pair.

The absence of an identifier in the case of a Pascal set is not surprising given the context in which these sets are used.

Type heap is special in Pascal. The user is not able to define objects of type heap: one such object is automatically instantiated when a program is run. Its operations are oriented towards manipulating individual members, and its very large cardinality and the style of its use demand the very different selection methodology. The heap operations **NEW** and **DISPOSE** can be likened to the dynamic processes of creation and deletion. If the heap is used to realize a user-defined data type then this is referred to as a dynamic realization. If the realization is based on one of the other data types then it is referred to as a static realization. Ultimately the terms static and dynamic refer to the memory space allocated when a data structure is realized: if the memory space necessarily remains fixed for the lifetime of the structure then we have a static realization; if different parts of memory may be allocated at different times, and perhaps in different quantities, then we have a dynamic realization. Both static and dynamic realizations of structured types will be developed in later chapters, and the approaches compared.

4

Type sequence: *realizing user-defined structured types*

Pascal provides the mechanisms for realizing structured types specified as **RECORD**, **SET**, **FILE**, **ARRAY** or *heap*. All user-defined structured types can be realized, ultimately, in terms of these basic structured types. As with the basic Pascal types, the user is saved the arduous task of mapping his specifications right down to the level of the hardware. Once again the price to pay is the lack of total control over an eventual realization, but, as we shall see, the constraints imposed are not severe.

4.1 REALIZATIONS

The specification of **SEQUENCE** stresses a totally ordered set of items. Any realization must therefore address the issues of:

 (i) An unknown number of items in the sequence.
(ii) An ordering function.

Conceptually, the ordering function could be any arbitrary Pascal function: the ordering is then implicit. In practice, the ordering is often explicitly defined: on insertion we identify the new item's successor or predecessor. We address the explicit situation, looking at both static and dynamic realizations. First let us introduce, in Pascal, the specification section for the type we will be realizing. This we do in Listing 4.1.

4.1.1 Static realization

Although an array is of fixed length, it is at least a sequence, and so satisfies the need for an ordering function. The fixed length characteristic, however, must be 'hidden' from the user. This can be achieved by asserting that the length of the array represents an upper bound on the number of items in the sequence, and not its actual size at any instance. As computer memory is finite there must be such a bound to any realization: we are merely making it more precise (and probably lower).

```
(* SPECIFICATION FOR SEQUENCE: of ITEM
    DOMAIN
      ITEM*
    OPERATIONS
      NEW              : − ( ): SEQUENCE
      EMPTY            : − (SEQUENCE): BOOLEAN
      FIRST, LAST,
      PREDECESSOR,
      SUCCESSOR,
      DELETE           : − (SEQUENCE): SEQUENCE
      INSERT           : − (SEQUENCE, ITEM): SEQUENCE
      SELECT           : − (SEQUENCE): ITEM
    SEMANTICS
      ⟨To be discussed in the text⟩

    (* END OF SPECIFICATION FOR SEQUENCE *)
```

Listing 4.1   Specifying **SEQUENCE** in a Pascal program.

We must now identify explicitly the 'last' item in the actual sequence; we take the first item to be identified by the base of the index for the array. As an example, let us suppose that the sequence is represented by an array of items (which has base index 1 and limit index *max*) together with the item identifier (index) for 'last'. This representation is an entity with two attributes: an item array and an item identifier. This leads to the following representation for type **SEQUENCE** (assuming type **INDEX = 1 .. MAX**):

```
TYPE SEQUENCE = RECORD
                  ITEMSET: ARRAY [INDEX] OF ITEM;
                  LASTITEM: INDEX
                END;
```

In this realization we find that the **LASTITEM** in facts tells us how many items are in the sequence, as the items are 'numbered' from 1 upwards. But how is an empty sequence to be represented? Let us consider two possibilities:

Representation R1

When a sequence is not empty, **LASTITEM** will identify the last item in the sequence. A boolean attribute '**ISEMPTY**' will be added to the representation to denote whether or not a sequence is empty.

Representation R2

LASTITEM will denote the number of items in a sequence. When **LASTITEM** is not zero it will also identify the last item in the sequence; when it is zero then the 'last' item is undefined.

With R1 we are storing the two pieces of information, concerning the 'emptiness' of the list and the identification of its last element, separately. This is the 'purer' approach where one fact is represented by one data item. R2 would probably require less memory (though not necessarily–suggest why) and may well be chosen on pragmatic grounds as it also requires fewer Pascal instructions in the implementation. We will leave the implementation of R1 as an exercise and modify our sequence representation in line with the requirements of R2.

Recall that each operation on a sequence actually operates on a sequence-pair rather than a sequence. This leads us to the following representation, where **CURRENTITEM** is the item-identifier of the pair:

```
TYPE SEQUENCE = RECORD
                ITEMSET: ARRAY [1..MAX] OF ITEM;
                LASTITEM: 0..MAX;
                CURRENTITEM:⟨type to be decided⟩
                END;
```

A typical instance of a sequence (in this case with seven items) can now be visualized as

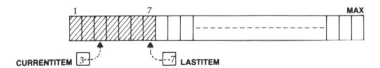

Having chosen a representation we now need to define the implementation; that is, we need to implement each of the specified operations. Let us take them in what will, with hindsight, be seen as a 'natural' order: one which forces important decisions to be made early.

NEWSEQ: – ():SEQUENCE

A sequence cannot be returned as the result of a Pascal function, so we will implement a procedure of the form

PROCEDURE NEWSEQ (VAR SEQ: SEQUENCE);

The semantics of **NEWSEQ** suggests that it should return an empty sequence. According to R2 this is represented by a **SEQUENCE** with **LASTITEM** set to 0. But what about the other fields?

The **ITEMSET** should never be accessed while the sequence is empty. It does not strictly need initializing. It can be argued that all variables should be initialized, even if this is a strictly redundant measure. The argument is based on the concept of the reliability of a system even in the presence of errors. This is a matter for a more advanced text: we will restrict ourselves, necessarily, to the most relevant issues. In short, **NEWSEQ** will not address the **ITEMSET** in our implementation.

CURRENTITEM is more of a problem. Strictly, the current item must always have a value between 1 and **MAX** when the sequence is not empty. Two pieces of information must be deducible from the specification before we can constructively proceed:

(i) What is the value of **CURRENTITEM** when the sequence is empty?
(ii) What is the value of **CURRENTITEM** before the first use of **FIRST**, **LAST**, **PREDECESSOR** and **SUCCESSOR**?

Rather than make arbitrary specification decisions now, we will delay discussion of the full static implementation of a general sequence using R2, until we have looked at special restrictions on type sequence for which the semantics are fully defined (Section 4.2). That should then give us enough insight to tackle the general case.

4.1.2 Dynamic realization

The ordering of items in the **ARRAY** representation was implied by their position in the array, that is, by the ordering of the indices which identify them. An alternative representation is one in which the identification of a **PREDECESSOR** and a **SUCCESSOR** is made explicit: that is, for each item in a sequence we explicitly store the item identifiers of the predecessor and successor items. An item in a sequence can now be depicted as

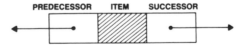

What form do the item identifiers take? In the case of arrays they are in the form of indices. If we receive items from the heap then they are in the form of pointers. We will build a sequence from elements taken from the heap, hence the term *dynamic representation*. A complete sequence can be depicted as

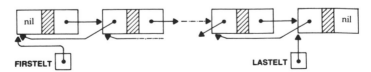

Notice that the first item has no *predecessor* (depicted by the special **nil** pointer) and the last item has no *successor*. We refer to an item together with its two associated item identifiers as an element. A sequence can be uniquely identified by **FIRSTELT** together with **LASTELT**. In actual fact, either one of these could be discarded: for example, the last element in a sequence can be identified by starting at **FIRSTELT** and repeatedly executing **SUCCESSOR** until no more successors exist.

The item identifier in a sequence-pair can itself be represented as a pointer to an element of the sequence representation. This gives us the following dynamic representation of a sequence:

```
TYPE SEQELT    = RECORD
                    DATA: ITEM;
                    PRED, SUCC:^SEQELT
                 END;
     SEQUENCE = RECORD
                    FIRSTELT, LASTELT, CURRENTELT:^SEQELT
                 END;
```

In this realization, the results of **FIRST**, **LAST**, **SUCCESSOR** and **PREDECESSOR** are all explicitly represented:

FIRST will set **CURRENTELT** to **FIRSTELT**
LAST will set **CURRENTELT** to **LASTELT**
SUCCESSOR will return the **SUCC** pointer
PREDECESSOR will return the **PRED** pointer

This is only true, of course, where the appropriate pointers are not nil. An attempt to perform a meaningless operation (for example, asking for the selection of the successor to the last element) generates what we call an *exception*: we have moved outside the world defined by the specification into 'uncharted waters'. The state which reflects a move outside the scope of the specification is called an *exception condition*. A programmer should handle these conditions by taking useful action rather than allowing the program to behave in a random (unspecified) manner. We will document exception conditions in the operations which can cause them. The best way to handle an exception depends upon the context in which the data structure is being used, so we will only address *exception handling* in general terms. Software engineering courses would address it in detail.

Procedure **INSERT** uses the **NEW** operation on the heap to obtain a new **SEQELT** object, which can then be inserted into the sequence by suitably adjusting the pointers. Once again, a discussion of the details of the implementation is delayed until we have presented the more fully specified restrictions of type sequence and developed their (simpler) realizations.

4.2 SOME IMPORTANT RESTRICTIONS

A sequence is a very general structure, with operations for:

- Identifying any constituent item, thus allowing its selection.
- Inserting a new item at any position.
- Deleting any of the items, in any order.

This generality is not always required, so restriction may be placed on the type. This would result in a new specification and hence a new type. The new type will be called a *restriction* of the old type. Restrictions may be achieved by

c1) Restricting the generality of one of the existing operations.
c2) Excluding an operation completely (an extreme form of c1).
c3) Limiting the domain of the type, that is only allowing a restricted set of sequences to be built.

We have already looked at Pascal files and arrays. A Pascal file has the following restrictions on a sequence:

c1) Insert must be at the end of a sequence.
c2) The following operations are absent:

> **LAST**
> **PREDECESSOR**
> **DELETE**

c3) There are no restrictions of this kind.

For a Pascal array the restrictions are as follows:

c1, c2) **INSERT** and **DELETE** are replaced by the weaker operation which substitutes one item for another (element assignment).
c3)   Only sequences of a given length are represented.

Three further restrictions are common and so worthy of note. Each is dealt with separately, first by specifying it and then by considering both static and dynamic realizations of it.

4.2.1 Type *stack*

The *stack* data type places the following restrictions on type sequence:

c1)   Insert must be at the end. **SELECT** always selects the *last* item.
c2)   **SUCCESSOR**, **FIRST** and **LAST** are not available.
c1, c2) **PREDECESSOR** and **DELETE** are replaced by one instruction.
c3)   No restrictions in this category.

These are the formal restrictions on type sequence which result in the new type stack, but what are their implications? Before formally specifying type stack we introduce its characteristics informally.

(a) Informal introduction to type stack

A stack is so named because it reflects the kinds of restrictions imposed in everyday life when one is confronted with a stack of objects. One restriction is that one may not attempt to take the item which is at the bottom (the *first* item in sequence notation: it was the first to be placed in the stack). Items can be added to the top of the stack (the end of the sequence) and removed from the top. It is easy to see that the last item placed on the stack must be the first to be removed. For this reason a stack is sometimes referred to as an LIFO data structure, this being an acronym for Last In First Out.

As this real-life model of a stack is so impressed in people's minds, it has become normal practice to adopt the terminology of 'top' and 'bottom' instead of the sequence terminology which it would otherwise inherit.

The operations on a stack take their name from a slightly different model: one typified by a coin-holder. A coin-holder holds a stack of coins, with only the top coin accessible: the rest are hidden in a plastic tube. To insert a coin one *pushes* the other coins down, thus putting the new coin on the top. When removing a coin, the spring at the bottom of the tube forces the other coins to *pop* up. Hence, **INSERT** is in fact called **PUSH** and the combined operation of **PREDECESSOR** and **DELETE** is called **POP**. Finally, we have mentioned the restriction that **SELECT** always selects the *last* item in the *stack*, that is the *top* item. Operation **SELECT** is therefore called, by convention, **TOP**.

We are now in a position to specify type **STACK**. To be precise, we will specify a **STACK** of **ITEM**s, where type **ITEM** is assumed to have already been defined (see Fig. 4.1).

(b) Using a stack

There are many uses of stacks in computer science, hence the need to specify the type. It finds application in memory management, the implementation of procedures and the analysis of expressions by a compiler, to name but a few areas. Of these, the implementation of procedures is the most straightforward example. When a procedure is called, the return address can be pushed onto a stack (**ITEM** must have been declared of type *address* in this case). If a procedure calls a further procedure then a new return address is pushed onto the stack, and so on. When the end of a procedure is reached, the address of the

```
                        Specification for STACK
    Domain
        ITEM*
    Operations
        NEWSTACK : – ():STACK
        EMPTY       : – (STACK):BOOLEAN
        PUSH        : – (STACK, ITEM):STACK
        POP         : – (STACK):STACK
        TOP         : – (STACK):ITEM
    Semantics
        As discussed in the text. A formal semantic definition
        will be given in Chapter 5.
```

Figure 4.1 Specifying type **STACK**.

instruction to return to can simply be accessed as the **TOP** of the stack. On return to this address a **POP** must be executed. This particular implementation of procedure returns can quite naturally deal with recursion.

(c) A static realization

The restrictions imposed in the definition of a stack significantly simplify its realization. In particular, only one end of the stack (the top) is active: the *bottom* is inactive and so can be 'anchored' in memory. If we choose to use an array to store the elements of a stack then we can assert that, if it exists, the bottom element of the stack is always located by the base index of the array. Let us define, as with a general sequence,

    ITEMSET: ARRAY [1..MAX] OF ITEM;

then **ITEMSET[1]** will always contain the bottom item of the stack, if one exists. The top of the stack must be identified by its index, but this also identifies the current item (see *sequence*). We therefore need only **TOPITEM**, which will take the place of both **CURRENTITEM** and **LASTITEM**:

    TOPITEM: 0..MAX

(we are using representation R2 as the basis for our realization). We therefore represent a stack as

    TYPE STACK = RECORD
                    ITEMSET:ARRAY [1..MAX] OF ITEM;
                    TOPITEM: 0..MAX
                END;

An empty stack will have **TOPITEM** equal to 0. A non-empty stack can be represented as:

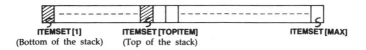

ITEMSET [1]   ITEMSET [TOPITEM]   ITEMSET [MAX]
(Bottom of the stack)   (Top of the stack)

It is not hard to catalogue the exceptions which can occur with this representation. We list them below, giving each a name and a summary of details.

Overflow

A stack as represented above can never contain more than **MAX** items. An attempt to store more than **MAX** items will lead to an exception condition. We note two things about this exception:

(i) It can only be caused by a **PUSH** operation, and so it must be detected in the code which implements **PUSH**.

(ii) It does *not* reflect a user mistake; the problem is due entirely to the limitations of the chosen representation. The user has not misinterpreted the specification and thereby misused the stack: his program may be perfectly correct but uses more memory than has been allocated for the stack. It is important to distinguish between misuse of a data structure and exceeding the limits of a given implementation.

Underflow

If a stack is empty it makes no sense to remove an item from it. An attempt to remove an item from an empty stack will lead to an exception condition. As before, we note two aspects of this exception:

(i) It can only be caused by a **POP** operation, and so it must be detected in the code which implements **POP**.

(ii) It *does* reflect a user mistake. There is no limitation of the system reflected here: it is a misuse of the stack and must be treated as such. In particular, the user should almost certainly be warned of this misuse.

Undefined

This exception refers to an attempt to select the top item of an empty stack: obviously there is no such item defined. We can therefore note:

(i) It can only be caused by a **TOP** operation, and so it must be detected in the code which implements **TOP**.

(ii) It *does* reflect a user mistake, so should be treated in a similar way to *underflow*.

In the chosen implementation we make the following concessions to Pascal:

● Operations **NEWSTACK**, **PUSH** and **POP** each return a **STACK** value. Therefore, they are implemented as procedures with var parameters. If we adopt the convention that var parameters are underscored then we can respecify these in the form

NEWSTACK (STACK)
PUSH (STACK, ITEM)
POP (STACK)

● For contrast we take **ITEM** to be defined as **CHAR**, so that **TOP** can be implemented as a function. (It may sometimes be necessary to define **STACK** examples with

TOP (STACK, ITEM)

We are now in a position to study the static implementation of a **STACK** data type given in Listing 4.2. The code is simple enough to be self-explanatory, but is it correct? How do we know we have implemented type **STACK** faithfully? This question needs very careful phrasing before we can even begin to tackle it, so we will delay any answers until we have brought some formality into our discussions. This we do in Chapter 5.

Although the code is simple it nevertheless has been documented. Apart from the documentation for a complete program (which will include all type specifications as well as general comments about structure and use) we should also incorporate comments in the code itself. These are for the guidance of those who one day may have to understand and 'maintain' the code. Anyone who has written a significant piece of code and then come back to it after some time will

```
(* Implementation of type STACK *)

Procedure Newstack(var s:Stack);
```

Listing 4.2 A static implementation of type **STACK**.

```
(* Initialise s to the empty stack *)

  begin
    s.topitem:=0
  end;

Function Empty(s:Stack):Boolean;

(* Return true if stack is empty, false otherwise *)

  begin
    Empty:=(s.topitem=0)
  end;


Procedure Push(var s:Stack;i:Item);

(* Place item i on top of stack s.
   Exception: overflow; s is full *)

  begin
    with s do
      if topitem<max
        then                       (* s is not full *)
          begin
            topitem:=topitem+1;    (* increment top *)
            itemset[topitem]:=i    (* deposit i *)
          end
        else                       (* s is full *)
          Report(overflow)         (* raise exception *)
  end;


Procedure Pop(var s:Stack);

(* Remove the top item from s.
   Exception: underflow; s is empty *)

  begin
    with s do
      if topitem>0
        then                       (* s is not empty *)
          topitem:=topitem-1       (* remove top item *)
        else                       (* s is empty *)
          Report(underflow)        (* raise exception *)
  end;

Function Top(s:Stack):Item;

(* Return the top item on s.
   Exception: undefined; s is empty *)

  begin
    with s do
      if topitem>0
        then                       (* s is not empty *)
          Top:=itemset[topitem]    (* return top item *)
        else                       (* s is empty *)
          Report(undefined)        (* raise exception *)
  end;
  (* end of implementation of STACK *)
```

realize how essential their documentation has become. It is even more important when maintaining codes written by other people.

We have adopted certain conventions for all codes presented in this book. It is not pertinent to discuss documentation in any serious way here, as this is not meant to be in any way a definitive guide to documentation; it is no more than an explanation of the style adopted:

- All comments are succinct.
- At the head of each procedure and function body we include, where appropriate:
    A general comment on what it does.
    A description of the arguments.
    A list of the exception conditions, with their meaning.
    Which other procedures/functions are called.
- Comments for imperative codes are imperative.
- Comments on the branches of conditions are descriptive.

In general, comments will be at a 'higher level' than the code itself, and so will not refer to it explicitly.

(d) A dynamic realization

The fact that only one end of a stack is active also simplifies the dynamic realization of this sequence restriction. At no time will any element except the last (top) be accessed: successor is a redundant concept and **SUCC** can be removed from **SEQELT** in the representation. As with the static representation, **FIRSTELT** and **CURRENTELT** are identified – we will refer simply to the top element – and **LASTELT** can be removed. Stack is now represented by the top element only (a pointer) and so a record is no longer required. This results in the following definitions:

```
TYPE STACKELT = RECORD
                    DATA: ITEM;
                    PRED:^STACKELT
                END;
     STACK    = ^STACKELT;
```

An empty stack will be represented by the nil pointer. A non-empty stack can be represented as:

All but one of the comments made concerning exception conditions with reference to the static case are true also in the dynamic realization.

The difference concerns the *overflow* exception: there is no arbitrary user-defined restriction made on the size of a stack. The *overflow* exception occurs only if the Pascal heap overflows, that is if insufficient space has been allocated for the whole program. The advantage of this can be seen when we declare several active stacks in a program. In the static representation, a stack will cause overflow if its allocated memory space is inadequate for the task in hand. There may well be several other stacks which have space allocated, but unused. In the dynamic representation, *overflow* will only be signalled if all available heap space has been utilized: in this case memory is truly full, and each stack is only holding the exact amount of memory space it requires.

As a stack is represented by a pointer variable, which is a simple type in Pascal, no concessions need be made in the implementation of a stack of **CHAR**. In particular, if function notation is used in the specification then we can use it in the implementation which follows. We choose, however, to adopt the same conventions as we were required to adopt in the static case. The reasons for this will be discussed fully in Chapter 5. In short, we are trying to make the stack look the same, as far as the rest of the program is concerned, whether we use a static, dynamic or hybrid representation. We therefore develop the dynamic implementation of a stack shown in Listing 4.3. The *overflow* condition has disappeared from the code: it has in fact been incorporated in a lower level, the implementation of the heap (see Chapter 6).

```
(* Implementation of type STACK *)

Procedure Newstack(var s:Stack);

(* Initialise s to the empty stack *)

  begin
    s:=nil
  end;

Function Empty(s:Stack):Boolean;

(* Return true if stack is empty, false otherwise *)

  begin
    Empty:=(s=nil)
  end;

Procedure Push(var s:Stack;i:Item);

(* Place item i on top of stack s. *)
```

Listing 4.3 A dynamic implementation of type **STACK**.

```
var
      temp:Stack;                    (* for new top element *)
   begin
     New(temp);
     with temp^ do
       begin
         data:=i;                    (* insert item i *)
         pred:=s                     (* with predecessor top of s *)
       end;
       s:=temp                       (* make temp the top of s *)
   end;

Procedure Pop(var s:Stack);

(* Remove the top item from s.
   Exception: underflow; s is empty *)

   var
        temp:Stack;
   begin
     if s<>nil
       then                          (* top elt exists: remove it *)
         begin
           temp:=s;                  (* temp refers to top of s *)
           s:=s^.pred;               (* remove temp from s *)
           Dispose(temp)             (* return it to the heap *)
         end
       else                          (* stack is empty *)
         Report(underflow)           (* raise exception *)
   end;

Function Top(s:Stack):Item;

(* Return the top item on s.
   Exception: undefined; s is empty *)

   begin
     if s<>nil
       then                          (* item exists *)
         Top:=s^.data                (* return its value *)
       else                          (* s is empty *)
         Report(undefined)           (* raise exception *)
   end;

(* end of implementation of STACK *)
```

4.2.2 Type *queue*

The **QUEUE** data type places the following restrictions on type sequence:

c1⟩ Inserts must be at the end. **SELECT** always selects the *first* item.
c2⟩ **PREDECESSOR**, **FIRST** and **LAST** are unavailable.
c3⟩ **SUCCESSOR** and **DELETE** are combined in one operation.

What are the implications of these restrictions on a sequence?

(a) Informal introduction to type queue

A queue is so named because it reflects the behaviour exhibited by a (disciplined) queue of people. The first person to enter the queue is the first to be served, and new additions to the queue join at the rear. A queue is therefore sometimes referred to as an FIFO data structure: First In First Out.

Once again, terminology is inherited from real-life queues rather than the sequence type, so we will refer to the **FRONT** and **REAR** of a queue in place of **FIRST** and **LAST**, respectively. Further, the operation to insert a new item is referred to as **JOIN** and the operation for **SUCCESSOR** combined with **DELETE** is termed **LEAVE**. Finally, the restriction that **SELECT** should always return the item at the front of a queue leads us to call this operation **FRONTITEM**.

We can now specify a **QUEUE** of **ITEM**s, in a similar manner as for type **STACK** (see Fig. 4.2).

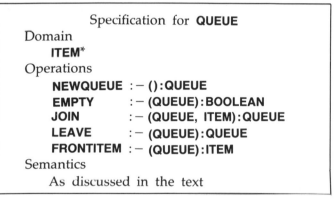

Figure 4.2   Specifying type **QUEUE**.

(b) Using a queue

Queues occupy the same role in computer science as they do in real life: they are useful structures for coordinating access to resources. In particular, queue items may represent processes. The queue itself is used in order to allow several processes to access a resource in a fair and ordered manner: first come first served. This may not always be the best way to organize the requests to use a resource (for example, a disk unit in a multiprogrammed environment) but in the absence of any other knowledge about a resource, it is a useful default. Another common occurrence of the queue data structure is in computer networks: these networks carry many 'packets' of information. These packets are stored in a queue at each node in the network, and 'forwarded' when a communication line is free. Again, in the absence of some knowledge of the importance of a particular packet, the queue is a fair and acceptable storage structure.

(c) A static realization

As with type **STACK**, let us assume that we are representing a **QUEUE** by

ITEMSET: ARRAY [1..MAX] OF ITEM;

Unlike a stack, a queue has no fixed end: we add elements to the rear and delete elements from the front. After five items have joined the queue and two items have left, the queue we are realizing will be represented as follows:

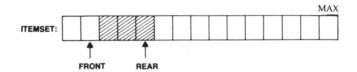

We have decided, merely as a convention, that *front* will contain an index one before the current front item in the queue. *Rear* will contain the index of the rear item of the queue. Hence, when the queue is empty, we have

FRONT = REAR

and the number of items in the queue at any given time is

REAR − FRONT

One important point should be noted about this realization: as items join the queue and others leave, the queue inexorably 'creeps' along **ITEMSET**. Eventually, **REAR** will hit **MAX** and a queue with less than **MAX** items will effectively have *overflowed*. There are two ways in which this can be remedied.

Remedy 1

If **FRONT = REAR** at any time (i.e. the queue becomes empty) then set **FRONT** and **REAR** to 0.

If **REAR** has the value **MAX** and a **JOIN** is requested, then move the queue back to the boundary of **ITEMSET**: the **FRONT** item is copied to **ITEMSET[1]**, the next to **ITEMSET[2]**, etc. This is obviously an expensive operation.

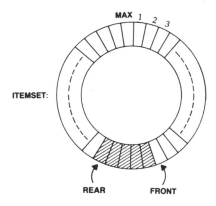

Figure 4.3 Realizing a queue using wrap-around.

Remedy 2

A less obvious, but more efficient implementation makes the representation circular: **ITEMSET[1]** is assumed to follow **ITEMSET[MAX]**. The queue can then 'chase its tail' around **ITEMSET**, with no copying necessary. This representation can be depicted as shown in Fig. 4.3.

In this representation, it is still the case that a queue is empty when

FRONT = REAR

but the number of items in the queue is now

REAR − FRONT   if **REAR > FRONT**
MAX + REAR − FRONT   otherwise

We adopt remedy 2, and hence the circular representation for a queue. In so doing we also adopt one minor problem, which we now consider. What is the interpretation of a queue represented by **ITEMSET** with **FRONT = REAR**? We know one interpretation: the queue is empty. Unfortunately there is another: the queue is **FULL**. Before we fully realize type **QUEUE** this ambiguity must be resolved. We could resolve it by explicitly representing the condition in a new attribute of queue:

STATE: (EMPTY, NORMAL, FULL)

but instead we adopt the convention that *overflow* will be signalled if a **JOIN** operation would result in **FRONT = REAR**. By calling *overflow* 'one item early' we resolve the ambiguity at the expense of being able to represent queues of size up to **MAX−1** only. We can now assert the following representation of a queue.

```
TYPE QUEUE = RECORD
              ITEMSET: ARRAY [1..MAX] OF ITEM;
              FRONT, REAR: 1..MAX
          END;
```

An empty queue will have **FRONT** = **REAR**. However, the front item is always in the next element to that indicated by **FRONT**. Assuming that we want the very first item to go into **ITEMSET[1]** (this is an arbitrary decision) we set **FRONT** to **MAX** for a new queue.

In the implementation of Listing 4.4 we make similar concessions to Pascal to those we made for **STACK**. We also assume again that **ITEM** is defined as **CHAR**. Hence we have

NEWQUEUE (QUEUE)
JOIN (QUEUE, ITEM)
LEAVE (QUEUE)

The exceptions are also similar, so we make only the following comments:

Overflow

An attempt to queue more than **MAX** − **1** items will lead to this exception. It can only be caused by **JOIN** and reflects a limitation of the representation rather than a user error.

```
(* Implementation of type QUEUE *)

Procedure Newqueue(var q:Queue);

(* Initialise q to the empty queue *)

   begin
     with q do
       begin
         front:=max;                    (* arbitrary *)
         rear:=max                      (* front=rear *)
       end
   end;

Function Empty(q:Queue):Boolean;

(* Return true if queue is empty, false otherwise *)

   begin
     with q do
       Empty:=(front=rear)
   end;
```

Listing 4.4 A static implementation of type **QUEUE**.

```
Procedure Join(var q:Queue;i:Item);

(* Join item i to queue q.
   Exception: overflow; q is full *)

  begin
    with q do
      begin
        if rear<>max              (* not at limit? *)
          then rear:=rear+1       (* increment rear *)
          else rear:=1;           (* circularity *)
        if rear<>front            (* queue not full *)
          then itemset[rear]:=i   (* join i to q *)
          else Report(overflow)   (* raise exception *)
      end
  end;

Procedure Leave(var q:Queue);

(* Remove the front item from q.
   Exception: underflow; q is empty *)

  begin
    if not empty(q)
      then                        (* front item exists: remove it *)
        with q do
          if front<>max           (* not at limit? *)
            then front:=front+1   (* increment front *)
            else front:=1         (* circularity *)
      else                        (* q is empty *)
        Report(underflow)         (* raise exception *)
  end;

Function Frontitem(q:Queue):Item;

(* Return the value of the front item of q.
   Exception: undefined; q is empty *)

  var
      f:1..max;                   (* index of front item of q *)
  begin
    if not Empty(q)
      then                        (* front item exists: return it *)
        with q do
          begin
            f:=front;             (* f indexes prior to true front *)
            (* increment f to index true front *)
            if f<>max
              then f:=f+1
              else f:=1;          (* circularity *)
            frontitem:=itemset[f]
          end
      else                        (* q is empty: error *)
        Report(undefined)         (* raise exception *)
  end;

(* end of implementation of QUEUE *)
```

Underflow

This can only be caused by **LEAVE**. The comments made earlier concerning stack underflow are also pertinent.

Undefined

This can only be caused by **FRONTITEM**. The comments made earlier concerning this exception are also pertinent.

We make one further comment about the style of programming adopted throughout the text. Whenever an 'unusual' condition needs to be catered for, we place the 'normal' condition code first. Hence, the increment code for **FRONT** and **REAR** appears before the 'unusual' circularity option in each case. Also, the code for non-exceptional cases always precedes that for exceptions. If this convention is not adopted then a person reading the code must browse through, in a complicated case, many lines of code catering for exceptional circumstances before he can see what normally happens.

(d) A dynamic realization

Predecessor is a redundant concept with queues, so we can remove **PRED** from the representation for a general sequence. A queue will therefore be represented as a linked list of elements which are very similar to those for **STACK**:

```
TYPE QUEUELT = RECORD
                  DATA:ITEM;
                  SUCC:^QUEUELT
               END;
```

As both ends of the queue are active we keep both *firstelt* and *lastelt* (we call them **FRONT** and **REAR**) in the representation of a **QUEUE**. *Currentelt*, however, is identified with **FRONT** and so can be dropped. This leads us to the representation

```
QUEUE = RECORD
           FRONT, REAR:^QUEUELT
        END;
```

A typical queue will now appear as

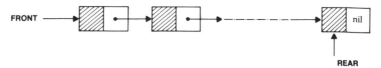

How will an empty queue be represented? As **FRONT** identifies the front element and **REAR** identifies the rear element, we must represent an empty queue by

FRONT = NIL
REAR = NIL

Only in the case of an empty queue will either of these be nil, so the test for **Empty** can simply check

FRONT = NIL

Before presenting a complete implementation, we develop the code for operation **JOIN**. We will see that inserting an item into an empty queue is a special case, for which we need to cater in a succinct manner.

Consider a non-empty queue of the form discussed above:

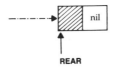

To add a further item we need to create a new queue element, chain it on as the successor of the current **REAR** element and then identify it as the new **REAR** element. We depict this sequence of operations in Fig. 4.4.

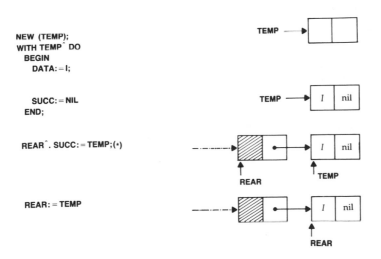

Figure 4.4 Joining an item to a queue: dynamic realization.

What happens if the queue is initially empty? In this case we wish to achieve.

The implementation above achieves this except in one detail: line (*) would attempt to link the new element as the successor of a non-existent rear element, instead of simply making it the front of the queue. This implies replacing line (*) by the line

FRONT : = **TEMP**

when the queue is empty. The implementation is therefore modified by including the following in place of (*):

IF the queue is not empty
    THEN REAR^. SUCC: = **TEMP** (* chain it at the rear *)
    ELSE FRONT: = **TEMP**   (* becomes the front element *)

We are now in a position to present a dynamic implementation of type **QUEUE**. This we do in Listing 4.5.

```
(* Implementation of type QUEUE *)

Procedure Newqueue(var q:Queue);

(* Initialise q to the empty queue *)

  begin
    with q do
      begin
        front:=nil;
        rear:=nil
      end
  end;

Function Empty(q:Queue):Boolean;

(* Return true if queue is empty, false otherwise *)

  begin
    Empty:=(q.front=nil)
  end;

Procedure Join(var q:Queue;i:Item);
```

Listing 4.5 A dynamic implementation of type **QUEUE**.

```
(* Join item i to queue q.
   Exception: overflow; q is full *)


   var
        temp:Qptr;                      (* for new rear elt *)
   begin
     New(temp);
     with temp^ do
       begin
         data:=i;                       (* insert item i *)
         succ:=nil                      (* with no successors *)
       end;
     if not Empty(q)
       then                             (* chain new element at the rear *)
         q.rear^.succ:=temp
       else                             (* or as front elt if q empty *)
         q.front:=temp;
     q.rear:=temp                       (* set new rear elt *)
   end;


Procedure Leave(var q:Queue);

(* Remove the front item from q.
   Exception: underflow; q is empty *)

   var
        temp:Qptr;                      (* to remove front elt *)
   begin
     if not empty(q)
       then                             (* front item exists: remove it *)
         with q do
           begin
             temp:=front;               (* temp is front of q *)
             front:=front^.succ;        (* remove this elt *)
             if front=nil               (* q now empty? *)
               then rear:=nil;          (* yes: reset rear *)
             Dispose(temp)
           end
       else                             (* q is empty *)
         Report(underflow)              (* raise exception *)
   end;

Function Frontitem(q:Queue):Item;

(* Return the value of the front item of q.
   Exception: undefined; q is empty *)

   begin
     if not Empty(q)
       then                             (* front item exists *)
         Frontitem:=q.front^.data       (* return it *)
       else                             (* q is empty: error *)
         Report(undefined)              (* raise exception *)
   end;

(* end of implementation of QUEUE *)
```

Note that the special case of an empty queue is reflected in the **LEAVE** code also: if the resulting queue is empty we must retrieve consistency by setting **REAR** to **NIL**. If this were not done, we would have **REAR** containing an unspecified identifier (the element it identified would have been returned to the heap). We could equally well have written

IF FRONT = NIL   (* **QUEUE is now empty?** *)
    THEN NEWQUEUE (Q) (* **yes reset it** *)

This is slightly less efficient, but one could argue that it is precise.

4.2.3 Type *deque*

The *deque* data type (Double Ended QUEue) places the following restrictions on type sequence:

c1⟩   Inserts must be at an end. **SELECT** must select either the first or last item.

c1, c2⟩ *Successor* and *delete* form one operation; *Predecessor* and *delete* form one operation.

(a) Informal introduction to type deque

All accesses on a deque must be at one end or the other, but this is the only restriction on a general sequence. The deque is, in fact, a fairly general data type (see Section 4.3). The restriction on access is strict enough to make implementation straightforward though less simple than for stack or queue. We specify deque in Fig. 4.5, and then discuss its operations with the idea of developing a suitable realization.

Specification for **DEQUE**
Domain
   ITEM*
Operations
   NEWDEQUE   : − ():DEQUE
   EMPTY   : − (DEQUE): BOOLEAN
   FIRST, LAST   : − (DEQUE):ITEM
   REMOVEFIRST, REMOVELAST : − (DEQUE):DEQUE
   NEWFIRST, NEWLAST   : − (DEQUE, ITEM):DEQUE
Semantics
   To be discussed in the text

Figure 4.5 Specifying the **DEQUE** data type.

As selection must take place at one end or the other, we introduce operations **FIRST** and **LAST**. **FIRST** (**LAST**) is equivalent to identifying the first (last) element and then selecting it. Insertions are performed by **NEWFIRST** (insert an item at the front) and **NEWLAST** (insert an item at the rear). **REMOVEFIRST** (**REMOVELAST**) will remove an item from the front (rear) of a deque.

(b) A static realization

Both ends of a deque are active, so our realization will be based on a similar representation to that used for a queue. A deque can migrate in either direction in memory, so the circularity condition must be strengthened. Note, in particular, that **FRONT** and **REAR** may be decremented (in operations **REMOVELAST** and **NEWFIRST**) as well as incremented (in operations **REMOVEFIRST** and **NEWLAST**). On decrementing we need to assert that

$$1 - 1 = max$$

to maintain the circularity. The implementation is now straightforward and we leave it as an exercise.

(c) A dynamic realization

Both predecessor and successor are necessary concepts for deques, suggesting that each element in a dynamic realization needs two element identifiers rather than one: in other words the deque elements, it appears, require the same representation as general sequence elements (see Subsection 4.1.2). If we attempt to release a deque using the dynamic queue representation we run into a problem with the implementation of operation **REMOVELAST**. Consider the example deque

To remove the last element we need to set **REAR** to identify element X in the diagram. The way the deque is constructed, this element (the predecessor of **REAR**) can only be identified by starting X at **FRONT** and repeatedly taking **SUCCESSOR** until the successor of X is **REAR**. It can be done, but it is inefficient. In fact, it is the only inefficient deque operation on this representation, but if it is frequently used then we may decide this is unacceptable (see Section 5.1).

We return to the general sequence representation of elements, and make the following definitions:

TYPE DEQUELT = RECORD
                            DATA: ITEM;
                            PRED, SUCC:^DEQUELT
                      END;
      DEQUE   = RECORD
                            FIRST, LAST:^DEQUELT
                      END;

We have what is referred to as a doubly linked list. As can be seen from the following example, such a list is now symmetrical and all operations can be performed efficiently:

    FRONT   REAR

An implementation of **NEWLAST** will suffice to indicate the use of double-linked representations (see Listing 4.6). The code should be compared with procedure **JOIN** in the implementation of a queue.

```
Procedure Newlast(var d:Deque;i:Item);

(* Join item i to front of deque d.
   Exception: overflow; d is full *)

   var
        temp:Deqptr;              (* for new last elt *)
   begin
     New(temp);
     with temp^ do
       begin
         data:=i;                 (* insert item i *)
         pred:=d.rear;            (* new predecessor to last *)
         succ:=nil                (* no successors *)
       end;
     if not Empty(d)
        then                      (* chain new element as the last *)
           d.rear^.succ:=temp
        else                      (* or as front elt if q empty *)
           d.front:=temp;
        d.rear:=temp              (* set new last elt *)
   end;
```

Listing 4.6   Adding an item to the rear of a deque.

4.3 **TYPE HIERARCHIES**

Each of the types introduced in Section 4.2 is a restriction of type sequence.

We can represent this fact as a hierarchy, with sequence at the top as it is the most general of the types:

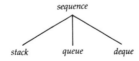

We can refine this diagram by considering type *deque* in a little more detail, in particular by considering type c2 restrictions of *deque*.

Restriction 1

Remove operations

> *first*
> *removefirst*
> *newfirst*

This results in a type for which all activity is at one end: the rear. It is, in fact, an LIFO data structure or *stack*.

Restriction 2

Remove operations

> *last*
> *removelast*
> *newfirst*

This restriction is the FIFO data structure, *queue*.

Restriction 3

Remove operations

> *removelast*
> *last*

This results in an Output Restricted deque (*ordeque*). The interesting aspect to this type is that an efficient implementation, using the same representation as for *queue*, can be developed: the troublesome operation *removelast* is not required.

If we include these facts, our hierarchy now appears as:

There are two further restrictions of type *deque* which we may wish to consider: one is a practical restriction, the other merely a theoretical issue.

Restriction 4

Remove operation

    newfirst

This is termed an Input Restricted deque (*irdeque*). It suffers from the same implementation problem as a deque: it needs a doubly linked dynamic representation if all operations are to be efficient.

Restriction 5

Remove all operations.

Such a restriction is as severe as one can impose and results in, by definition, an unusable type. It is useful only in a type diagram – which is now a lattice. It is the lattice *bottom* ($\perp$):

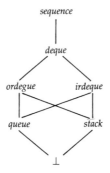

The diagram tells us that any algorithm written to operate on a type, say T, can also operate on any type S which is superior in the hierarchy. Hence, any algorithm which manipulates a *queue* can be written to operate equally well on a *deque,* but not necessarily on a *stack.* We return to this aspect when we briefly consider generic programming in Section 5.4.

4.4 TYPE *sequence* REVISITED

We transferred our attention from the general sequence data structure to the more restricted examples because of the lack of precise definition of certain key features. In particular, we had not specified the semantics of **INSERT** and **DELETE**, or fully specified which item is identified under given conditions. These specifications are complete for the restrictions defined in Section 4.2, which is why we were able to consider implementations.

There are many ways in which our specification of a sequence can proceed: an item may be inserted as the predecessor or successor of the current item; the sequence resulting from an insert may identify the newly inserted item or the same item as prior to the insertion; delete may delete the current item, its predecessor or its successor and so on. Each of these options will probably have been taken by system specifiers at some time. The most common general sequence data structure in use is the text editor: all systems have one, but all too few systems use the same specification of sequence. Rather than arbitrarily making a choice of semantics we discuss the implications, for the various realizations, of certain choices.

4.4.1 Static realization

The ordering of items in a sequence is implied by their position in an array which represents it. We have seen that this constraint is of little consequence when only the 'ends' of a sequence are active, but when arbitrary changes can be made to a sequence, the implicit constraint is too severe. In practical terms, when an item is inserted between two sequence elements we are redefining the sequence ordering and so must reorganize memory to reflect this: items must be moved to make room for the new item. If we choose to insert an item as the predecessor of the current item (a choice of semantics) and successor items are moved to make way for it (a choice of implementation) then we arrive at an insertion algorithm of the form shown in Listing 4.7. Note that the newly inserted item also becomes the current item (a choice of semantics).

If we make the convention that an empty sequence is represented by

LASTITEM = **0**
CURRENTITEM = **1**

```
Procedure Insert(var seq:Sequence;i:Item);

(* Place item i as the predecessor of current of seq.
   The new item becomes the current of seq.
   Exception: overflow; seq is full *)

   var
        this:1..max;                    (* item identifier within seq *)
   begin
     with seq do
       if lastitem<max
         then                           (* seq is not full *)
           if not Empty(seq)
             then
               begin
                 for this:= lastitem downto currentitem do
                   itemset[this+1]:=itemset[this];(* move this item *)
                 itemset[currentitem]:=i;          (* insert new item as current *)
                 lastitem:=lastitem+1
               end
             else                       (* i is the only item hence last item *)
               begin
                 itemset[1]:=i;
                 currentitem:=1;
                 lastitem:=1
               end
         else                           (* s is full *)
           Report(overflow)             (* raise exception *)
   end;
```

Listing 4.7   Insertion in a sequence.

then the case of an empty sequence ceases to be special, and the code can be simplified accordingly (see the listing).

Deletion can also be achieved by moving items in memory. This can be an expensive operation, so a variation on the implementation can be used. It involves the use of 'null' items: when an item is deleted it is merely replaced by a null value. If, for example, the sequence contains text characters, then any of the non-printing 'special' characters (including ASCII null) could be used. This complicates the implementation of the other operations, but does have the advantage of postponing the movement of items until a later time (for example, when the array is clogged with nulls). At such a time, a single 'pass' over the array, moving items down in memory as we proceed, can remove all nulls (a process known as compaction). The postponement and grouping of expensive reorganizations in this manner is an option which must be considered when a chosen implementation is performing unacceptably. Modifying an implementation or changing a representation to respond to poor performance statistics is a process known as *tuning*. This process is discussed in Section 5.1.

4.4.2 Dynamic realization: Singly linked

In the single-link representation of sequence elements we have

```
TYPE SEQELT = RECORD
                DATA: ITEM;
                SUCC:^SEQELT
              END;
```

The predecessor operation is not explicitly catered for and becomes expensive, so this is very much a representation for algorithms which process the sequence primarily from first to last (a common situation).

(a) Insertion

(i) Insert an item as the successor of the current item

This is a straightforward operation, similar in nature to the **JOIN** operation on a queue. The difference is that the new item will have the successor to the current item as its successor, as opposed to having no successor. If we temporarily ignore the case in which the sequence, **SEQ**, is empty we arrive at Fig. 4.6. If we wish the newly inserted item to become the current item, we must add

SEQ.CURRENTELT : = **TEMP**

The alteration needed to accommodate the case of an initially empty sequence is left as an exercise.

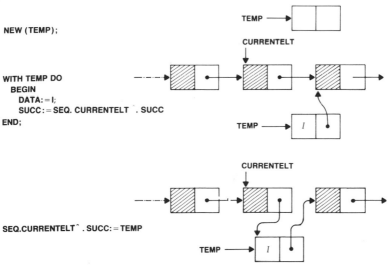

Figure 4.6 Inserting a new successor item in a sequence.

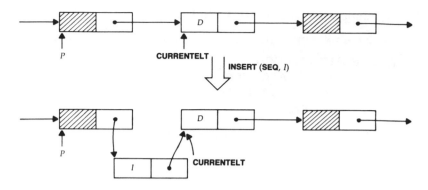

Figure 4.7   Inserting a new predecessor item: conceptual.

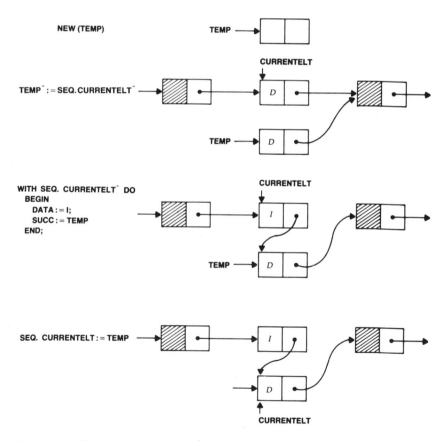

Figure 4.8   Inserting a new predecessor item: actual.

(ii) Insert an item as the predecessor of the current item, which remains the current item

This is definitely not a straightforward operation. We are effectively giving the item which is the predecessor of the current item (call it *P*) a new successor (Fig. 4.7).

The problem is: how do we identify *P*?

Solution 1. Start from the **FIRSTELT** of **SEQ** and repeatedly take the successor until the successor is **CURRENTELT**. The time taken will depend on the position of **CURRENTELT** in the sequence.

Solution 2. Insert an element as the successor of **CURRENTELT** (as in (i) above). Copy the item from the current element (i.e. *D*) into this new element. Copy *I* into the current element. Finally, make the new element the current element (Fig. 4.8).

Once again, the special case of the empty sequence is left as an exercise.

(b) Deletion

(i) Delete the successor item to the current item

This specification is the simplest to implement on the singly linked realization. If such an item exists, we need only one instruction in Pascal to achieve the result: two further instructions are required to ensure the return of the freed element to the heap:

```
WITH SEQ DO
  BEGIN
    TEMP: = CURRENTELT^. SUCC;          (*identify elt to dispose*)
    CURRENTELT^.SUCC: = TEMP^. SUCC;    (*remove elt from SEQ *)
    DISPOSE (TEMP)                      (*return it to heap*)
  END
```

If there is no successor we can specify either of two possible outcomes: an exception condition is generated or no action is taken. The latter is perfectly acceptable in the text-editor systems mentioned (except that a 'side effect' may be induced to notify the user, for example a 'bleep' on the terminal: as far as the state of the system is concerned, nothing has happened).

(ii) Delete the current item

This operation in many respects mirrors the problems encountered with (a)(ii) above. Basically, we need to be able to give the predecessor element a new successor. The two solutions mentioned in (a) have parallels in the deletion case.

Solution 1. Start from **FIRSTELT** and follow **SUCC** links. Having found the predecessor we perform a delete as in (b)(i).

Solution 2. Provided the current element has a successor, we can achieve a deletion of the current element by overwriting it with a copy of its successor and then deleting the successor as in (b)(i). Hence we have:

```
TEMP: = CURRENTELT^. SUCC;    (* identify successor *)
CURRENTELT^: = TEMP^;         (* copy it *)
DISPOSE (TEMP)                (* dispose of original *)
```

Solution 2 is certainly the most efficient in most circumstances (when would it not be?), but does not allow us to delete the last element of a sequence. This problem can be overcome either by using Solution 1 in this situation (a 'special case' formulation) or by circumventing the problem: we can insist that a sequence is represented by a singly linked list with a dummy last element which is never deleted (a *trailer*). An empty list is now represented by a single (dummy) element.

The use of a dummy element to alleviate 'boundary-condition' problems is a common technique which we will meet again in this text. Frequently the dummy element is the 'first' in the representation: it is then sometimes referred to as a *header* element. We will use headers and trailers in diverse contexts, but almost invariably where boundary conditions are a problem.

4.4.3 Dynamic realization: doubly linked

The presence of a predecessor link removes the problems encountered with single linking. All reasonable specifications for insertion and deletion can be accommodated efficiently, that is with no scanning. Each operation will require more code in its implementation, however, because now both **SUCC** and **PRED** links must be maintained. Listing 4.8 shows an implementation of **DELETE** for a specification in which the predecessor of current is deleted, if it exists. No action is taken if it does not exist. The diagram can be used to help in visualizing the necessary steps involved.

4.4.4 Dynamic realization: circular linked

The last element in the singly linked dynamic representation of a sequence usually has its **SUCC** field set to **NIL** in Pascal. In the circular-linked representation we set it to **FIRSTELT**. By convention, a

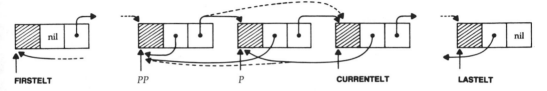

FIRSTELT   PP   P   CURRENTELT   LASTELT

```
Procedure Delete(var seq:Sequence);

(* Delete the predecessor to current of seq, if it exists *)

    var
        p,                      (* predecessor to current *)
        pp:Seqptr;              (* predecessor to p *)
    begin
      if not Empty(seq)
        then p:=seq.currentelt^.pred
        else p:=nil;            (* no predecessor *)
      if p<>nil                 (* predecessor exists? *)
        then                    (* yes: delete it *)
          with seq do
            begin
              pp:=p^.pred;           (* p's pred: may not exist *)
              currentelt^.pred:=pp;  (* extract p from pred ordering *)
              if pp<>nil             (* p has a predecessor? *)
                then                 (* yes: extract p from succ ordering *)
                  pp^.succ:=currentelt
                else                 (* no: current is first elt *)
                  firstelt:=currentelt;
              Dispose(p)
            end
    end;
```

Listing 4.8   Deletion in a doubly linked realization of a sequence.

single pointer is used which identifies the last element in the sequence:

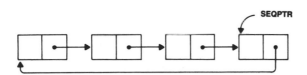

We no longer need both **FIRSTELT** and **LASTELT** as each can be obtained from **SEQPTR**:

LASTELT = SEQPTR
FIRSTELT = SEQPTR^.SUCC

A general sequence is therefore represented by **SEQPTR** together with **CURRENTELT,** and its restrictions (Section 4.2) can be represented by **SEQPTR** above. If we define a 'generic' element as

```
ELT = RECORD
        DATA: ITEM;
        PTR:^ ELT
      END
```

(where **PTR** has previously been called **SUCC** in the case of **QUEUE** and **PRED** in the case of **STACK**) then the following operations with their implementations are of particular interest to us.

(1) Insert an item as the *first*.
   The basis of the implementation is

```
NEW (TEMP);
WITH TEMP^ DO
  BEGIN
    DATA: = I;
    PTR  : = SEQ^.PTR
  END;
SEQ^.PTR: = TEMP
```

This differs from the **PUSH** operation given for **STACK** only in so far as **S** in **PUSH** is replaced by **SEQ^.PTR** in **INSERT**.

(2) Insert an item as the *last*.
   The implementation of (1) is the basis for this operation. The implementation is completed by adding

```
SEQ: = TEMP
```

as the final instruction.

(3) Delete the *first* item.
   Procedure **LEAVE** (Subsection 4.2.2(d)) can be used as a point of comparison for this implementation:

```
TEMP : = SEQ^.PTR;
SEQ^.PTR : = TEMP^.PTR;
DISPOSE (TEMP)
```

These operations are important because together they give the basis for implementations of *stack*, *queue* and *ordeque*.

(1) + (2) + (3):   *ordeque*
(2) + (3):   *queue*
(1) + (3):   *stack*

In each case the empty-sequence case must, of course, be catered for.

5
More formal aspects

In our introduction to the study of data structures we have attempted to state explicitly all factors which are involved in their development. We have deduced that only data-structure specifications need be known before algorithms can be developed which use those data structures, and that their realization can be treated as a separate exercise, and may involve system-dependency. In this chapter we give pointers towards a rigorous and more formal approach to these issues. We discuss three aspects in particular. Firstly, we consider the task of choosing a suitable realization for a specified data structure. This involves a comparative study of static and dynamic realizations, and also introduces the possibility of hybrids. Secondly, we tackle the important issue of formally specifying the semantics of a data structure. The implementor must have a rigorous description of a data structure from which to work: any imprecision can lead to expensive redesign late in a software production cycle. Thirdly, we need some way of arguing convincingly that a realization is correct, that is, that a realization meets a specification. It should be borne in mind that this chapter aims only to promote rigour: it does not attempt to advance any single formal methodology. In particular, algebraic specification techniques do currently have severe limitations when used for complex data structures, but their elegance in the cases we study does lead to a certain clarity in proofs of correctness.

5.1 CHOOSING A REALIZATION

A given specification can be realized in any number of different ways. Even after the major decision whether to use a static or dynamic realization has been resolved, we have seen that many subsidiary questions still remain. Should we use double linking, or circular single linking? Is packing desirable for an array? Does it matter if **DELETE** is inefficient? We cannot begin to answer these questions until we have decided exactly what it is we wish to achieve, and just as importantly, how well a given realization achieves it. We are in need of some quantification. Several measures can be used to compare realizations, but ultimately no single one can be used alone: a judicious compromise is invariably required, making use of as much system and usage information as is available. There is no substitute for experience and expertise in this area.

5.1.1 Criteria

(a) Efficiency measures

There are two major criteria by which implementations are judged: space requirement and time requirement. The relative importance of the criteria is dependent upon the environment in which the program is to run. In general, there is a trade-off between these two measures of efficiency: we can often lower time requirements by increasing space requirements and vice versa. This space/time trade-off will be met frequently in subsequent chapters. The space requirement of a representation can be presented as a function of the number of items in the data structure: we may, for example, find that a particular dynamic representation of a stack requires $3n + 1$ bytes of memory to represent a stack of n items. An implementation of an operation has its own space and time requirements, known as its space-complexity and its time-complexity. These are determined by a process known as complexity analysis, and must be calculated for each operation in a realization before its full characteristics are known. Once again they can usually be presented as a function of n. The study of complexity analysis should form part of a theory of algorithms course: it is not covered in this text. Some comments are made in Subsection 5.1.2, and results will be presented where appropriate, but no formal derivations will appear. Suitable references appear in the Bibliography.

Once the time-complexities of each of the operation implementations has been calculated, the overall time-efficiency (E) of a realization can be deduced. Conceptually E is a measure of

$$\sum_i p_i t_i$$

where p_i is the proportion of total operations on the data structure accounted for by the use of operation i, and t_i is the time cost for operation i. E will be a function of n. The aim of an implementor is to minimize E for expected n.

In practice, E is not as useful a measure as one might hope. There are often explicit constraints which take precedence over any measure of efficiency (see (b)), and the true measure of E is normally dependent on the actual data involved – something which we may only be able to test experimentally (see Section 5.1.4). Even if it is never enumerated, E is conceptually in the background when we state a preference for one realization over another.

(b) Critical operations

Irrespective of the general (or average) behaviour of a realization, there may be constraints which must take priority over the measure E. For example, it may be known that one particular operation is time-critical whereas a second is space-critical. These are known as implementation requirements, and play a similar role with respect to performance as specifications do with respect to correctness: a realization must satisfy its specification to be correct; it must satisfy its requirements. to be acceptable.

A typical example of a constraint can be conjectured for the **SET** data structure. The set may be used primarily for the storage and retrieval of data items, with a constraint that the test on set membership (operation **IN**) must be performed within a specified time. It is frequently the case that in these circumstances no constraint is placed on the related operation **INSERT**. This is useful because, up to a point, the more time we are able to spend on inserting an object in a data structure, the faster we can make its retrievel. Such trade-offs between operations are not uncommon.

(c) Average-case/worst-case performance

We have mentioned the general behaviour of a realization, which is quantified by E. This measure is based on the average-case performance of the implementation: the expected time spent on operations on the data structure given knowledge about the expected number of data items, their spread of values, etc. For critical operations we are often required to perform a worst-case analysis which, for given n, will tell us the maximum time, over all possible data sets, that we can expect for a given operation. Requirements may be based on average- and/or worst-case performances.

5.1.2 Static versus dynamic: some comparisons

The realizations developed in Chapter 4, for a sequence and its restrictions, can act as the basis of a brief critique of the relative merits of dynamic versus static representations. The critique can be used as a guide to some major factors which enter into an analysis when alternative realizations are assessed.

(a) Space analysis

The static realizations of a heap have no 'administrative' data associated with each data item in the structure, so it could be asserted that minimum storage is used. On the other hand, the dynamic realizations have an overhead of one (or two) pointer values per data item. It could be argued, therefore, that static realizations are more space-efficient, but this argument is too simplistic for two reasons:

(i) Memory is usually allocated to data items in whole units, where a unit refers to the unit of addressability (word). On many systems a pointer requires less than one word of memory, and a data item may not require a whole number of words. For example, we may find that a data item can be represented in one and a half words thus leaving a spare half word for a pointer. In this case an element will use the same number of words (two) whether it is stored in an array or stored as a linked element.

(ii) Sequential realizations require space to be claimed fully before it is used: space for the maximum size of sequence must be allocated. This is not an issue if only one sequence is in use: we may as well allocate free memory to an array as to the heap. If, however, there are several sequences active in parallel then a different picture emerges. Static allocation results in memory exhaustion when, in fact, one sequence hits its limit – even if other sequences are empty. Dynamic allocation will only result in memory exhaustion if the heap is exhausted; in this case exhaustion is actual.

These two factors together suggest that neither system is inherently better than the other: the choice, as always, depends on the circumstances. This becomes even more apparent when we consider hybrid realizations in Subsection 5.1.3.

(b) Time analysis

The time analysis of a realization involves the scrutiny of each operation implementation, in order to determine its complexity. We start by checking those operations cited in the requirements: if these are not satisfied then we need go no further. If the requirements are satisfied then the realization is acceptable: it remains to determine whether it is the best of the acceptable realizations under consideration. We may compare a realization R favourably with a realization P in one of two related ways:

(i) The time analysis of each implementation in R is uniformly as good as or better than the corresponding one in P.
(ii) $E(R) < E(P)$, where E is computed either theoretically or experimentally.

Each of the operations on a stack and a queue are implemented in constant time in each of the realizations. The comparison must therefore proceed to a lower level: how large is the constant in each case? The answer to this largely depends on the efficiency of the heap operations and the cost of array accesses. We defer analysis of these until Chapter 6. The general sequence operations of **INSERT** and **DELETE** are, however, rather different. Each of these operations can be performed in constant time in the dynamic implementation developed: their cost is independent of the sequence size, n. In the static case, an **INSERT** requires that all elements with higher index than **CURRENT** are copied to move them 'along' the array in order to make room for the new element. On average this will require $n/2$ elements to be moved, each, say, with cost K. The total cost of this implementation of *insert* is thus

$$\frac{Kn}{2} + c_1 \quad (K \text{ and } c_1 \text{ are constants})$$

For large n this will compare unfavourably with the constant cost for dynamic realizations. Similarly, **DELETE** results in elements being copied to move them in memory. Even if the copying (compaction) is delayed, as suggested in Section 3.3, we still only lower the constant associated with the time analysis function:

$$Kn + c_2 \quad (K \text{ and } c_2 \text{ are constants})$$

This again compares unfavourably, for large n, with the dynamic case.

The use of the rider 'for large n' is important. There are many situations in which n is not large, in which case the constants may have more impact than the n. If, however, n is very large then the constants c_1 and c_2 become insignificant, and we are concerned only with, in the latter case, Kn.

The dominant term in an expression when n is very large ('approaches infinity'), of which Kn above is an example, is of special interest. It represents what is called the asymptotic behaviour of the expression with respect to n. For large n all the lesser terms can be ignored for the purposes of comparing one expression with another, i.e. one implementation with another in our case. This *asymptotic* behaviour of algorithms is the preserve of complexity theory. We denote the most significant term (as n becomes very large) by o-notation, in this case

$$o(Kn)$$

In some cases we are not even interested in the size of the constant associated with the dominant term: we are more interested in whether the cost of the operation is constant, increases in proportion to the number of elements, increases with the square of the number of elements, etc. This is denoted by *O*-notation, in this case

$$O(n)$$

This is referred to as the order of complexity of an algorithm. The most common orders, with the lowest complexity first, are

$$O(1), \quad O(\log n), \quad O(n), \quad O(n \log n), \quad O(n^2) \quad O(2^n)$$

where $O(1)$ represents constant cost. The lower the order of complexity, the better the asymptotic behaviour of an implementation.

5.1.3 Hybrid realizations

The realizations we have discussed so far are pure: each data structure is represented by a separate array of items or by linked elements each containing a single item. There is scope for relaxing these conditions to provide useful hybrid alternatives. We look at each alternative in turn.

(a) Modified static

We relax the constraint that a data structure is represented by a separate array. The motivation for this is the desire to signal *overflow* only when all available space in memory is actively in use, as opposed to just that section rigidly ascribed for a given structure. The method used represents several structures by a single array. Consider two stacks represented in pure static form:

VAR S1, S2: STACK;

S1:   S2:

S1[1]   S1[max] S2[1]   S2[max]

Overflow will occur if an attempt is made to **PUSH** an item onto a full stack, say **S1**, irrespective of the condition of **S2** (which may even be empty). A simple modification can easily overcome the problem in this case: represent both in the same array **S**:

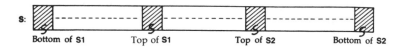

S:

Bottom of S1   Top of S1   Top of S2   Bottom of S2

The stacks grow towards each other in **S**, so that overflow occurs if a **PUSH** is attempted on either stack when

$$Top\ of\ \textbf{S2} = Top\ of\ \textbf{S1} + 1$$

This will only occur when **S** is genuinely full. This idea only works, of course, for two stacks. For two queues or multiple stacks we must be more sophisticated in our implementation and some copying, to move a stack in memory, will be necessary.

Note that **S1** and **S2** must be implemented slightly differently: **PUSH** implies that **TOPELT** must be incremented for **S1** but decremented for **S2**. This suggests that an extra attribute should be introduced into the representation of a stack to indicate in which direction it is to grow.

(b) Modified dynamic

Here, we relax the constraint of one item per element in a dynamic realization. The problem with the pure approach stems from the repeated calls on *heap* operations, which may be expensive. In the modified dynamic realization we define elements which can store several items each:

```
TYPE STACKELT = RECORD
                DATA:ARRAY [1..BLOCKSIZE] OF ITEM;
                PRED:ˆSTACKELT
              END;
```

A stack must now be represented by both an element pointer and an index: the first indicates in which element the top item is found and the second indicates which **DATA** item within that element is the actual top item:

```
TYPE STACK = RECORD
             TOPITEM:1..BLOCKSIZE;
             LAST:ˆSTACKELT
           END;
```

An empty stack will be represented by the pair

(*blocksize*, **NIL**)

This realization is explored more fully in the Exercises.

Analysis of space requirements depends somewhat on the factors mentioned in (a). We can assert that no more than the space for (*blocksize* − 1) items will be reserved but unused by a stack at any given time. We can reach a compromise, therefore, between space and time requirements. If we increase *blocksize* we will increase potential space demands but decrease time demands (there will be fewer calls on the *heap* operations). If we decrease *blocksize* we will decrease space demands (unless *blocksize* becomes so small that the space taken by the **PRED** pointer becomes significant) but increase time demands. In the limiting cases we see that

$$blocksize = 1 \quad \Rightarrow pure\ dynamic\ representation$$
$$blocksize = max \Rightarrow pure\ static\ representation$$

and we have a very flexible realization indeed.

In representing a general sequence, the advantages are not so clear. The **INSERT** and **DELETE** problems remain, but in a different form. An insert may result in the introduction of a new element, which will have ($blocksize - 1$) item spaces unused. These must presumably be set to *null*. A large number of partially filled elements may co-exist in a sequence representation, giving a much higher potential ratio of reserved space to used space. Some form of compaction could be periodically performed to remove null values and return freed blocks to the heap.

5.1.4 Tuning

Once a data structure is in use in an actual program we can investigate its actual as opposed to theoretical behaviour. To do this, we perform a profile analysis. The profile will give us experimental evidence of the performance of a realization, for various values of data set size (n). We would expect the asymptotic behaviour to accord with the complexity studies, though this may not happen until n is larger than any anticipated data set: some implementations have indicated $O(n)$ behaviour experimentally when an $O(n \log n)$ complexity has been derived. There is no inconsistency here: the machine architecture is simply such that very large values of n are required before the asymptotic behaviour is exhibited.

A profile will give experimentally obtained values for E. For a given n these values may vary according to chosen data sets, so care must be taken to produce suitable test data. The ideal is to run the system under expected conditions: use it, and collect profile statistics which correspond to actual use. The aim is to build up a true time and space study of a realization so that requirements can be checked and realization problems detected.

If a requirement is not met, or evidence suggests that a realization can usefully be improved, then a representation and/or implementation may be adjusted. This process is known as tuning. As an example, we may have a modified dynamic realization for a stack with blocksize B. After profiling the program we may deduce that a large blocksize would be advantageous, and modify the realization accordingly. The performance characteristics of each procedure in an implementation may be of more benefit at this stage than an overall value for E, unless alternatives are still being tried.

5.2 FORMAL SPECIFICATION OF TYPES

A specification comprises definitions of domain, operations and semantics for a data type. So far we have specified the semantics of types only informally, an unsatisfactory arrangement because the correctness of a program must be claimed with respect to a specification: if the specification is informal then so must any correctness assertion be. A formal specification overcomes this problem. Such a specification will be stated using a precise notation based on some well-known mathematical foundation: probably an algebra or a calculus. As we are aiming to promote the use of formality rather than investigate formal specification methods, a simple example only will be used. As algebraic specification methods deal adequately with this example and also lend themselves to simple proof techniques, we use such a method in this section.

5.2.1 Algebraic specification

The specification method introduced by Guttag in 1975 forms a base from which many, more complex methods have been developed. An algebraic specification for a type includes a set of axioms from which the total behaviour of the type can be deduced. These axioms must, for example, constrain the LIFO nature of a stack, or the FIFO nature of a queue. Any expression involving operations on a type can be reduced to a canonical form: a form which most simply represents values of the type in question. For example, the value of a stack can be uniquely represented by an expression involving *push* operations on a *newstack*. Our axioms must therefore allow

$push\,(pop\,(push\,(push\,(newstack,\ a),\ b)),\ c)$ (*)

to be reduced to its canonical form

$push\,(push\,(newstack,\ a),\ c)$

The axioms themselves are given in the form of rewrite rules: given an expression of one form it may be rewritten in a simpler form. One of these axioms for a stack concerns its LIFO nature, and is necessary for the transformation above. It is the axiom that, given an item i and a stack S, then the expression

$pop\,(push\,(S,\ i))$

can be rewritten as simply

S

To see how this works, let us simplify (*) using this axiom. Define

$S = push(newstack, a)$

(*push* always gives a stack as a result, so this is type-legal). Define

$i = b$

Then

$$pop(push(push(newstack, a), b))$$
$$= pop(push(S, i))$$
$$= S$$
$$= push(newstack, a)$$

Hence (*) can be rewritten as

$Push(push(newstack, a), c)$

A stack, or any other data structure, is only used in an algorithm as some kind of temporary store for item information: a stack value as such is of no interest, only which item will be delivered next by a stack or whether the stack is empty (a boolean value). The axioms must therefore be complete, so that item values and boolean values can be returned from expressions involving stacks. These are the ultimate forms of simplification: the stack operations disappear entirely from the expression. We need, then, axioms which can reduce

$top(push(push(newstack, a), c))$

to

c

and

$empty(push(newstack, a))$

to

false

Before looking at type stack more closely, we introduce some terminology.

Constructor functions

Those operations which are used in the canonical representation of values of a type. They must return values of the type in question.

Example 5.1
newstack and *push* for type *stack*.

Extender functions

Those operations which return a value of the type in question, but are not constructor functions.

Example 5.2
pop for type *stack.*

Output functions

Those operations which act on a value of the type in question and return a value of a different type (already defined).

Example 5.3
top and *empty* for type *stack.*

These distinctions are useful when determining when a set of axioms is complete (no more are needed to fully define the type), a topic which we must leave unexplored in this text.

5.2.2 A specification of type stack

Guttag's specification method involves a statement of form for operations (as we have already presented with each type introduced) together with a statement of axioms. We specify a *stack* of *items* in Fig. 5.1. Note that *pop(newstack)* is defined to be *newstack,* but could

```
Operations
    NEWSTACK := ():STACK
    EMPTY      := (STACK):BOOLEAN
    PUSH       := (STACK, ITEM):STACK
    POP        := (STACK):STACK
    TOP        := (STACK):ITEM
Semantics
    For all s: stack; i: item let
        empty(newstack)  = true
        empty(push(s, i)) = false
        pop(newstack)     = newstack
        pop(push(s, i))   = s
        top(newstack)     = undefined
        top(push(s, i))   = i
```

Figure 5.1 A complete specification for type **STACK**.

justifiably have been **undefined**. Once a value of **undefined** is returned we are outside the specification, so it is better to remain within the specification by using this axiom. By contrast, *top* (*newstack*) is definitely undefined.

It is not difficult to convince oneself that these axioms do indeed characterize a stack and no other data type. They are complete and also consistent (any expression will be reduced to a unique canonical form irrespective of the order in which the axioms are applied). If an implementation of a stack satisfies these axioms then that implementation is correct. It is this issue to which we now turn.

5.3 PROVING THE CORRECTNESS OF A REALIZATION

A realization consists of a representation together with an implementation. Each of these must be given a notation which will allow correctness arguments to be made. We will suggest notations for representations appropriate to each case considered. The notation for an implementation we already have: the Pascal language. We make a simple transformation of the code, however, before a proof is tackled. The changes we make to the program code in order to simplify our proofs are of two kinds: we represent data variables in the notation chosen, so that the values resulting from Pascal instructions can be expressed; and we remove code relating to exception conditions as these are outside the specification. In each case we will show the implementation transformation which results. Remember that a proof is a convincing argument, and that that is all we are aiming to present. It is inappropriate here to present proofs based exactly on the Pascal code itself, or to take the formal treatment down to the lowest levels of deduction. The flavour of proof techniques should still reside.

5.3.1 A static realization

In its static realization, a stack is represented by an ordered pair $[A, t]$. The first of the pair represents the **ITEMSET** array used to store actual items on the stack; the second represents the **TOPITEM** and indicates how many items are on the stack. We know one invariant (a fact: something which is always true):

$$0 \leqslant t \leqslant \max$$

As a notation, we can refer to the value a variable had on entry to an operation by using a bar, viz.

We may therefore meet such statements as

$t := \bar{t} + 1$ (* equivalent to **t**: = **t** + 1 in Pascal *)

This will be useful in some proofs of correctness.

The first step is to present the transformed implementation; check this for yourself against the original:

$$newstack([A, \ t]) \equiv t := 0$$
$$empty([A, \ t]) \quad \equiv empty : = (t = 0)$$
$$pop([A, \ t]) \quad \equiv \text{if } t > 0$$
$$\qquad\qquad \text{then } t := \bar{t} - 1$$
$$push([A, \ t], i) \quad \equiv t := \bar{t} + 1;$$
$$\qquad\qquad A[t] := i$$
$$top([A, \ t]) \qquad \equiv \text{if } t > 0$$
$$\qquad\qquad \text{then } top := A[t]$$

Recall that the Pascal implementation insisted on **NEWSTACK**, **POP** and **PUSH** using a **VAR** parameter, instead of a value parameter with the result returned as a function value. In the first step of our proof we reverse this limitation and so replace assignment statements by representing instead the value of the function which would result. In the case of *newstack* we have

$$newstack : - \ () : stack$$

which is implemented as

$$newstack \equiv [A, \ 0].$$

If we treat the other operations similarly, each can be replaced by an algebraic expression: these expressions can then be checked with regard to the algebraic specification.

$$empty([A, \ t]) \equiv t = 0$$
$$pop([A, \ t]) = \text{if } t > 0 \text{ then } [A, \ \bar{t} - 1]$$
$$\qquad\qquad\qquad \text{else } [A, \ \bar{t}]$$

(the expression 'if b then i else j' has the value i if b is true and the value j otherwise).

$$push([A, \ t], \ i) \equiv [A : A[\bar{t} + 1] = i, \ \bar{t} + 1]$$
$$top \ ([A : A[t] = i, \ t]) \equiv \text{if } t > 0 \text{ then } i$$

Note that the expression

$$A: \ A[t] = i$$

represents an array in which the element identified by t has the value i. We are now in a position to tackle the proof.

The proof consists of demonstrating that each axiom in the specification is true for the implementation. If the specification is complete then only a true implementation will satisfy all the axioms. We take each axiom in order, as presented in Subsection 5.2.2.

Let $s = [A, t]$ be a *stack* and i be an *item*.

1. *empty* (*newstack*)
   $\equiv empty \ ([A, \ 0])$
   $\equiv 0 = 0$
   $\equiv$ **true**

Hence *empty* (*newstack*) $\equiv$ true for the implementation.

2. *empty* (*push* (*s*, *i*))
   $\equiv empty \ (push) \ [A, \ t], \ i))$
   $\equiv empty \ ([A:A \ [t+1] = i, \bar{t}+1])$
   $\equiv \bar{t}+1 = 0$
   but $0 \leqslant \bar{t} \leqslant$ Max, so $\bar{t}+1 > 0$

Hence *empty* (*push* $([A, \ t], i)) \equiv$ false for the implementation.

3. *pop* (*newstack*)
   $\equiv pop \ ([A, 0])$
   $\equiv$ if $0 > 0$ then $[A, -1]$ else $[A, \ 0]$
   $\equiv [A, 0]$
   $\equiv newstack$

Hence *pop* (*newstack*) $\equiv newstack$ for the implementation.

4. *pop* (*push* (*s*, *i*))
   $\equiv pop \ (push \ ([A, \ t], \ i))$
   $\equiv pop \ ([A:A \ [\bar{t}+1] = i, \ \bar{t}+1])$
   $\equiv$ if $\bar{t}+1 > 0$ then $[A, \ (\bar{t}+1)-1]$
   $\qquad\qquad\qquad$ else $[A, \ (\bar{t}+1)]$
   $\equiv [A, \ \bar{t}]$, as $\bar{t}+1 > 0$

Hence *pop* (*push* (*S*, *i*)) $\equiv S$ for the implementation.

5. *top* (*newstack*)
   $\equiv top \ ([A, \ 0])$
   $\equiv$ if $0 > 0$ then $\ldots$
   its value is therefore not defined.

Hence *top* (*newstack*) $\equiv$ undefined for the implementation.

6. *top* (*push* (*s*, *i*))
   $\equiv top \ (push \ ([A, \ t], \ i))$
   $\equiv top \ ([A:A[\bar{t}+1] = i, \ \bar{t}+1])$

$\equiv$ if $\bar{i}+1>0$ then i

$\equiv i$

Hence *top* (*push* (*S*, *i*))$\equiv i$ for the implementation.

We have therefore shown that we have a true implementation of type *stack*: one which completely satisfies the specification.

5.3.2 A dynamic realization

A stack in this realization is represented by a list of items, *S*. A list of items has a head item, say *i*, and a tail, say *T*, which is itself a list of items. We can therefore denote *S* thus:

$S:[i, T]$

If we form a new list *Q* by putting a new item, *j*, as the head of the list then we have

$Q:[j, S]$

which could also be written as

$Q:[j, S:[i, T]]$

An empty stack is represented by the empty list [ ].

With this notation, we can transform the dynamic implementation in a similar manner to Subsection 5.3.1. Again, this should be compared with the original (Subsection 4.2.1 (d)).

$$newstack \equiv [\,]$$
$$empty(S) \equiv S = [\,]$$
$$push\ (T,\ i) \equiv S:[i, T]$$
$$pop\ (S:[i,\ T]) = \text{if } S <> [\,] \text{ then } T$$
$$\text{else } S$$
$$top\ (S:[i,\ T]) \equiv \text{if } S2 <> [\,] \text{ then } i$$

We have moved from Pascal code to algebraic expression in one step this time. You might like to produce the intermediate code for yourself if you are in any doubt about the method.

As before, the axioms are taken in order. For each axiom, we demonstrate that the implementation satisfies it.

Let $S:[i, T]$ be a stack, and *i* be an *item*.

1. *empty* (*newstack*)

$\equiv empty\ ([\,])$

$\equiv [\,]=[\,]$

$\equiv$ **true**

Hence *empty* (*newstack*)$\equiv$ true.

2. *empty* (*push* (*S, i*))
    $\equiv empty\ (P{:}[i,\ S])$
    $\equiv [i,\ S]=[\ ]$
    $\equiv$ **false**

Hence *empty* (*push* (*S, i*)) $\equiv$ false.

3. *pop* (*newstack*)
    $\equiv pop([\ ])$
    $\equiv$ if $[\ ]<>[\ ]$ then ?? else $[\ ]$
    $\equiv [\ ]$
    $\equiv newstack$

Hence *pop* (*newstack*) $\equiv$ *newstack*.

4. *pop* (*push* (*S, i*))
    $\equiv pop\ (P{:}[i,\ S])$
    $\equiv$ if $[i,\ S]<>[\ ]$ then S else P
    $\equiv S$

Hence *pop* (*push* (*S, i*)) $\equiv S$.

5. *top* (*newstack*)
    $\equiv top\ ([\ ])$
    $\equiv$ if $[\ ]<>[\ ]$ then ??

The value of this expression is not defined.
Hence *top* (*newstack*) $\equiv$ undefined.

6. *top* (*push* (*S, i*))
    $\equiv top\ (P{:}[i,\ T])$
    $\equiv$ if $[i,\ T]<>[\ ]$ then i
    $\equiv i$

Hence *top* (*push* (*S, i*)) $\equiv i$.

The implementation satisfies all the *stack* axioms and is therefore correct.

This is as far as we wish to take correctness proofs in the text. A proof of correctness for a hybrid stack realization is the subject of one of the exercises.

5.4 LONG-LIVED PROGRAMS: DATA INDEPENDENCE

It is unquestionably true that a well-structured program is easier to verify and to maintain than its unstructured counterparts. The separation of data-type realization from the program which uses it is an essential aspect of this structure. An algorithm is generally longer lived than the particular realization of the data types to which its realization (the program) is interfaced. If we follow the rules laid down in the preceding chapters, we will find that a date-type operation, as implemented, will be called using the same procedure/function name and with syntactically identical arguments no matter which realization is in use. The calls on data-type operations are independent of the realization chosen for the data type. This concept is known as data independence. Data independence is the cornerstone of successful large systems: without it a system must be treated as a whole, and not as independent components. Any change, however minor, could have dramatic and widespread implications in such an environment. Data independence is a theoretical issue which has very important pragmatic ramifications.

5.4.1 Programming for data independence

The rules for achieving data independence in a program are few and simple. They are listed below, with comments.

(i) An operation on a data object must look the same syntactically, irrespective of the realization associated with its type.

Hence, if a stack operation is realized as a procedure with the stack as a var parameter, this should be so for any future realization of stack for that program. This is very important: it means that changing a realization is restricted to changing the stack definition only: no part of the main program is affected.

(ii) Objects of a given type, say T, must only appear as arguments defined to be of type T.

A very strongly typed language would enforce this automatically. Pascal is not strong enough in its type enforcement, so this must be checked independently of the compiler.

(iii) No realization details should appear outside the realization itself.

Once again, Pascal is too weak to insist that the only operations performed on, say, a **STACK** are those defined in its specification. Given a dynamic realization, the Pascal compiler will turn a blind eye to such statements as

while S < > nil do (∗)

for **S** of type stack. Such statements would destroy data independence: change the realization to static and the compiler will object to (∗). The implications of a change should not propagate outside the realization.

Consider the simplest use of a stack to reverse a sequence of

```
(* Representation of Stack in here *)

var
     valuestack:Stack;
     value:Char;

(* Implementation of Stack in here *)

begin (* Test program *)
  Newstack(valuestack);
  while not Eoln do
    begin
      read(value);
      Push(valuestack,value)
    end;
  while not Empty(valuestack) do
    begin
      Write(Top(valuestack));
      Pop(valuestack)
    end;
  Writeln
end.
```

Listing 5.1 Using the stack data structure.

characters. We will assume that the characters are stored in a Pascal file, and the reverse sequence is to be printed. We present the code in Listing 5.1. The **valuestack** is only ever used as an argument to **STACK** operations. No reference is made in the code to the realization being used. We have obeyed the rules of data independence. A realization of the **STACK** can be introduced *post-facto*, and no artificial constraints are imposed on this realization. It can be dynamic, static or hybrid: the program will work equally well with each.

5.4.2 Generic programming

It is common practice in computer science to 'tailor' a program to fit specific circumstances: a new version of the program code is generated for each application which uses it. The situation is typified by sort routines: thousands of sort routines are in existence, each based on one of a few basic algorithms. However, the odds are that if you wish to perform a sort in a program, you will be required to write your own!

Further, if you wish to sort different types of data items in a program, there is a strong probability that you will have to incorporate a sort routine for each type.

Some systems do provide generic sort routines, sometimes called sort packages. The principle used is that of defining the parameters of a sort: the system will use these parameters to perform a correct sort. The parameters used would include:

- Size of a data item.
- Details of the key for the sort.
- Where the input file is.
- Where to store the result.

This principle can be extended to general program modules: if they are of general use they should be written in such a way that they need be coded only once. A particular application will then require only the parameters to be defined.

As a simple example, a typical sort routine may require only the following operations to be performed on the set of items to be sorted:

swap: − (*item id, item id, set*)
compare: − (*item, item*): *boolean*

To use the sort routine we need only provide implementations for these operations on our data structure. The sort routine itself is generic.

6
Basic structured types: realizations

The static and dynamic realizations so far presented have been based on array and heap structures, respectively. We have specified these structures, but have not yet considered their own realizations: ultimately all realizations must be mapped to the linear structure which is memory. Even though array and heap are provided in Pascal it is still worth investigating them. One reason for this is that whoever writes compilers must be aware of these details. A further, more general reason, concerns the lack of control given to a programmer relying on the Pascal system provided: he may wish to by-pass the inevitable restrictions by implementing his own operations. We look at various possible realizations for both *array* and *heap*.

6.1 ARRAY

The most fundamental operation required for an array determines the address of a data item given its index (or indices, if multidimensional). Two obvious ways of doing this are by calculation (discussed in Subsection 6.1.1) and table look-up (Subsection 6.1.2). Less obvious methods, for more complex representations, are covered in Subsection 6.1.3.

6.1.1 Mapping functions

A mapping function is a function which takes indices as arguments and returns an address as its result. Each array has its own mapping function. The elements of the array must be stored consecutively in memory for this method. We consider arrays of one dimension first, and then show how the technique generalizes to multiple dimensions.

(a) One dimension

As the one-dimensional array is the data structure which most closely models actual memory, we can expect a fairly straightforward implementation. This we develop by example.

Example 6.1
For the simplest case let us take an array, **X**, of items each of which is of unit size. The origin of indexing is 0 and the limit is 7.

   var X:array[0..7] of Integer;

We store the known facts about the array (its parameters) in what is called a dope vector. Apart from the details mentioned above, the dope vector will contain an entry to signify the base address (*BA*) of the array, which is the address in memory of its first element. Let this be 200:

1	(Number of dimensions)
200	(Base address, *BA*)
0	(Origin of indexing, o)
7	(Limit of indexing, *l*)
1	(Element size, *s*)

Dope vector:

The mapping function for **X**, MF_X, must take an index between 0 and 7 as an argument and return the address of the appropriate element. It is not hard to see that in this case

   $MF_X(i) \equiv 200 + i$

Our first approximation to a general mapping function, M, becomes

   $M(i) \equiv BA + i$

Example 6.2
Let us take a similar array to **X**, but with origin of indexing 2 instead of 0. All other parameters remain the same.

   var Y:array[2..7] of Integer;

We have the situation in which the first element in **Y** has address 200 and is referred to as **Y[2]**.

   $MF_Y(2) \equiv 200$

Again, it is not hard to see that the address of the element with index *i* is offset from the base address, 200, by $(i-2)$. Hence

$$MF(2) = 200 + i - 2$$

Our second approximation to M, for an **array [o..I] of Item,** is therefore

$$M(i) = BA + i - o$$

Note that $BA - o$ is a constant. If we let $\overline{BA} = BA - o$ then the function becomes $\overline{BA} + i$. The value of $\overline{BA}$ should be stored in the dope vector, rather than BA.

Example 6.3
Let **Z** have the same parameters as **X** except for the size of an item, which is 2. The original mapping function was

$$200 + i$$

because the ith element was i memory units removed from the base address. Now that each item has size 2, we can deduce that element i should in fact be $2 \times i$ memory units from the base address:

$$MF_Z(i) = 200 + 2 \times i$$

In general we can deduce the following mapping function for arrays of one dimension declared as

var A: array[o..I] of Item;
$$M(i) \equiv BA + (i - o) \times s$$
$$\equiv BA - o \times s + i \times s$$

Take $\overline{BA} = BA - o \times s$ (a constant)

$$M(i) \equiv \overline{BA} + i \times s$$

The dope vector, in the general case, can be depicted as

1
$BA - o \times s$

o
l
s

(b) Two dimensions

In developing a mapping function for two dimensions we demonstrate the general technique which can be used for n-dimensions, for any n. The particular array we will consider is

A:array[o1..I1,o2..I2] of Item;

There is no longer a trival mapping to memory, but there are two obvious storage possibilities. We first consider the one represented by

A:array[o1..l1] of array[o2..l2] of Item

In this case the elements of each row are stored consecutively in memory:

This ordering is known as *row-major* or *lexicographic* and is implied in Pascal. Let us analyse **A** from the viewpoint of a one-dimensional array, which we already know about.

Array **A** is of the form

array[o1..l1] of compound-object;

What is the size of a compound object? For the moment let us denote it by $s2$. We know that the address of the first element in the ith row of **A** is

$$M_A^1(i) = BA + (i - o1) \times s2$$

But what does $M_A^1(i)$ give us? It gives us the base address (BA^2) of another array, declared as

array[o1..l2] of Item.

(Note: BA^2 does not denote BA squared; the 2 is merely a superscript.) How do we address the jth element of this array? Once again we have a one-dimensional case:

$$M_A^2(j) = BA^2 + (j - o2) \times s$$

But we know that

$$BA^2 = BA + (i - o1) \times s2$$

Hence

$$M_A(i,j) = BA + (i - o1) \times s2 + (j - o2) \times s$$

Finally, we need the value of $s2$, the size of a compound object. This compound object is an

array[o2..l2] of Item

so has

$$o2 - l2 + 1$$

items of size s. Therefore

$$s2 = (o2 - l2 + 1) \times s$$

and we conclude that

$$M_A(i, j) = BA + ((i - o1) \times (l2 - o2 \times 1) + j - o2) \times s$$

In order to simplify this, let

$$\dim 2 = (l2 - o2 + 1) \qquad \text{(a constant)}$$

and

$$\overline{BA} = BA - (o1 \times \dim 2 + o2) \times s \quad \text{(a constant)}$$

Then

$$M_A(i, j) = \overline{BA} + (i \times \dim 2 + j) \times s$$

The dope vector for **A** would be of the form

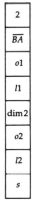

2
$\overline{BA}$
$o1$
$l1$
dim 2
$o2$
$l2$
s

Example 6.4

B:array [2..15, −1..3] of Item;

(* stored in locations 200 onwards; items of size 3 *)

$$\dim 2 = 3 - (-1) + 1 = 5$$
$$\overline{BA} = 200 - (2 \times 5 - 1) \times 3 = 173$$
$$M_B(i, j) = 173 + (i \times 5 + j) \times 3$$

For arrays of higher dimension, the process is repeated to obtain the required functions. No new concepts are involved.

An alternative storage strategy for arrays is that termed *column-major* or *reverse lexicographic*, a scheme adopted by FORTRAN. Under this scheme, the elements of **A** would be stored in memory as follows:

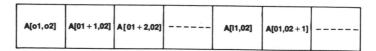

It is as if the array had actually been declared as

array[o2..l2] of array[o1..l1] of Item

The mapping function can therefore be obtained by interchanging **o1** with **02** and **l1** with **l2**.

6.1.2 Access tables

An access table is a table of values which represent partial evaluations of the appropriate mapping function. The approach is designed to trade space for time: by partially evaluating the function we make array accesses cheaper, but these partial evaluations must be stored in memory. The access table itself is an array of one dimension, but it has item size 1 and so has a simple mapping function. Arrays with equally simple mapping functions do not benefit from an access table approach.

Consider array **Z** above. Its mapping function is

$$M_Z(i) = 200 + 2 \times i$$

An access table for **Z** would contain the value of $M_Z(i)$ for each value of i, viz.

AT_Z:

200
202
204
206
208
210
212
214

An access to **Z[i]** now becomes an access to the memory location with address $AT_Z[i]$, that is the address stored in location

$$\overline{BA}_{AT} + i$$

We have removed the need to multiply by 2 when evaluating an address. This is a marginal saving: in general, access tables will be significantly more beneficial. Also it should be noted that, in machine language, the access of memory location

$$\overline{BA}_{AT} + i$$

can be achieved using indexing on $\overline{BA}_{AT}$, and so performed in one instruction.

The advantage of access tables becomes more apparent when considering multiple dimensions. We consider the case of two dimensions, using array **B** as our example.

$$\begin{aligned} M_B^1(i) &= 200 + (i-2) \times 15 \\ &= 170 + i \times 15 \end{aligned}$$

Using the one-dimensional case as a guide, we can construct an access table

$AT_B^1[2..15]$:

200
215
230
⋮

which contains the base addresses of each row. Each row is declared as

array[−1..3] of Item

for which we have the mapping function

$$\begin{aligned} M_B^2(j) &\equiv BA' + (j+1) \times 3 \\ &\equiv BA' + 3 \times j + 3 \end{aligned}$$

The base address is itself dependent on i, and is given by access table 1. We may therefore deduce that access table 2 should be defined by

$AT_B^2[-1..3]$:

0
3
6
9
12

The address of element **B[i, j]** can now be obtained as

$$AT_B^1 [i] + AT_B^2 [j]$$

each component of which can be accessed in one instruction.

It should be noted that access table 2 is only necessary because items are not of unit size; if they were then the table would be superfluous and the access to element **B[i, j]** would be by calculating

$$AT_B^1 [i] + j$$

The extension of the above to multiple dimensions follows a similar pattern.

An alternative form of access to element **B[i, j]** is represented by

$$AT_B^2 [AT_B^1 [i] + j]$$

This obviously requires the access tables to be set up differently. The advantage of this form of access is that machines supporting multilevel indexing and indirection can achieve it in one instruction. The disadvantage is that more space for access tables is required. We take as our example

C:array[−1..3, 2..15] of Item;

which is a transposition of array **B**. The reason will be discussed after the basic description. The idea is to set up access tables as in Fig. 6.1. The size of AT_C^1 is dim $1 = l1 - o1 + 1 = 3 - (-1) + 1 = 5$. The size of AT_C^2 is dim $1 \times$ dim 2. (If a three-dimensional array were in use, then the third access table would be of size dim $1 \times$ dim $2 \times$ dim 3, etc.)

Access table 1 actually provides addresses of elements in access table 2, in fact the addresses in access table 2 of the first entries for each row. Access table 2 contains the actual addresses of elements of **C**. The

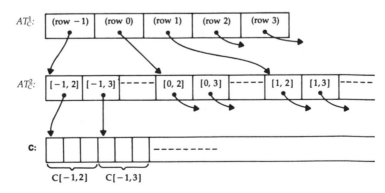

Figure 6.1 Iliffe access tables.

exercises explore this method further. The tables are known as Iliffe access tables, after their originator.

To return to the point about space overheads, we note that the total extra storage space required for access tables is minimized if the first dimension represented is the smallest, and the others are in increasing order of size. There is therefore less of a space overhead for **C** in lexicographic ordering than for **B**. It is not uncommon to have differences in size of several magnitudes, so the effect of ordering on space demands can be significant.

Finally, we note the flexibility which the use of access tables allows, because apart from the speed benefit, they provide a level of indirection in element access which can be exploited.

(i) Consider AT_B^1: if an algorithm calls for the interchange of two complete rows in **B** we can effect this by simply interchanging two elements of AT_B^1. Similarly, if we are interchanging elements of **C** (an operation very common in sorting) we may achieve this simply by interchanging elements of AT_C^2 which are smaller.

(ii) Some applications call for the use of arrays with rows of uneven length. An access table can be set up which reflects this property. An equivalent mapping function would be unrealistic.

(iii) Access tables can contain any addresses: elements do not have to be stored contiguously in memory; elements may even be stored on backing store (say disc). We may, for example, keep as many rows in memory as there is room for. AT_C^1 may contain an address which is distinguishable either as a memory address or as a disc address.

This flexibility can sometimes make the difference between feasibility and infeasibility for a system.

6.1.3 Sparse arrays

In a sparse array a large proportion of the elements are zero, but those which are non-zero are randomly (or at least, unpredictably) distributed. Many applications involving sparse arrays use examples which are too large to be represented in the standard way. Some way of compacting the information contained in an array is needed. Two methods are presented in this subsection, a further method being discussed in Section 15.1. The most appropriate representation will depend, as usual, on the details of the algorithm using the array.

(a) Bit-map

Information concerning whether an array element is zero or non-zero can be represented in 1 bit of memory. In the majority of cases this is all that is required: if the bit is zero then the value zero can be returned. Extra information is required for the non-zero elements. With this in mind, we suggest the following representation for a sparse array

D:array[o1..l1, o2, l2] of Item

D≡a bit-map

B:array [o1..l1, o2..l2] of 0..1

+a value-array

V:array[0..max] of Item

+the index in **V** of the last non-zero element of **D**

TOP:0..max

No more than max+1 non-zero values are expected at any point in time. **V** will contain the non-zero values, in lexicographic order.

Example 6.5

$$\begin{bmatrix} 0, & 7, & 0 \\ 0, & 0, & 2 \end{bmatrix}$$

can be represented by

$$\mathbf{B}{:}\begin{bmatrix} 0, & 1, & 0 \\ 0, & 0, & 1 \end{bmatrix} + \mathbf{V}{:}[7, 2]$$

To estimate the saving in space, let us assume that array **D** in fact has 128000 integers, each represented by a 32-bit word. The array has approximately 5% non-zero values. The suggested representation would require

128000 bits = 4000 words for **B**
128000 × 5% = 6400 words for **V**

The total space requirement is therefore 10400 words: less than 10% of the standard requirement for the array.

Having represented the array we now need to implement the array operations of selection and element assignment. Consider selection first, of element **D[i,j]**:

if B[i,j] = 0

    then return the value 0
    else find the index in **V** of the required value, say **k**, and return
      V[k]

The **then** part is simple enough to translate directly into Pascal, but how do we find the appropriate index in **V** for the **else** clause? The answer to this is not difficult, but the algorithm is slow. It involves counting the number of '1' bits in **B** which precede the '1' bit representing **B[i,j]**. In the worst case, all 128000 bits must be tested. The only saving grace is that this will only occur 5% of the time. By trading more space for a faster time we may be able to reduce significantly the cost of the **else** clause. To do this we introduce a table which contains '1' counts for the first element of each row: in other words, for each row **i** the table contains a count of the number of '1' bits preceding bit **B[i,o2]**. With this method, no more than $(o2 - l2 + 1)$ bits need to be scanned on any selection operation.

Element assignment presents its own problems. We can distinguish four different cases for the assignment **D[i, j]**: = **VAL:**

(i) **D[i,j]** = 0; **VAL** = 0.
(ii) **D[i,j]** < > 0; **VAL** < > 0.
(iii) **D[i,j]** = 0; **VAL** < > 0.
(iv) **D[i,j]** < > 0; **VAL** = 0.

Case (i). No action called for: this is a redundant operation.

Case (ii). Assume that the non-zero value is stored at position **k** in array **V**: this can be calculated in the same way as for selection. The operation becomes **V[k]**: = **VAL**.

Case (iii). Let **k** be the number of '1' bits preceding **B[i,j]**. We wish to store **VAL** in **V[k]**, but **V[k]** will probably be occupied. To make room for **VAL**, we move all the entries in **V** after **V[k − 1]** to the next position. We can then enter **VAL**:

```
for I: = TOP down to k do
    V[I + 1]: = V[I];
V[k]: = VAL;
TOP: = TOP + 1
```

The appropriate bit in **B** must, of course, be set to 1. This algorithm is correct as long as **V** does not overflow.

Case (iv). This case can be treated exactly as case (ii) but would result in **V** storing zero elements, as well as non-zero elements. This may be acceptable for a while, but a 'purge' of **V** would be in order periodically. To purge **V** we need to work from **V[0]** and remove all zero elements (not forgetting to change their respective **B** bits to zero) by overwriting with non-zero elements (see the Exercises). A straightforward implementation of case (iv) would simply set **B[i,j]** to 0 and shift all elements above **V[k]** down one position (the opposite of case (iii), viz.

```
for I: = k + 1 to TOP do
  V[I – 1]: = V[I];
TOP: = TOP – 1;
```

this is equivalent to a 'purge' after every such operation).

(b) Coordinates

In this representation we do not represent zero elements at all. The non-zero elements are represented (in the case of two-dimensional arrays) by triples of the form

(row index, column index, value)

Example 6.5 would therefore be represented by the two triples

(1, 2, 7)
(2, 3, 2)

We can describe the representation as

```
T: array [1..max] of record
                     row:o1..I1;
                     col:o2..I2;
                     val:Item
                   end;
   TOP:0..max;
```

If we perform a space calculation on the same basis as for bit-maps, and assuming that both indices can be packed into one word, we arrive at

$$128\,000 \times 5\% \times 2$$

or 12 800 words for **V**. This is 10% of the standard requirement for the array.

Operations on this basic representation are slow. A selection requires a sequential scan of the triples, attempting to match **i** and **j** with **row** and **col**. A match will eventually be found if the element is non-zero, but all triples must be checked before a value of zero is returned. Element assignment is no better: we must search the triples to establish whether the element is there. We have the same four cases as before:

Case (i). Do nothing.
Case (ii). Overwrite the val field with the new value.
Case (iii). Increment **TOP** and set **T[TOP]** to (i, j, val).
Case (iv). Overwrite the triple with **T[TOP]** and decrement **TOP**.

We have used a sequential representation for the triples, but a linked allocation may well be better. In particular, the introduction of an access table to a linked allocation scheme can significantly improve performance. Notice that row numbers need no longer be kept explicitly:

```
T = record
       col:o2..l2,
       val:Item;
       next:^T
    end
AT:array[o1..l1] of^T;
```

Example 6.6

$$\begin{bmatrix} 0 & 0 & 0 & 0 \\ 0 & 3 & 0 & 7 \\ 0 & 5 & 0 & 0 \end{bmatrix} : \textbf{array[1..3,1..4] of Integer;}$$

Searches need now only be through the elements of a given row. This representation is also good for processing elements by row. The equivalent could obviously be designed for column access.

6.2 HEAP

Memory can be visualized as a single block of contiguous locations. A realization for a *heap* must take this single block and allocate small sections of it as requested in the operation *new*. The representation must allow us to identify which subblocks have been allocated (we refer to *used* blocks) and which have not (*free* blocks). The free blocks are usually linked together in a sequence called the *free list*.

In general, used blocks can be of any size. This reflects the fact that elements of any type can be created by **NEW**. Before considering the general case we look first at the simplified case where all used blocks are of the same size. This is not unrealistic in some list-processing situations.

6.2.1 Uniform element size

If all heap elements are of the same size, *s*, then the memory space allocated to the heap can be divided into free blocks initially. When operation **NEW** is performed, any free block can be allocated. The identifier returned will be the memory address of the first word in the block. The block must be removed from the list of free blocks. As blocks are not **DISPOSEd** of in any particular order, it makes sense to link them together in the free list. The links will be the identifiers, which are memory addresses. The heap is therefore initialized as

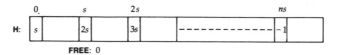

Each block is of size s. The value of the 'link' field is shown: it gives the address of the next element in the free list.

When a block is allocated, all s memory locations can be used: links are only needed for free blocks. The variable **FREE** contains the address of the *front* element of the free list, and so is initially 0. Consider the operation of **NEW(P)**:

> **P: = FREE;** (∗ return identifier of an element in the free list ∗)
> **FREE: = H[FREE]** (∗ remove the element from the free list ∗)

The operation **DISPOSE(P)** is equally simple:

> **H[P]: = FREE;**
> **FREE: = P;**
> **P: = −1**   (∗ set P to nil ∗)

These operations are, in fact, very reminiscent of operations *push* and *pop* for a stack implemented using single links. In fact, our memory addresses (indices in array **H**) are nothing more than representations of pointers. We conclude that the free list is organized as a stack which is realized using a single-linked representation, with pointers represented as indices in an array **H**.

6.2.2 Non-uniform element size

The simplification of heaps to uniform element size led to an elegant and very efficient realization. In the more general case this simplification is unacceptable, and we must adopt a totally different implementation strategy. We can no longer usefully divide memory initially into free blocks. Instead we declare that the free list comprises one block, which is the total space available. When a call is made on **NEW** the strategy is to allocate a part of a free block sufficient for the call. The free block will be reduced in size, or in the extreme case will be removed from the free list. **DISPOSE** will return a block to the free list, linking it as before. Repeated

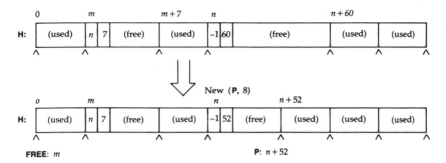

Figure 6.2 The effect of **NEW** on a heap.

use of **NEW** and **DISPOSE** will result in more and more, smaller, blocks appearing in the free list. We depict this in Fig. 6.2, for the case

NEW (P,8)

which calls for a block of size 8 to be allocated, and its identifier returned in **P**. The size of the large free block has been reduced by 8, a fact reflected in the size field, which appears in every free block.

The implementation of **NEW(P,s)** is of the form

Scan the free list to find a block of size $z \geqslant s$;
  let its address be n
Reduce the block to size $z - s$
Return $n + z - s$ in **P**

When we reduce the size of the block we may decide that $(z - s)$ is too small to be usable: in particular it may become smaller than any defined data type, or too small to still contain link and size data in the free list. In such cases we allocate the whole block instead of splitting it, and remove it entirely from the free list.

If we now dispose of item **P** we can see a further problem which must be overcome. First the diagram resulting from **DISPOSE(P,8)**:

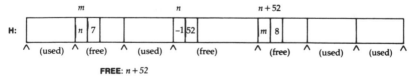

We see that a straightforward '*push*' of the block onto the free list does not return us to our original diagram: we now have two adjacent free blocks instead of one large block. In this particular case we wish to go further and coalesce the blocks. We cannot always do this of course: a further block could have been allocated after **P**, so a used block would be interposed between the free blocks at n and $n+52$. We need some method of checking blocks which are adjacent in memory, to see if they are free.

Having outlined a realization for a general heap we have, then, two residual problems: how to decide which block to use on a call of **NEW**; and how to check adjacent blocks in memory (not neighbouring blocks in the free list) to see if they are free. We take each of these in turn.

(a) Block allocation

We know that a block is chosen which is large enough to service a request. There are three major strategies, however, for deciding which of the many suitable blocks to choose.

(i) Best-fit policy: Find the smallest block large enough to satisfy the request

It may be advantageous to order the list on increasing size, to facilitate this policy. At first sight this seems a reasonable aim: if you require a block of size s then use the one which is nearest in size. The residual effect, however, is to leave a block of size $(z-s)$ on the free list, where $(z-s)$ is minimized. The policy therefore leads to a 'clutter' of small blocks, and hence a fragmentation of memory.

(ii) Worst-fit policy: Find the largest block and use it

It would be advantageous to order the free list on decreasing size for this policy. This policy certainly appears to steer clear of the problem in (i), but once again a possibly troublesome side-effect results. Large free blocks are quickly broken up leading to a narrow spectrum of block sizes. If a large block is requested, it may well be that the request cannot be satisfied.

(iii) First-fit policy: Allocate from the first block found which is large enough

The free list must not be ordered on size for this policy: its advantage lies in the random nature of allocations. The free list is made circular, and a scan is made starting from the successor block to the one used on the previous call to **NEW**. A reasonable spectrum of block sizes ensues, so this policy is the best one to use in the absence of any other information.

(b) Coalescing of blocks

We consider two methods by which the neighbours of a free block can be checked for possible coalescing. The first requires no change to the representation already introduced.

(i) Ordered free list: Order the free list on block address

The first-fit policy does not demand any order for the blocks on a free list. If we choose to order the free list by address we should still find it randomly ordered as far as size is concerned and so the benefits of first-fit are not lost. When a block is returned to the free list we scan to find its correct insertion point: let Q refer to the block which has the next lowest address to the returned block, **P**. Let **R** be the successor of **Q** in the free list. We need to perform the following:

> **if Q**+size **(Q)**=**P**   (∗ **Q** is a neighbour? ∗)
>   **then** coalesce **Q** with **P**
>   (∗ i.e. size **(Q)** is increased by size **(P)** ∗) and make **P** refer to it;
> **if P**+size **(P)**=**R**
>   **then** remove **R** from the free list
>   coalesce **P** with **R** and make **P** refer to it
>   insert **P** in the free list

If no coalescing is performed then **P** is merely inserted in the free list, as a new free block.

(ii) Tagged blocks

The difficulty of checking the status of a neighbouring block can be overcome if we insist that every block (whether used or free) has special tags in its first and last words. The tag must include a bit which is *set* if the block is used and *unset* if the block is free. Free blocks must also have the size field stored in the tag. The free list is doubly linked in order to make list operations simple. The representation of free and used blocks is depicted below:

free block:

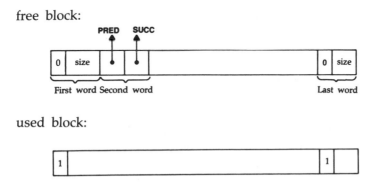

used block:

(we have made the 1-bit tag the first of a word in each case: this is beneficial if this 'sign' bit can most easily be checked). The overhead of this method is merely the two tag bits, necessary for bookkeeping, which are set aside in the used blocks. The resulting advantage is a fast implementation of the code for coalescing.

Consider the operation

DISPOSE(P, s)

where **P** refers to a block in memory depicted below:

The left-adjacent block has its tag in **W[P − 1]**, and the right-adjacent block has its in **W[P + s]**: we do not need to search the free list to check their status. The algorithm can be outlined as follows:

```
if  W[P − 1].tag = 0                    (* left-adjacent block free? *)
  then  Q: = P − W[P − 1].size;
     remove Q from the free list;
     coalesce Q with P and make P refer to it;

if  W[P + s].tag = 0
  then  remove the block at (P + s) from the free list;
     coalesce it with P and make P refer to it;
  insert P into the free list
```

The full details of the tagged-block method are presented in Knuth's volume.

(iii) Buddy system

Each of the above methods has allowed allocated blocks to be of any size, and has allowed returned blocks to coalesce with either neighbour. In the buddy system each block is constrained to have a size which is a power of 2, and has a single defined block (its buddy) with which it can coalesce. A block of size 2^j will originally have been formed by splitting a block of size 2^{j+1} into halves. The halves, if they at any time become complete and free, can be coalesced. The advantage of the method is that, given the address of a block and its size, the address of a required buddy can be simply calculated. A 1-bit tag is needed in the first word of each block, to denote whether a block is used or free. The blocks of a given size are chained together in a doubly linked circular list, to simplify the algorithms for new and dispose. We present a diagram of the representation in Fig. 6.3, and the pseudo-code for

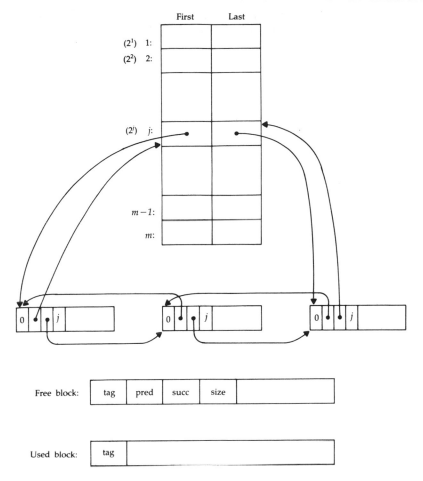

Figure 6.3 Data structures for the buddy system.

NEW and **DISPOSE** below. The links are in fact memory addresses, as before.

New (P, 2^k) ::   choose the smallest j such that $2^k \leq 2^j$ and the j-list is
                    non-empty;
                    take a block off the j-list; call it **R**;
                    while $j <> k$ **do**
                       set j to $j-1$;
                       split the block and place one half on the j-list (which
                          was empty);
                       call the other half **R**;
                    set **P** to **R**

Dispose (P, 2^k):: **while P** has not been added to a free list **do**
if Buddy **(P)** is used or of a different size
then place **P** onto the k-list
else combine with its buddy and call the new block **P**;
set k to $k+1$

The buddy of a block with address P can be found in the following way:

$$Buddy\ (P) = \begin{cases} P+2^k & \text{if } P \bmod 2^{k+1}=0 \\ P-2^k & \text{otherwise} \end{cases}$$

PART TWO

Parametrized data structures

7

Parametrized data structures: introductory comments

7.1 INTRODUCTION TO PARAMETRIZED TYPES

Type *stack* has been completely specified in Subsection 5.2.2. It is interesting to note that the type *item* was irrelevant to the specification details: we could substitute any type without changing one character in the specification itself. Type *stack* is an example of a parametrized data type, the parameter, in this case, being the type for which *item* is to stand. This idea is very useful because, without it, we would have to introduce a new specification for each variant of *stack*: one for a stack of integers, one for a stack of characters and so on. The use of parameters for procedures plays a parallel role: we do not have to introduce one procedure for swapping a with b and another for swapping c with d; if a, b, c and d are compatible, we merely introduce two parameters to the swap procedure.

The fact that a specification can be parametrized, thereby catering for a whole set of actual data types, does not mean that realizations can be parametrized also. Some languages, including Ada, even go this far. In general a different realization for each parameter is more likely to be required.

A parametrized data type will have a specification which lists the parameters in the usual way. For example

    Specification for *stack* (*item*)
        Domain
         item*
        etc.

A realization must be specific – an actual parameter will be supplied:

    Realization of **STACK (INTEGER)**
        ⋮

The *array* data type is parametrized to a greater extent. We must provide as a parameter not only the type of an element, but the type of the index also. In Subsection 3.2.2 we specified type **BITVECTOR**, for which these types were made explicit. A more general specification would be headed

Specification for *array* (*indextype, elementtype*)

where *indextype* is any ordinal type and *elementtype* is any type whatsoever (including an *array*). Each array declared in a Pascal program will supply its own parameter values, thereby generating a new instance of the generic type. A realization for each is also generated, in the form of a dope vector, associated mapping function (or access vectors) and memory block.

All of the structured types presented in Part One, with the exception of the special case *heap*, are more generally specifiable as parametrized types. We have briefly considered *stack* and *array* as typifying the approach to these structures. From now on we explicitly parametrize type specifications as appropriate. One class of parametrized types which we have not yet discussed is based on the graph of graph theory. This we briefly discuss before proceeding.

7.2 SOME CONCEPTS FROM GRAPH THEORY

In graph theory, a graph consists of a set of nodes, N, and a set of edges, E. An edge is an unordered pair of nodes, which is said to connect the two nodes. An example of a graph is

$$G = (\{1, 2, 3, 4\}, \{(1, 2), (2, 3), (3, 4), (2, 4)\})$$

which can be depicted as

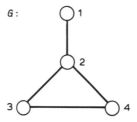

If two nodes are connected by an edge we say that they are adjacent. If we start from a node n_1, and repeatedly move to adjacent nodes until we reach n_2, then the corresponding edges form a path in the graph from n_1 to n_2. For example, if we start at node 1 in G, and move to node 2, then node 4, we see that edges (1, 2) and (2, 4) form a path from node 1 to node 4. The nodes passed through on a path must be distinct, with the exception that the same node may designate both the start and the end of the path. A path which has the same node as its start and end is called a cycle. An example of a cycle is

$$(2, 3), (3, 4), (2, 4) \quad (\text{Note: } (2, 4) \equiv (4, 2))$$

which is a path starting and ending on node 2.

A graph is said to be connected if a path exists between each pair of distinct nodes in the graph. It is said to be directed if the edges are directed, that is, if their constituent nodes are ordered. A directed graph is often depicted with arrows giving the direction of the edges. For example, if G were ordered it would be depicted as

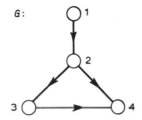

This selective view of some concepts from graph theory is sufficient for the data types we will be specifying in the coming sections. General graphs are the subject of Chapter 10. A special restriction on a graph, called a tree, is discussed in Chapter 8.

8
Type tree

A tree is a restriction on type graph. It is defined in graph theory as follows.

Definition

A *tree* is a connected, undirected graph with no cycles.

For the most part this definition is too broad for the data type normally referred to in computer science as a tree. In fact, the trees most commonly encountered are more specifically related to a rooted tree.

Definition

A *rooted tree* is a connected, directed graph in which each node has one predecessor, except a unique node called the root which has no predecessors.

This definition uses the concept of a predecessor. A node n_2 is said to have a predecessor n_1 in a graph G if the arc (n_1, n_2) is in G. Although a node will have only one predecessor in a tree, it may have many successors: adjacent nodes for which it is the predecessor.

Definition

The *degree of a node* in a tree T is the number of successors of that node in T.

Two types of node are distinguished, according to their degree.

Definition

A node of a tree T which has zero successors is called a *leaf* node of T. All other nodes are called *branch* nodes.

Trees are so called because their botanical counterparts make good models. For historical reasons trees in computer science are always depicted 'upside down' as demonstrated below. Nodes are labelled with their degree purely for demonstration purposes. For the same reason branch nodes are depicted ○ and leaf nodes □:

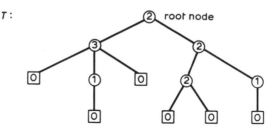

The definition of degree, above, applies to individual nodes. An important, related concept is that of the degree of a tree:

Definition

The *degree of a tree T* is the maximum degree over all nodes in *T*.

The degree of *T* above is 3.

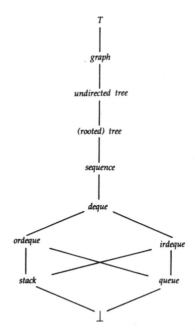

Figure 8.1 Type hierarchy for *graph* restrictions.

If we restrict type tree by insisting that its degree must be 1, then we have a structure, S, with the following characteristics:

- Each node of S has one predecessor, except one which we call the root.
- Each node of S has one successor, except one which we call the leaf.

Allowing for slight changes in terminology, we can assert that S is a *sequence*. We conclude that *sequence* is a restriction of *tree*, which may now be added to our type hierarchy. For completeness we also add *graph* and *undirected tree* (Fig. 8.1).

An important property of trees is that there is only one path between any two nodes. In particular, there is only one path from the root node to each other node in the tree.

Definition

Let the number of edges in the path from the root node of a tree T to a node n in T be L. Then the *level* of n in T is defined to be $L + 1$. The root node is ascribed the level 1.

Once again, a related definition pertains to the whole tree:

Definition

The *height* of a tree T is the maximum level over all nodes in T.

As an example, the height of the tree depicted above is 4, this being the level of several leaf nodes and no node having greater level.

There are many other terms which are used in discussing trees. Most of them are borrowed either from botanical trees or family trees. We proceed to define those which are most common. In all cases T refers to a tree and n, n_1, n_2 refer to nodes.

Definition

A *forest* is a set of disjoint, rooted trees.

Definition

Let n_1 be the predecessor of n_2 in T. Then n_1 is referred to as the *parent* of n_2 in T, and n_2 is referred to as the *child* of n_1 in T.

Definition

If n_1 and n_2 have the same parent in T then n_1 and n_2 are said to be *siblings* in T.

Definition

Let n_1 be on the path from the root node of T to n_2 in T. Then n_1 is an *ancestor* of n_2 in T and n_2 is a *descendant of n_1* in T.

We have defined a rooted tree in the first paragraph of this chapter.

There are, in fact, several equivalent definitions available each stressing a different facet of a tree structure. One of these alternative definitions will be particularly useful to us:

Definition

A (rooted) *tree T* is either null or a set of nodes with a distinguished node r called the root. The remaining nodes in T are partitioned into d disjoint subsets, called *subtrees* of T, each of which is a (rooted) tree. (The value d is the degree of r in T.)

This definition is recursive: it defines a tree in terms of subtrees which are themselves trees. The tree data structure is therefore frequently referred to as a recursive data structure. The definition places emphasis on the nodes in a tree: the edges are implied. For example, we know that

(r, n)

is an edge in T if n is the root of a subtree of T. A complete (recursive) definition of edges in terms of nodes can easily be developed: the definition of tree is indeed equivalent to our former definition.

We introduce one more general definition before looking in more detail at the definition and use of trees in computer science.

Definition

An *ordered tree*, O, is a rooted tree in which the subtrees are ordered. If we call the subtrees $O_1, O_2, \ldots, O_d$ then we say that O_i is to the left of O_j and O_j to the right of O_i if $i < j$. O_1 is referred to as the leftmost subtree.

8.1 BINARY *tree*

A binary tree is a tree of degree 2 which differs from an ordered tree of degree 2 in the following respect: an ordered tree has subtrees which are ordered; a binary tree has subtrees which are named left and right.

Definition

A *binary tree* is either null or is an ordered triple (L, r, R), where r is a distinguished node called the root node and L and R are binary trees called the *left* and *right* subtrees, respectively.

The distinction is pedantic for nodes within a tree which are of degree 0 or degree 2. The difference is apparent only when we consider nodes of degree 1. Let B be a tree of two nodes, n_1 and n_2, with n_1 as the root node. If B is ordered then this definition is sufficient to determine the unique tree

However, if B is a binary tree we are still left with two distinct interpretations

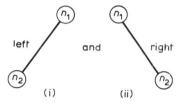

Although in some applications these two trees may be semantically equivalent, in the majority they convey very different information. In case (i) we say edge (n_1, n_2) has *left orientation*; in case (ii) it has *right orientation*.

8.1.1 Specification

Binary tree, or *bintree*, is a parametrized data type. The parameter to be supplied is its node-type. In general we will say that a binary tree comprises *node*s and specify *bintree* accordingly. The details of the specification are presented in Fig. 8.2.

One further operation which we may need in a Pascal environment is that of tree assignment. If **B1** and **B2** are binary trees, then

   ASSIGN(B1, B2)

will have no effect on **B2**, but will result in **B1** satisfying the following:

   $left(\text{B1}) = left\ (\text{B2})$
   $right\ (\text{B1}) = right\ (\text{B2})$
   $root\ (\text{B1}) = root\ (\text{B2})$

Operation *compose* is the only one worthy of further comment. It takes

```
                  Specification for BINTREE (NODE)
Domain
    (bintree, node, bintree) ∪ null   (* an ordered triple *)
Operations
    Newbintree  :—  ( ): bintree
    isnull      :—  (bintree): boolean
    left, right :—  (bintree): bintree
    root        :—  (bintree): node
    compose     :—  (bintree, node, bintree): bintree
Semantics
    For all S, T: bintree; n: node let
      isnull (newbintree) = true
      isnull (compose (S, n, t)) = false
      left (newbintree) = undefined
      left (compose (S, n, T)) = S
      right (newbintree) = undefined
      right (compose (S, n, T)) = T
      root (newbintree) = undefined
      root (compose (S, n, T)) = n
```

Figure 8.2   Specifying type **bintree (node)**.

three arguments: the first will become the *left* subtree of the resultant tree, the second will become its root and the third will become its *right* subtree. These facts are represented in the semantic definition, in axioms 4, 6 and 8. The specification can be shown to be both complete and consistent. Its formal nature caters for a formal proof of the correctness of any realization.

8.1.2 Traversals

A tree traversal is an ordering of the set of items in a tree. An algorithm is a traversal algorithm if it visits (processes) each node in the tree once. There are many traversal algorithms of use, each resulting in a different tree traversal for a given tree. We consider only three. It should be noted that, because we have a full specification for type *bintree*, we can write procedures for traversals before we give any thought to possible realizations for *bintree*. The specification is a fixed reference point in the system.

(a) Pre-order traversal

In a pre-order traversal of a tree, the root node is always visited before any other node. The pre-order traversal algorithm can be expressed as

```
Procedure Preorder (t:Bintree);
  begin
    if not Isnull(t)
      then
        begin
          Visit(Root(t));
          Preorder(Left(t));
          Preorder(Right(t))
        end
  end;
```

If we take as an example the tree T:

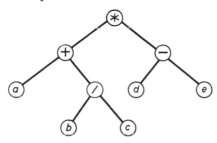

which represents the arithmetic expression $(a+(b/c))\times(d-e)$, we can see that the algorithm will progress as shown in Fig. 8.3. The pre-order traversal of T visits the nodes in the order

$\quad * + a / b c - d e$

This is the *polish* notation for the expression, otherwise known as prefix notation.

(b) In-order traversal

In an in-order traversal of a tree, the root is visited after the nodes in its left subtree but before the nodes in its right subtree. This definition leads to the following procedure implementation:

```
Procedure Inorder (t: Bintree);
  begin
    if not Isnull (t)
      then
        begin
          Inorder (Left (t));
          Visit (Root (t));
          Inorder (Right (t))
        end
  end;
```

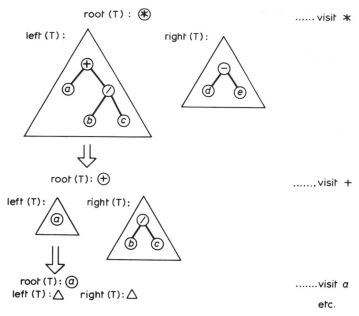

Figure 8.3 The operation of a pre-order traversal.

The in-order traversal of T visits the nodes in the order

$$a + b / c * d - e$$

This is infix notation (note that brackets would be needed before this could be given the same semantics as the original arithmetic expression).

(c) Post-order traversal

In this traversal, the nodes of the left subtree are visited first, then the nodes of the right subtree and finally the root node itself.

```
Procedure Postorder (t:Bintree);
  begin
    if not Isnull(t)
      then
        begin
          Postorder(Left(t));
          Postorder(Right(t));
          Visit(Root(t))
        end
  end;
```

This results in the following traversal for our example:

$a\ b\ c\ /\ +\ d\ e\ -\ *$

which is post-fix notation or *reverse Polish.*

(d) Tree walks

The operation of a tree traversal can be visualized more easily if we consider going for a walk around the tree, starting to the left of the root node and keeping as close to the tree as we can at each stage. The process is depicted in Fig. 8.4.

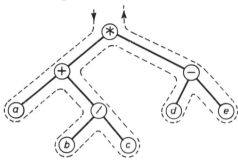

Pre-order: visit a node on passing to its left on the walk
In-order: visit a node on passing underneath it on the walk
Post-order: visit a node on passing to its right on the walk

Figure 8.4   Tree walks.

8.1.3 Some special cases of binary trees

There are many special cases of binary trees which have been defined. The three major sorts are defined here.

Definition

A *strictly binary tree* is a binary tree in which every branch node has degree 2.

An example of strictly binary trees is discussed in Section 8.4. For the following definition let h stand for the height of a binary tree.

Definition.

A *complete binary tree* is a binary tree in which all leaf nodes are at level h or level $h-1$.

It is occasionally insisted that all leaf nodes at level h are the leftmost in the tree. This is true for the tree defined in Section 8.3. The third sort of binary tree requires a prior definition before it can be presented.

Definition

The *balance* of a binary tree is the difference in height between its left and right subtrees.

We will see, in using trees, that the efficiency of an algorithm is often determined by the height of a tree. In order to enforce 'bushy' rather than 'straggly' growth, a binary tree may be restricted to being 'balanced':

Definition.

A binary tree is said to be *k-balanced* if the magnitude of its balance is at most *k* and its left and right subtrees are also *k*-balanced.

We will refer to a 1-balanced tree simply as a *balanced binary tree*. Such a tree is discussed in Subsection 14.1.2.

8.2 *N-ARY tree*

An *N*-ary tree is an ordered tree of degree *N*. We refer to an ordered tree of degree 2 as a 2-ary tree to distinguish it from a binary tree. We will only have to process *N*-ary trees in very restricted circumstances in this text, and so a formal specification is not developed. In particular, any *N*-ary tree can be represented by an equivalent binary tree.

To realize an *N*-ary tree as a binary tree we take the following steps:

(i) Introduce edges, with right orientation, between each node and its right sibling.
(ii) Remove all edges from parent node to child node, except that between a parent node and the root of its leftmost subtree, called the eldest child. This edge is given left orientation.

The root of the original tree is the root of its equivalent binary tree.

Example 8.1

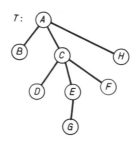

After step (i) we have

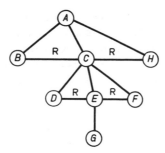

where the orientation is given as a label on an edge. After step (ii) we have

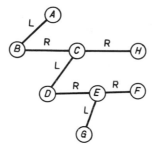

which, when drawn conventionally (and without the labels), becomes the equivalent binary tree to T:

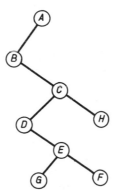

The equivalent binary tree contains exactly the same information as the original. Instead of explicitly representing parent: child relationships between nodes we represent a parent: elder-child relationship together with sibling relationships. It is not difficult to see that the original tree can be reconstructed: no information has been lost.

8.3 **REALIZATIONS**

Trees are of such importance in computer science that their realizations are many and varied. Each representation will be oriented towards specific algorithms with a defined mix of operations. Most algorithms require free movement between nodes in a tree, whether this be in order to traverse the tree, or merely to identify required nodes. Paths may be traced top down, starting at the root and moving to the leaves, or bottom up from a leaf to the root. For traversals we need to be able to move both up and down the tree. Many realizations support only one of these directly. A plethora of algorithms have been developed to counteract this problem. We consider some of these in conjunction with the representations which support them.

The realizations we consider are largely for binary trees. Some direct realizations of N-ary trees are present, but for the large part we assume that equivalent binary trees would be used.

8.3.1 **Dynamic representations**

Our definition of a binary tree is recursive: a binary tree consists of... a binary tree.... A Pascal compiler would not be able to sort out a conundrum of the form

```
TYPE  BINTREE = RECORD
                  ROOT:NODE;
                  LEFT, RIGHT:BINTREE (*?!*)
                END;
```

even though this accurately represents our intention. The problem is that the compiler does not know how much space to allocate to such an object: neither do we, accurately, except in very specific cases. We are forced to consider the details of a representation at a lower level, and this we now do.

(a) Basic dynamic

If we keep our basic *record* construction as a basis for representing a **BINTREE** we can overcome the problem of recursion by making references indirect. Instead of actually storing the subtrees in the record representing a **BINTREE**, we will simply identify them. A **BINTREE** is to be represented by a pointer to a tree element:

```
TYPE BINTREE = ^ELT;
     ELT     = RECORD
                 ROOT:NODE;
                 LEFT,RIGHT:BINTREE
               END;
```

By introducing this indirection we have taken all doubts about size out of the definitions. Each object in the system is of known, fixed size.
    The binary tree

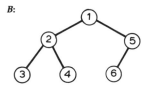

can be represented by a structure which we depict in Fig. 8.5. A leaf node will be stored in an element which has both **LEFT** and **RIGHT** pointers set to **nil**.

    For the implementation we follow the specification semantics. We therefore define implementations for **NEWBINTREE** and **COMPOSE** first (Listing 8.1).

Proof.

$$isnull\,(newbintree) \qquad = isnull\ (nil)$$
$$= (nil = nil)$$
$$= \textbf{true}$$
$$isnull(compose\,(L,\ n,\ R)) = isnull\,(temp)$$
$$= isnull(\textbf{New})$$
$$= \textbf{false}$$

(We know that **New** will never return a nil pointer.)
    The other functions are presented without analysis. Convince yourself of their validity.
    Now that we have a realization we can actually try the traversal procedures already developed. Unfortunately, we have not yet shown how to input a tree. To give a flavour of the use of *newtree* and *compose* in actually constructing a binary tree, we detail such a function for reading

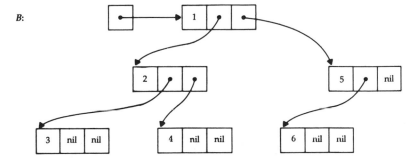

Figure 8.5 Dynamic representation of a binary tree.

```
(* Implementation of type BINTREE *)

Function NewBintree:Bintree;

(* return an empty tree *)

  begin
    NewBintree:=nil
  end;

Function Compose(l:Bintree;n:Node;r:Bintree):Bintree;

(* Compose a new tree out of L, n and R, and return it *)

  var
      temp:Bintree;                    (* for newly composed tree *)
  begin
    New(temp);
    with temp^ do
      begin
        root:=n;
        left:=l;
        right:=r
      end;
    Compose:=temp
  end;

Function Isnull(b:Bintree):Boolean;

(* return true if b is empty, false otherwise *)

  begin
    Isnull:=(b=nil)
  end;

Function Left(b:Bintree):Bintree;
  begin
    if not Isnull(b)
      then Left:=b^.left
  end;

Function Right(b:Bintree):Bintree;
  begin
    if not Isnull(b)
      then Right:=b^.right
  end;

Function Root(b:Bintree):Node;
  begin
    Root:=b^.root
  end;

(* end of implementation for BINTREE *)
```

Listing 8.1   Dynamic implementation of **BINTREE**.

```
Function Intree:Bintree;
  var ch:Char;
  begin
    read(ch);
    if ch in operators
      then                                (* branch node: an operator *)
        Intree:=Compose(Intree,ch,Intree)
      else                                (* leaf node: an operand *)
        Intree:=Compose(NewBintree,ch,NewBintree)
  end;
```

Listing 8.2 Building an expression tree from prefix input.

expression trees in prefix notation. The algorithm in Listing 8.2 assumes a set

VAR OPERATORS:SET OF CHAR;

which has been initialized by the command

OPERATORS: = ['*','/','+','−'];

It does not cater for errors in the input. Try this by inputting a tree and then printing its traversals. This can be done by simply defining procedure **VISIT** to be **WRITE**:

procedure Visit(n: Node);
begin Write(n) end;

If we wish to modify the function **INTREE** so that it detects input sequences which are not prefix trees, the changes can be simply incorporated. If we keep a count of

(number of operators read) − (number of operands read)

then function **BINTREE** should terminate with a count of − 1 and with no more characters left to read (eof = true). If eof becomes true before the count reaches − 1, or if the count reaches − 1 with eof false, the input data is in error.

(b) Traversal considerations

During the course of a tree traversal we need to move up a tree as well as down it. The representation of trees in (a) explicitly provides links for moving down a tree. How do the traversal algorithms cope with moving back up?

To answer this important question let us first depict a tree which has been partially traversed. The incomplete traversal is shown alongside the tree.

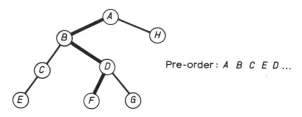

Pre-order: *A B C E D ...*

The darkened edges show a path from the root to the node currently being visited. When *F* has been visited, edge *DF* will be retraced and edge *DG* followed. In other words, after a subtree has been fully visited a return is made to the parent node. If the right subtree has yet to be traversed then the right root is visited, otherwise a return is made to the parent again. Hence, after *G* has been visited, control first returns to *D* and, as *D*'s subtrees have both been traversed, thence back to *B*. The path shown therefore shows all possible nodes which may be returned to in the future. Further, it shows the order in which they will be returned to: *D* first, then *B* and then *A*. This path can be fully represented by a *stack* of *nodes*. When a subtree has been fully traversed its root is popped from the stack. When a subtree is first visited its root is pushed onto the stack.

A stack is implicitly used in recursive algorithms. In procedure **PREORDER**, each time a call is made to itself the current value of **T** is pushed onto a stack. Upon procedure exit, the prior value of **T** is restored from the top of the stack, which is then popped. Movements up the tree are therefore 'hidden' in the details of recursion. The overhead is the space needed by the stack itself, but the simplicity of the procedure is hard to better. The use of a recursive procedure for processing a tree is not surprising given the recursive nature of its definition. Without recursion we need explicit stacks. A generic 'traverse' procedure (Listing 8.3) illustrates the point well. In this procedure, if we define procedures **a** and **b** to be null then we have a post-order traversal: if **b** and **c** are null we have a pre-order traversal and so on. Its iterative equivalent is also given.

If we are working in a language which does not provide recursion, this version (or a suitable form of it in the language being used) can be

```
Procedure Traverse(t:Bintree);

(* Recursive traversal of a Binary tree *)

begin
   if not Isnull(t)
      then
```

Listing 8.3 Recursive and iterative traversals of a bintree.

```
                begin
                  A(Root(t));
                  Traverse(Left(t));
                  B(Root(t));
                  Traverse(Right(t));
                  C(Root(t))
                end
            end;


Procedure Traverse(t:Bintree);

(* Iterative traversal of a Binary tree *)

    var
        finished:Boolean;
        progress:Stage;                    (* prelude,interlude or postlude *)
        st:Treestack;
        sp:Stagestack;
    begin
      progress:=prelude;
      while not finished do          t<>nil
        if not Isnull(t)
          then
            case progress of
              prelude:  begin
                          A(Root(t));
                          Pusht(st,t);Pushp(sp,interlude);
                          t:=Left(t)
                          (* progress=prelude for new subtree *)
                        end;
              interlude:begin
                          B(Root(t));
                          Pusht(st,t);Pushp(sp,postlude);
                          t:=Right(t);
                          progress:=prelude    (* for new subtree *)
                        end;
              postlude: begin
                          C(Root(t));
                          if Emptyt(st)
                            then finished:=true
                            else
                              begin
                                t:=Topt(st);Popt(st);
                                progress:=Topp(sp);Popp(sp)
                              end
                        end
            end (* case *)
          else
            begin
              t:=Topt(st);Popt(st);
              progress:=Topp(sp);Popp(sp)
            end
    end;
```

used. It can, of course, be simplified quite easily to result in code for the special cases of pre-order, in-order and post-order traversal.

(c) Threading

The implicit or explicit stack used in tree traversals is necessary in order to allow movement up the tree. We now investigate a first method of traversing such a tree without the need for a stack. Clearly this could be done by incorporating a *parent* pointer in each tree element, but the extra space needed to represent a tree would probably rule this out.

Consider a binary tree of N nodes represented as in (a). Such a tree will have $2N$ pointers, only $N-1$ of which will be non-**nil**. There are therefore $N+1$ **nil** pointers in the tree. A **nil** pointer represents an empty subtree, but this information can be represented in 1 bit. If this is done, then the other **nil** pointers can be used instead to identify nodes higher in the tree. The resulting tree is called a *threaded* tree. The pointers originally required to represent the binary tree are referred to as *links*, the pointers which were **nil**, but instead are being used for threading, are called *threads.* To allow efficient traversal algorithms to be developed, some convention for threading must be developed. We give one such convention in this section.

Convention

Make a left thread identify the predecessor node in in-order.
Make a right thread identify the successor node in in-order.

With this convention, threads always identify ancestor nodes. The element containing the first node in in-order will have no predecessor and so its **LEFT** field will be **nil**. Similarly, the **RIGHT** link of the element containing the last node in in-order will be **nil**. An example, shown in Fig. 8.6, will clarify the situation.

The new representation of a tree element can be defined as follows:

```
TYPE TAG  = (LINK, THREAD);
     ELTID =^ ELT;
     ELT  = RECORD
              ROOT: NODE;
              LTAG, RTAG: TAG;
              LEFT, RIGHT: ELTID
            END;
```

The **TAG** fields require only 1 bit of memory each. **LTAG** has the value **LINK** if **LEFT** identifies a subtree (is a link) and **THREAD** otherwise. **RTAG** is associated with **RIGHT** in a similar manner. We first consider how to

T:

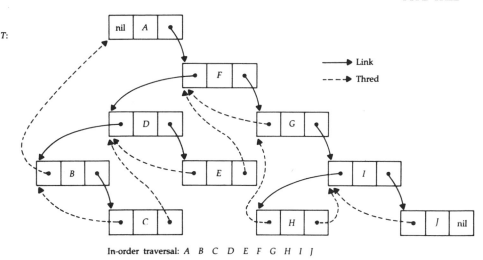

In-order traversal: A B C D E F G H I J

Figure 8.6 A threaded binary tree.

perform an in-order traversal of a threaded tree, and then how to construct one.

An in-order traversal always traverses the left subtree of a tree before visiting its root. This implies an algorithm which will repeatedly follow left links as far as it can. Our example tree has a null left subtree, so its root (A) is the first to be visited. Let us denote the element containing the node currently being visited by **CURRENT**. As we have just visited the root node, we next wish to traverse the right subtree. We must therefore follow the right **LINK** (if one exists) and then implement our repetition of following left links in order to find the *next* node in in-order. Let **S** be an **ELTID**. We can implement our algorithm by

```
S: = CURRENT^.RIGHT;
while S^.LTAG = LINK do
  S: = S^.LEFT;
CURRENT: = S
```

If we perform this on tree T with **CURRENT** initially identifying the element with node A, we find that the second node in in-order is B. Repeat the steps and we arrive at C. The statements in fact form the basis for our algorithm. To complete the algorithm we need to consider the case of visiting the root of a tree with no right subtree: in this case no subtrees remain to be traversed, so we must use the **THREAD** provided to move back up the tree. We have defined right threads to identify successors in in-order, so if the **RIGHT** pointer is a **THREAD** (as it is in the

```
Function Successor(current:Bintree):Bintree;

(* Return the successor to current in inorder.
   Current must identify an element of a tree threaded in inorder.
   Exception: undefined; no successor exists in the tree *)

var
     s:Bintree;                    (* cursor in the tree *)
begin
  if current<>nil
    then
      begin
        s:=current^.right;
        if current^.rtag=link
          then                    (* right subtree exists: follow left links *
            while s^.ltag=link do
              s:=s^.left;
        successor:=s
      end
    else Report(undefined)
end;
```

Listing 8.4 In-order successor in a threaded tree.

case of the element containing node C) we simply perform

S: = CURRENT ˆ.RIGHT

to identify this successor. We can now present a function (Listing 8.4) which, given the identifier of an element in a threaded binary tree, will deliver the element containing the successor node in in-order. A full traversal now takes the form:

(i) Identify the **FIRST** element and call it **CURRENT**.
(ii) Repeatedly use **SUCCESSOR** to identify successors.
(iii) Finish when no successor exists.

This is a straight transcription of the algorithm for processing the elements of a sequence (Section 3.3):

identify *first* of sequence;
while *not* ⟨*end* of sequence⟩ **do**
  begin
    Process (selected item);
    identify *successor* in sequence
  end;

We can write the remaining routines and hence use this program to traverse the tree. We will have developed a facet of tree which mimics a *file* and so can be used in algorithms developed for processing files (Listing 8.5). Functions **FIRST** and **SUCCESSOR** can be modified to

```
Function First(b:Bintree):Bintree;

(* Identify the element in b which is visited first in inorder *)

   var
        l:Bintree;                        (* cursor in tree *)
   begin
     l:=b;
     if not Isnull(l)
       then
         while l^.left<>nil do
               l:=l^.left;
     First:=l
   end;

Function Select(current:Bintree):Node;

   begin Select:=current^.root end;

Function Eos(current:Bintree):Boolean;
   begin Eos:=(current=nil) end;


Procedure Inorder(b:Bintree);

(* Print the inorder traversal of b, a threaded tree *)

   var
        current:Bintree;                  (* tree cursor *)
   begin
     current:=First(b);
     while not Eos(current) do
       begin
         Write(Select(current));
         current:=Successor(current)
       end;
     Writeln
   end;
```

Listing 8.5   Processing the nodes of a threaded tree in sequence.

provide a pre-order traversal of a tree threaded in the same way as the above. The details are left as an exercise.

To build a threaded tree we need to modify only our **COMPOSE** function in order to set up threads correctly. Let the compose function have trees L and R as arguments, together with a new node n. After **COMPOSE** we have the tree

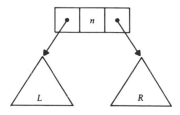

Its inorder traversal is

$$traversal(L); n; \ traversal(R)$$

so the threading within L and R remains virtually untouched. The only changes are as follows:

- The last element in L now has a successor: the new root element.
- The first element in R now has a predecessor: the new root element.

We have already developed a function which returns the element in L which contains the **FIRST** node in in-order. We can develop a similar function **LAST** to return the element containing the last node in in-order. In the case where L and R are both non-null we need only add the following two statements to function **COMPOSE**:

```
LAST (L)^.RIGHT:=temp;
FIRST (R)^.LEFT:=temp;
```

The first of these need only be performed if L is non-null; if it is null then no threading is implied by the new left subtree. This is similarly true for R. Each of the above statements must therefore be made conditional.

The resulting function is Listing 8.6.

If a tree is given a special *head* element, the iterative scans for **FIRST (R)** and **LAST(L)** can be avoided. The tree head would have the form

```
RECORD
  FIRST, LAST, TREE:^ELT
END
```

and can be set up, as far as example T is concerned, with

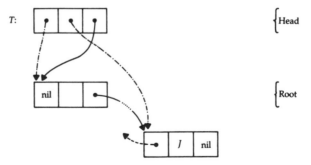

(d) Traversal: unthreaded revisited

We have investigated the threading of a tree in order to facilitate traversals with no space overhead other than the 1-bit tags. Algorithms do exist which work in a similar fashion but on trees which are not threaded. We look at one such algorithm now.

```
Function Compose(l:Bintree;n:Node;r:Bintree):Bintree;

(* compose a new threaded tree out of l,n and r and return it *)

   var
        temp:Bintree;                  (* for newly composed tree *)
   begin
     New(temp);
     with temp^ do
       begin
         root:=n;
         left:=l;
         right:=r
       end;
     if not Isnull(l)
       then
         begin
           temp^.ltag:=link;          (* left pointer is a link *)
           l:=Last(l);                (* identify successor      *)
           l^.right:=temp;            (*    and construct a thread *)
           l^.rtag:=thread
         end
       else                           (* convention: set to thread *)
         temp^.ltag:=thread;
     if not Isnull(r)
       then
         begin
           temp^.rtag:=link;          (* right pointer is a link *)
           r:=First(r);               (* identify predecessor     *)
           r^.left:=temp;             (*    and construct a thread *)
           r^.rtag:=thread
         end
       else                           (* convention: set to thread *)
         temp^.rtag:=thread;
     Compose:=temp
   end;
```

Listing 8.6 Constructing a threaded tree.

The methodology used in algorithms for traversing standard dynamic trees involves the inversion of the links in the trees. On moving down the tree from root to leaf, each link is inverted thereby giving a path from leaf to root. On retracing this path the links can be restored to their original direction. A 1-bit tag is needed for each element, to say whether the path to follow back up the tree is via the *left* or *right* links. The overall procedure embodies a case statement with three branches:

Prelude: To move to a non-null left subtree.
Interlude: To visit the root and then move to a non-null subtree.
Postlude: To retrace a path up the tree.

It is presented in Listing 8.7 in its documented form. The new representation for tree element is

TYPE TAGVALUE = (L, R);
**   BINTREE   = ^ ELT;**

```
Procedure Inorder(t:Bintree);

(* Print the nodes of t in inorder using constant space overhead.
   Assumes all tags are initially set to l (upleft) *)

   var
       pred,                            (* predecessor on path to current *)
       curr,                            (* current node on path *)
       succ:Bintree;                    (* prospective successor elt on path *)
       progress:(prelude,interlude,postlude);
   begin
     if not Isnull(t)
       then
         begin
           pred:=nil;
           curr:=t;
           progress:=prelude;
           repeat
             case progress of
               prelude:  begin
                           succ:=curr^.left; (* try left subtree *)
                           if succ<>nil      (* exists? *)
                             then            (* yes: follow link and invert it *)
                               begin
                                 curr^.left:=pred; (* invert link *)
                                 pred:=curr;       (* move left *)
                                 curr:=succ
                                 (* progress already prelude *)
                               end
                             else            (* no: visit the root next *)
                               progress:=interlude
                         end;
               interlude:begin
                           Visit(curr^.root);
                           succ:=curr^.right; (* try right subtree *)
                           if succ<>nil       (* exists? *)
                             then             (* yes: follow link and invert it *)
                               begin
                                 curr^.tag:=r;     (* signal right inversion *)
                                 curr^.right:=pred;(* invert link *)
                                 pred:=curr;       (* move right *)
                                 curr:=succ;
                                 progress:=prelude (* traverse this subtree next *)
                               end
                             else             (* no: need to retrace path *)
                               progress:=postlude
                         end;
               postlude: begin
                           if pred^.tag=1      (* retrace on left? *)
                             then              (* yes: follow left back-link  *)
                               begin          (*      and restore it.        *)
                                 succ:=pred^.left;
                                 pred^.left:=curr; (* restore link *)
                                 curr:=pred;       (* and retrace path *)
                                 pred:=succ;
                                 progress:=interlude(* left traversed:visit root
                               end
```

Listing 8.7 Traversal of a tree using link inversion.

```
              else
                begin
                  succ:=pred^.right;
                  pred^.tag:=1;      (* restore tag  *)
                  pred^.right:=curr;(*  and link     *)
                  curr:=pred;        (* retrace path *)
                  pred:=succ
                  (* progress=postlude: whole subtree traversed *)
                  (*                     so retrace further.     *)
                end
            end
      end (* case *)
    until (pred=nil)and(progress=postlude)
  end
end;
```

```
ELT        = RECORD
               ROOT: NODE;
               TAG: TAGVALUE;
               LEFT, RIGHT: BINTREE
             END;
```

Other traversal algorithms of this nature do exist. Many are studied in Knuth's volume and several, including a version of **Inorder** above, appear in Standish (see the Bibliography).

(e) Trees with data at leaves only

An important class of trees has data at the leaves only: an example is discussed in Section 8.4. A typical tree has the form

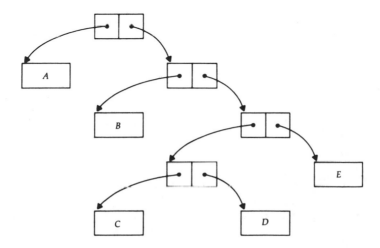

It can be seen that, rather than having two pointers *and* a data item in each element, we now require two pointers *or* a data item. A branch node must be distinguished from a leaf node by a binary **TAG**:

> **TYPE TAG** = (LEAF, BRANCH);

The type of an element will depend on whether it is a leaf or a branch: it is a variant record type.

```
LEAFTREE =  ^ ELT;
ELT         = RECORD
                 CASE SORT:TAG OF
                   LEAF:(ROOT:NODE);
                   BRANCH:(LEFT, RIGHT:LEAFTREE)
              END;
```

An empty tree will still be represented by a nil pointer. Operations **LEFT** and **RIGHT** will each return a **LEAFTREE**, which is of course a restriction on a **BINTREE**. The new implementation of **COMPOSE** demonstrates the use of this representation (Listing 8.8).

```
Function Compose(l:Leaftree;n:Node;r:Leaftree):Leaftree;

(* Compose a new leaf tree, from n or l and r, and return it *)

   var
        temp:Leaftree;                  (* for newly composed tree *)
   begin
      if Isnull(l) and Isnull(r)        (* new node a leaf? *)
         then                           (* yes: store n *)
           begin
             New(temp,leaf);            (* new leaftree of sort leaf *)
             with temp^ do
               begin
                 sort:=leaf;
                 root:=n
               end
           end
         else                           (* no: create a branch to l and r *)
           begin
             new(temp,branch);
             with temp^ do
               begin
                 sort:=branch;
                 left:=l;
                 right:=r
               end
           end;
      Compose:=temp
   end;
```

Listing 8.8 Constructing a leaftree.

For leaftrees, the function **ROOT** is only defined for trees with **SORT** = **LEAF** and must be implemented accordingly. Functions **LEFT** and **RIGHT** must return **nil** (a *null* tree) if supplied with such a tree.

(f) Parent notation

This is equally applicable to both static and dynamic realizations. We choose to consider its static form, which we do in Subsection 8.3.2(a).

8.3.2 **Static representations**

We consider two static representations for trees, each oriented towards specialized processing requirements. The first can, in fact, be used for general *N*-ary trees; the second is specifically for complete trees.

(a) Parent notation

Each node in a tree has a unique parent node, except for the root. A tree can be represented by an array, each element of which represents a node and its parent:

```
TYPE INDEX = 1..MAX;
     ELT   = RECORD
               ITEM:NODE;
               PARENT:INDEX
             END;
     TREE  = ARRAY[INDEX] OF ELT;
```

The parent field of the root node of the tree is set to identify itself. Hence the tree

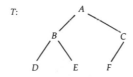

can be represented by the array

	1	2	3	4	5	6		max	
T:	C	D	E	F	A	B			{Item
	5	6	6	1	5	5			{Parent

This representation is efficient in terms of storage, but is inconvenient for top-down traversal. It is used when bottom-up traversal is required. In particular, Subsection 9.1.2 presents one algorithm which uses such trees to determine whether two nodes are in the same tree, when a forest of trees is represented in the same array. This is achieved by moving up the trees to find if the two nodes have a common ancestor: we discuss this use further in that section. Note that no ordering is represented in these trees.

(b) Positional notation

With arrays and sequences, static realizations relied on the uniformity of the structure to allow the use of functions instead of pointers for moving between elements. In general, a tree is not regular enough for efficient mappings to be developed: much space could be wasted by allocating relative positions in memory before the shape of a tree is known. However, the class of complete trees does not have this problem. A representation for complete N-ary trees can be developed which allows easy movement between parents and children. It is as easy to move up such trees as it is to move down them. We develop the positional notation for binary trees.

Let T be a complete binary tree. Store the nodes in an **array [1..MAX] of NODE**, in level by level order. In other words, store the root node in element 1, then store the level 2 nodes in left to right order, then the level 3 nodes, etc. Our earlier example is complete, and so can be used to demonstrate this process (Fig. 8.7). The index of A is 1. The index of its left child is 2, and of *its* left child is 4. In general, given a node with index i we can assert that its left child has index

$$2 \times i$$

and its right child is always next to its left child, i.e. it has index

$$2 \times i + 1$$

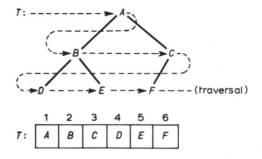

Figure 8.7 Positional notation for a tree.

Conversely, the parent of a node *i* will have index

   i div 2

which will deliver the value 0 in the special case that node *i* is the root of the whole tree. Each of these functions can be computed very quickly.

As the representation is sequential, and as position is important, the trees are unlikely to be built using function *compose*. This would require significant copying. More generally we find algorithms which fill the array sequentially, swapping node values if the particular function

```
(* Implementation of type TREE        *)

Function Newtree:Tree;
  begin Newtree:=0 end;

Function Isnull(t:Tree):Boolean;
(* return true if t is empty, false otherwise *)
  begin
    Isnull:=(t=0)
  end;

Function Left(t:Tree):Tree;
  var
      l:Integer;                        (* prospective index of left subtree *)
  begin
    if not Isnull(t)
      then
        begin
          l:=t*2;                       (* try left subtree   *)
          if l<=rep.limit               (* exists ?           *)
            then Left:=l                (*    then return it  *)
            else Left:=0                (*    else return null *)
        end
  end;

Function Right(t:Tree):Tree;
  (* very similar to Left *)

Function Parent(t:Tree):Tree;
  begin
    if not Isnull(t)
      then Parent:=(t Div 2)
  end;

Function Root(t:Tree):Node;
  begin
    if not Isnull(t)
      then Root:=rep.nodes[t]
  end;

(* end of implementation for TREE *)
```

Listing 8.9 Implementing type **TREE** using positional representation.

which determines the desired structure of the tree demands it. An algorithm of this kind is presented in Subsection 8.5.3. A realization incorporating all the non-constructor functions is developed in Listing 8.9. A tree is fully represented by the pair

$(curr, rep)$

where *curr* is the index of the root of the tree currently being considered, and *rep* identifies the array being used and the index of the last element in it. For simplicity we drop *rep* from the pair, making it implicit. This cannot be done in general, but is useful here as Pascal cannot return records from functions.

```
(* REPRESENTATION for TREE *)
   TYPE TREE = 0..MAX;
      (* all TREE indices pertain to REP.NODES where REP is a
         HEAP.. *)
         HEAP = RECORD
                     LIMIT:0..MAX;
                     NODES: ARRAY [1..MAX] OF NODE
                 END;
(* END of REPRESENTATION for TREE *)
   VAR
        REP: HEAP;
```

8.3.3 Tree compression

We have viewed tree representations from the standpoint of their ability to support key operations. In many cases we wish to be able to represent a tree without reference to any possible use: we may wish to transmit the tree over a computer network, or store it for later reconstruction. In these circumstances we are interested only in those representations with minimum required bits of information. Having found one, we need conversion algorithms which map from this compressed form to one of the more easily processed forms considered earlier. If the tree is a complete tree, then positional notation is suitable for a compressed representation: it has truely minimal storage requirements as only node information is actually present. We therefore turn our attention to more general trees.

The information contained in a tree is of two kinds: node data and shape information. The node data can be represented by a tree traversal: level by level for complete trees, pre-order for the forms below. In the case of complete trees, the shape is represented by the ordering of the node data. In the more general case we need a separate shape data structure. We consider this initially for general N-ary trees and then for strictly binary trees.

(a) N-ary tree

The shape of an ordered tree can be represented by a pre-order traversal in which the number of children of each node is represented rather than the node data, which is to be represented separately. Unary notation is used for the counts. In unary, a sequence of 1 bits is terminated by a 0 bit. The number of 1 bits gives the count of the subtrees. Thus

    1110 represents 3
    0   represents 0

If we take the 3-ary tree

its pre-order traversal is

    P: A B C D E F G H

and its shape traversal is

    S: 110 1110 0 0 0 110 0 0
        (A   B   C D E F   G H)

The shape is called a *terminating binary sequence* because the sequence is known to terminate when a count of the zeros exceeds a count of the ones. Tree T can be successfully transmitted by first sending S and then sending P. If a node contains a single character then this can be sent using ASCII encoding. In general, node data must be encoded itself in a suitably compressed form.

(b) Strictly binary tree

Each node in a strictly binary tree has either two children or none: it is either a branch node or a leaf node. This information can be coded in 1 bit of information, using 1 for a branch and 0 for a leaf.

A pre-order traversal which delivers this bit of information on visiting a node is sufficient to dictate the shape.

Example 8.2

Pre-order traversal, P: $A\ B\ C\ D\ E$
Shape traversal, S: $1\ 1\ 0\ 0\ 0$

This is again a terminating binary sequence, with the same termination property as in (a). Tree T can be uniquely reconstructed from $P + S$.

A tree can be converted to this compressed notation by an appropriate code in place of **VISIT** in a pre-order traversal. Two traversals would be necessary to produce S followed by P, but it may be just as convenient to intersperse S with P and perform only one traversal. This would be of the form

$$1\ A\ 1\ B\ 0\ C\ 0\ D\ 0\ E$$

for tree T above. The code to replace **VISIT** would be

if Isnull (Left (T))
 then Sendbit (0)
  else Sendbit (1);
Send (Root (T))

where **Sendbit** and **Send** are defined in an appropriate manner. When required, tree T can be reconstructed with the function in Listing 8.10.

```
Function Decode:Bintree;
   var
        shape:Sort;                  (* shape bit *)
        item:Node;                   (* data value *)
   begin
     Fetch(shape,item);              (* fetch the first pair *)
     if shape=branch
       then                          (* form subtrees and compose *)
         Decode:=Compose(Decode,item,Decode)
       else                          (* compose a leaf node *)
         Decode:=Compose(NewBintree,item,NewBintree)
   end;
```

Listing 8.10 Reconstruction of a compressed tree.

It remains to define procedure **Fetch**, which will return the next pair from the input sequence. For the sake of clarity, function **Decode** does not attempt to recover from errors in the input.

8.4 HEAP *tree*

Rather confusingly, and not untypically, computer science has given the same name to two different concepts: type *heap* as discussed in Section 3.5, and a complete tree with special properties. It is this latter meaning on which we now elaborate.

Let T be a complete binary tree, each node of which has a unique identifier called a *search key*, or *key* for short. As the tree is complete, it can be represented in positional notation. Let the node which has index i in the positional representation have key k_i. Then a tree of six nodes can be depicted

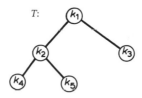

Such a tree is a heap if:

(i) The root node has a value not greater (less) than either of its children.
(ii) Each subtree is a heap.

As can be seen, a heap can be defined using either the greater than or the less than relationship. For the time being we will assume our heap to be defined using the former in its definition.

As we are using positional notation we can translate this, for a tree of n nodes, into

(i) $k_i < k_{2i}$, $\forall i \epsilon \{1 \ldots n \text{ div } 2\}$.
(ii) $k_i < k_{2i+1}$, $\forall i \epsilon \{1 \ldots (n-1) \text{ div } 2\}$.

Because of these definitions, we can assert that:

• The keys on any path from the root to a leaf will be increasing.
• The root node will have the smallest key in the heap.
• The keys of nodes at a given level are in no defined order.

It is the second of these facts which makes heaps of interest to us, together with the fact that if the root node is replaced by a node with arbitrary key then the resulting tree can be transformed back into a heap in $O(\log n)$ time (i.e. time proportional to the height of the tree). These properties allow us a fast method of extracting keys in increasing order.

Before use can be made of a heap, we need to formulate the following algorithms:

A1: Given a set of nodes with defined keys, form a heap.
A2: Given two subtrees which are heaps, and a node with random key, form a new heap from them.

Algorithm A2 is called *sift*, and is the basis of algorithm A1 and the algorithm to remove nodes in key order. It is the one we consider first, acting on a tree T.

Let T be a (possibly null) heap within T. This will be the left subtree of a new heap. Let R be a heap with T (R will be null if L is null, and may be null if L is not): R will be the right subtree of the new heap. The root of L (if it exists) will have index $2 \times i$; the root of R (if it exists) will have index $2 \times i + 1$ for some i. Let tree T be represented as in Subsection 8.3.2(b), but with **REP.NODES** having a new definition

> **array [0..max] of Node:**

with **NODES[0]** set to have a key value larger than any key in the tree. This *sentinel* will be useful in algorithm heaporder, below. It defines a key value for a null tree.

The root of the newly formed heap will have index i. Procedure **SIFT** will compare key_i with key_{2i} and key_{2i+1}:

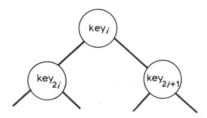

The smallest of the three must be the new root, and so must be swapped with the current root if necessary. We therefore need

> **function heaporder (var REP: HEAP; i, L, R: TREE): TREE;**
> (* **will return** ix where $key_{ix} = \min(key_i,\ key_L,\ key_R)$.
> if $ix <> i$ then will swap key_i with key_{ix} in *REP* *)

Given this procedure the **SIFT** routine follows naturally (Listing 8.11).

By repeated use of **SIFT** a heap can be built in **REP** from an initially unordered set of keys, the algorithm proceeds as follows

> Load **REP.NODES** with nodes in any key order
> Sift trees $n, n-1, \ldots, 2, 1$ in that order

Notice that procedure **SIFT** insists that, on entry, the left and right subtrees of tree i are already heaps. This is clearly true in the case of null trees, so the algorithm above will always ensure that the constraint is

```
Procedure Sift(var rep:Heap;i:Tree);

(* Given that Left(i) and Right(i) are both heaps,
   form a heap at i. All trees are in rep.        *)

  var
       l,r:Tree;                    (* Left and Right subtres of i *)
       t:Tree;                      (* Tree which had smallest root key *)
  begin
    l:=Left(i);
    r:=Right(i);
    t:=Heaporder(rep,i,l,r);
    (* t now identifies the tree with which the root of i was exchanged *)
    if t=l                          (* exchanged with l? *)
       then Sift(rep,l)             (* yes: l must be re-formed *)
       else                         (* no, but check r *)
          if t=r                    (* exchanged with r? *)
             then Sift(rep,r)       (* yes: r must be re-formed *)
  end;
```

Listing 8.11 Sifting a heap from position *i*.

satisfied. We can, in fact, go further: a tree with only one node must be a heap. We need therefore only call **SIFT** for trees

$$n \text{ div } 2, \ n \text{ div } 2 - 1, \ \ldots, \ 2, \ 1$$

Given a set of nodes already stored in **REP** we therefore present the algorithm in Listing 8.12 for forming a full heap.

Finally, we develop the algorithm for extracting nodes in key order. We know that the root node has the smallest key, so this can be extracted with no problem. What should replace it? Any node could be chosen, as **SIFT** can be used to re-form a heap with the now smallest element (previously the second smallest) at the root. The best thing to do is take the element from position **LIMIT** and decrease the **LIMIT** by 1. We arrive at algorithm **SUCC** which removes a node from the heap on each call, and **SELECT**, which returns the value of the root node of a heap (Listing 8.13). Note that we make **REP** a **var** parameter in **SELECT**.

```
Procedure Formheap(var rep:Heap);

(* form the nodes in rep into a heap in positional representation *)

  var
       t:Tree;                      (* next tree to be sifted *)
  begin
    rep.nodes[0].freq:=infinity;
    for t:=(rep.limit Div 2) downto 1 do
      Sift(rep,t)
  end;
```

Listing 8.12 Forming a heap.

```
Procedure Succ(var rep:Heap);

(* Reduce the heap by removing its root element *)

   begin
     with rep do
       if limit>0                    (* heap not empty? *)
         then                        (* no: remove root node *)
           begin
             nodes[1]:=nodes[limit];(* replace root with leaf *)
             limit:=limit-1;         (* reduce size            *)
             Sift(rep,1)             (* and reform heap.       *)
           end
   end;

Procedure Select(var rep:Heap;var val:Node);
   begin
     val:=rep.nodes[1]
   end;
```

Listing 8.13   Removing the root from a heap.

If we did not, then a costly copy would be taken. This is another Pascal feature which interferes with our intentions! We return to heaps in Subsection 13.2.1.

8.5 AN EXAMPLE: FILE COMPRESSION

We take a file compression study as an example of the use of trees. We will generate a tree representing the codes to be allocated to each character in a set, in order to minimize the length of a piece of text formed using that set. The scenario we shall take is a computer network over which files of character data are to be sent. Network charges are assumed to be proportional to the length of a message, so text compression is to be used. Clearly, the most frequently used characters in the set should be allocated the shortest codes, and the least frequently used the longest.

8.5.1 Principles

Consider a file of text which uses the characters below, with their respective frequencies:

A	25
C	10
D	30
E	20
space	15

A standard encoding would allocate 3 bits per character, resulting in an overall text length of $3n$ (assuming n characters in the text). An algorithm ascribed to Huffman builds an encoding tree from the bottom up, leaving the least frequently used characters at higher levels. Each character is initially stored in a tree of height one, giving a forest of such trees. Each tree in the forest is given a frequency, which initially is the character frequency associated with the root character.

On each iteration the two trees with lowest frequency are **COMPOSED** into a new tree with a frequency value which is the sum of those for the two subtrees. A leaftree is thus built which will eventually contain all characters and have a frequency of 100.

The leaftree for the example given is built as follows:

Pass 1

Compose a tree from C and space, with frequency 25. The forest will now be

Pass 2

Compose E with the new tree:

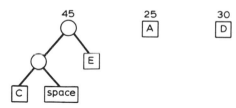

Note that E could equally well have been composed with A: the algorithm generates an optimal code set, but this may not be unique.

Pass 3

Compose A with D:

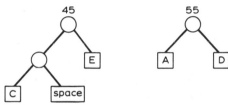

Pass 4

Compose the remaining trees:

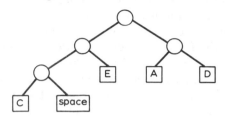

We then allocate codes to the characters in the set which relate to the paths from the root node to the characters. If the path uses a left child then a code of 0 is indicated: a move to the right indicates a 1.

To give an example, the path to the space character moves left, left again and then right. The space character is therefore allocated the code 001. The characters with their associated frequencies and codes are now

A	25	10
C	10	000
D	30	11
E	20	01
space	15	001

If we take as our text the sentence

A DEAD DECADE

our encoding of this will be

10001110110110011101000101101

which is 29 bits long. Using an equal number of bits per character we would need 39 bits. In general, we can say that the text as described will require Σ_i (freq$_i \times$ length$_i$) for $i \epsilon$ {A, C, D, E, space}

$$= (0.25 \times 2 + 0.1 \times 3 + 0.3 \times 2 + 0.2 \times 2 + 0.15 \times 3)n \text{ bits}$$
$$= 2.25n \text{ bits}$$

This compares with $3n$ originally. The saving can be considerable for large n.

The solution used in the given environment is therefore the following one. To send a file F over the network we:

(i) Generate a frequency count of each character used in the file.
(ii) Form an encoding tree from these data.
(iii) Use the tree to allocate codes to the characters.
(iv) Transmit the encoding tree.
(v) Transmit the file, mapping each character to its new code.

Step (iv) can be achieved by tree compression (Subsection 8.3.3): the characters sent will be in their standard (ASCII) coding.

The receiving node will perform a reverse mapping by reconstructing the encoding tree and decoding the text data using it. Once the tree has been constructed we start at the root and move left if an incoming text bit is 0, right if it is 1. The first part of our example message is

10...

so we move right, then left. We have reached a leaf node: this means that we have our first character (in this case A). We return to the root, ready to receive the next character. In this way the whole text can be decoded (decompressed).

8.5.2 Huffman's algorithm

The algorithm for building an optimal encoding tree, ascribed to Huffman, is not surprisingly referred to as Huffman's algorithm. The codes developed from this tree are likewise referred to as Huffman codes. The tree itself is even referred to as a Huffman encoding tree. A high-level presentation of Huffman's algorithm is given below.

Huffman's algorithm

Let F be a forest of binary leaf trees each of which initially consists only of the root node, which is of course a leaf. For each tree t in F associate a relative frequency, tf. (For the encoding example, this frequency will be that associated with a given character which is stored as the value of the root node – the only node – in each tree.)

    Let t_1, t_2 and T be trees;
    While more than one tree exists in F **do**
      begin
        select t_1 in F such that $t_1.f$ is minimum in F;
        remove t_1 from F;
        select t_2 in F such that $t_2.f$ is minimum in F;
        remove t_2 from F;
        construct T with
          Left $(T) = t_1$
          Right $(T) = t_2$
          $T.f = t_1 f + t_2.f$
        insert T into F
      end;

The final tree remaining in F will be the required optimum tree.

8.5.3 **Turning the algorithm into a program**

We wish to turn Huffman's algorithm into a Pascal program. To do this we need to:

(i) Identify the data structures involved.
(ii) Implement the operations from the algorithm in terms of operations on the data structures.

If we take the data structures first, it is not difficult to identify:

- *Tree:* A leaftree data structure.
- *Forest:* A structure which contains *trees* as elements.

We have investigated leaftrees in Subsection 8.3.1 (e), so we concentrate on the *forest*.

Each element of the forest is a tree which has an associated frequency. The only operations on a forest, once it has been constructed, are:

(i) Remove an element with lowest frequency.
(ii) Insert a new element.

We have seen in Section 8.4 that type *heap* is designed exactly with these operations in mind. Let us represent a *forest* as:

- A *heap*.
- Each node being a leaftree.
- Each node having a key value which is the associated frequency of its leaftree.

The operations on *forest* F in the algorithm can now be construed as follows:

Create F initially: Create a set of trees, each with a single node which is a character.
Form a set of nodes in the prospective heap F – each will be a pair (*tree, frequency*).
Use procedure **FORMHEAP** on F.
Select from F: *Use* **SELECT**.
Remove from F: Use **SUCC**.

The final operation, making a tree an element of F, needs more thought. The preceding operation on F is the removal of the root node, for which we are suggesting the use of **SUCC**. If instead we combine these operations, we arrive at a simple implementation in which the old root is replaced by a newly created leaftree and the heap is re-formed (procedure **Replace** of Listing 8.14). We use the representation for leaftrees given in Subsection 8.3.1 (e), using **CHAR** instead of **NODE**, and the representation of a heap as given in Subsection 8.3.2 (b), with

```
TYPE NODE = RECORD
              TREE : LEAFTREE;
              FREQ : INTEGER
         END;
```

If the character table is initially input from a Pascal file as (*character, frequency*) pairs, we can produce the Pascal version of Huffman's algorithm in Listing 8.14. Procedure **FORMHEAP** has a time compexity of

```
Function Huffman(var table:Text):Leaftree;

(* Read a set of (character,frequency) pairs from file table and
   return an optimal encoding tree for the set.    *)

  const
       dummy=' ';

  var
       t1,t2:Node;             (* receive pairs from the heap *)
       t :Node;                (* to construct new node *)
       ch:Char;                (* character input from file *)
       f :Heap;                (* a set of nodes, representing a forest *)
begin
  Reset(table,'TEMP');
  f.limit:=0;
  while not eof(table) do
    with f do
       begin                   (* create new node from (ch,freq) pair *)
         limit:=limit+1;                                 (* new node *)
         Readln(table,ch,nodes[limit].freq);         (* read freq *)
         nodes[limit].tree:=Compose(NewLeaftree,ch,NewLeaftree)(* set leaftree *)
       end;
  Formheap(f);
  while f.limit>1 do            (* more than one tree in forest? *)
    begin
       Select(f,t1);           (* lowest freq node is t1 *)
       Succ(f);                (* remove t1 from forest *)
       Select(f,t2);           (* lowest remaining is t2 *)
       with t do
         begin                 (* construct a new pair *)
            tree:=Compose(t1.tree,dummy,t2.tree);      (* branch: no root *)
            freq:=t1.freq+t2.freq
         end;
       Replace(f,t)            (* replace t2 with new pair *)
    end;
  (* f now contains a single pair or is empty *)
  if f.limit<>0
    then
       begin
         Select(f,t1);         (* remaining node in t is root of full tree *)
         Huffman:=t1.tree      (* return optimal tree *)
       end
    else                       (* no text in original file *)
       Huffman:=NewLeaftree
end;
```

Listing 8.14 Constructing a Huffman encoding tree.

$O(n \log n)$, which dominates in Huffman's algorithm. It is therefore itself of $O(n \log n)$.

8.5.4 A file compression program

For the complete file compression program we need a data structure for the character table, which we will call a codetable. We define this table as follows:

TYPE CODETABLE = array[CHAR] of CODE;

As it is indexed on character, there is no need to store the characters themselves. The code for character 'A' will be stored in the appropriate elements of a codetable **CODES**, that is

CODES['A']

and so on. The codes themselves are sequences of bits, or 0/1 values. We need to know the length of each code, so **CODE** will be a structure of the form

CODE = record
        LENGTH:0..MAX;
        BITS: array[1..MAX]of 0..1
    end;

```
Procedure Sendcompressed(var textf:Text);

(* Transmit a compressed version of the text in file textf *)

    var
        codetree:Leaftree;          (* the encoding tree *)
        codes:Codetable;            (* character codes *)
        c:Code;                     (* an individual encoding *)
        table:Text;                 (* for (char,freq) pairs *)
        ch:Char;
    begin
        c.length:=0;                (* initialise code c to null *)
        if not Eof(textf)
            then
                begin
                    Count(textf,table);      (* generate frequency count *)
                    codetree:=Huffman(table);(* form encoding tree *)
                    Encode(codetree,c,codes);(* allocate codes to characters *)
                    Sendtree(codetree);      (* transmit encoding tree *)
                    Sendtext(textf,codes)    (* transmit compressed text *)
                end
    end;
```

Listing 8.15 File compression and transmission.

The frequency and codes are never required together. When we develop a frequency counting program we use a structure

FREQ:array[CHAR] of INTEGER

instead of the codetable.

Our skeleton file compression procedure is now of the form given in Listing 8.15. Each of the procedures in the body of the if statement will be developed in turn, to complete our implementation.

Count::   This is a simple procedure which processes file **TEXTF** sequentially. Each time a character is read, its associated frequency count is updated. Finally, (*character, frequency*) pairs are written to file **Table** for all characters with non-zero count. The details are left as an exercise.

Encode::   Generate character codes in **Codes** from the encoding tree **Codetree**. **Prefix** represents, at any one time, a path from the root of **Codetree** to the subtree currently being processed. This path is expressed in 0/1 terms and so represents a prefix code for characters in the current subtree. See Listing 8.16.

Sendtree::   **Codetree** is a strictly binary **leaftree**, so the code in Subsection 8.3.3(b) must be altered accordingly. In particular, the root character is only sent when a leaf node is encountered and recursion is curtailed at leaf nodes. See Listing 8.16.

Note that when the tree is reconstructed using procedure **Decode** in Subsection 8.3.3(b), the procedure **Fetch** must return a dummy character in **Item** when it encounters a branch node. This parallels the behaviour of **Sendtree**.

Sendtext::   Another simple procedure which processes file **TEXTF** sequentially. Each time a character is read, its associated code is sent bit by bit, as stored in **Codes**. This is again left as an exercise.

The complete program will have three data types (structures) specified:

Codetable
Leaftree
Heap

Each can be realized, as suggested, with the procedures grouped in an implementation for each. These are followed by the main procedures above. The body of the main program for the data compression is the single statement

SENDCOMPRESSED (TEXT)

```
Procedure Sendtree(codetree:Leaftree);
  begin
    if Isnull(Left(codetree))           (* a leaf? *)
      then                              (* yes: send 0 then character *)
        begin
          Sendbit(0);
          Send(Root(codetree))
        end
      else                              (* no:  send 1 then the subtrees *)
        begin
          Sendbit(1);
          Sendtree(Left(codetree));
          Sendtree(Right(codetree))
        end
  end;

Procedure Encode(codetree:Leaftree;prefix:Code;var codes:Codetable);

(* Generate codes in code table from code tree.
   Prefix represents the path from the root node to codetree,
   expressed in 0/1 terms.      *)

  begin
    if Isnull(Left(codetree))
      then                              (* leaf found: prefix is complete code *)
        codes[Root(codetree)]:=prefix   (*         for the root character.     *)
      else                              (* branch node: process its subtrees.  *)
        with prefix do
          begin
            length:=length+1;                   (* extend prefix...       *)
            bits[length]:=0;                     (*    by 0                *)
            Encode(Left(codetree),prefix,codes); (*      for left subtree  *)
            bits[length]:=1;                     (*    by 1                *)
            Encode(Right(codetree),prefix,codes) (*      for right subtree *)
          end
  end;
```

Listing 8.16   Support procedures for file compression.

It would be of benefit to develop the program fully to investigate its construction. Those (few) procedures and functions for which code is not given should be developed and tested first.

We leave data type *tree* for the moment. Other *tree* variants are discussed in Chapter 14.

9
Type set *revisited*

Type *set* is a parametrized data type; the parameter specifies the type of element in the set. Rather than specify type *brochure* in Section 3.2 as a totally separate type specification, it would be truer to specify a general type *set* with *brochure* as an instance. We then have

> Specification for *set* (*item*)
> Domain
>   *item**
> Operations
>   + , *, − : − (*set, set*): *set*
>   etc.

with a separate definition

> *brochure* = *set* (*colour*)

We postulate a further operation of the form

> *select* : − (*set*) : *item*

rather than rely on an exhaustive check using the *in* operator. This will allow us to postulate sets with elements of any specified type. We assume that repeated invocations of *select* will return different elements of the set, so that a *foreach* loop can easily be constructed. The elements will, in general, be returned in an unspecified order.

   The elements of a set may be of any type. A forest, for example, is a set of trees; the workforce of a factory may be represented by a set of social security numbers and so forth. Without loss of generality we postulate a set of integers,

> *intset* = *set* (*integer*)

Any Pascal compiler would report an error if we attempted a straight Pascal realization, so we must create new realizations for *intset*. As with all data types, it is the mix of operations which determine whether a realization is good or not. If we develop several alternatives, then a judicious choice of the 'best' can be made as and when the environment is specified. We develop a few possible realizations below, but some good contenders have to be deferred until Part Three of the book.

9.1 REALIZATIONS

A vector of bits, one for each possible member of a set, has already been considered (Section 2.2). Such a representation is clearly infeasible when an element type has high cardinality, and in particular for *intset*. Two feasible approaches to representing a general set are now described.

9.1.1 Sequence

If we represent a *set* as a sequence, then each of the *set* operations must be implemented in terms of sequence operations. If the sequence order is not based on the member values then this representation is said to be unordered: if the members are stored in lexicographic order in the sequence, then it is said to be ordered. Each of these possibilities favours a different set of operations. For example, operation *compose* ([] in Pascal) with m members is $O(m)$ for an unordered sequence representation but $O(m\log m)$ for an ordered sequence, as the algorithm must use an $O(m\log m)$ sort routine (Chapter 13). However, the intersection operation (*in Pascal) on two sets, with m_1 and m_2 members, respectively, is $O(m_1 + m_2)$, or linear, for an ordered sequence but more complex for an unordered sequence. In fact, for the unordered case it is best to order the set with smaller membership (say the set with m_1 members, the sort taking $O(m_1 \log m_1)$ time) so that each member from the larger set can be checked more quickly. Each member from the larger set can be checked in $O(\log m_1)$ time (Subsection 2.2.2) giving a total of $O(m_2 \log m_1)$. The full intersection operation therefore takes time

$$O((m_1 + m_2) \log (m_1))$$

9.1.2 Tree

Consider a set of disjoint sets (two sets are disjoint if they have no member in common, that is, if their intersection is null). These can be represented by unordered trees. For example, the sets $([e_1, e_3, e_9, e_{10}, e_{11}], [e_5, e_6], [e_7])$ could be represented by

This representation is only efficient for algorithms using particular set manipulations, but such algorithms are not uncommon. One is presented below.

If, in turn, the trees are represented in parent notation then the following operations can be efficiently implemented.

(i) *Set-union:* Given two element identifiers, form the union of the two sets of which they are members.
(ii) *Which-set:* Given an element identifier, identify the root of the tree representing the set of which it is a member.

The root of a tree can be used as a set identifier. Two elements are members of the same set if and only if *Which-set* returns the same value for each.

We assume that the elements themselves can be identified efficiently, probably by use of some other structure. The algorithm using disjoint sets can therefore supply the identifier as an argument. We consider each of the operations.

Which-set :: (*element-id*) : *element-id*

The tree is in parent notation (Subsection 8.3.2(a)), so we assume that a function

Parent : − (*element-id*) : *element-id*

is available (its implementation is trivial). We assume that the parent of a level-1 node is *null* (0 for static representations, nil for dynamic). *Which-set*, in its simplest form, can now be written as

```
(* set-id = element-id *)
Function Which-set (e: Element-id): Element-id;
(* return the identifier for the set containing e *)
  begin
    while Parent (e) <> null do
      e: = Parent (e);
    Which-set := e
  end;
```

(We are using the fact here that copies are taken of value parameters, so

Changing **e** in the procedure does not affect the actual parameter supplied.) An alternative implementation of **Which-set** is considered after the **Set-union** operation.

Set-union :: *(element-id, element-id)*

The trees representing sets are unordered, and in fact their shape is irrelevant. The following three trees all represent the same set:

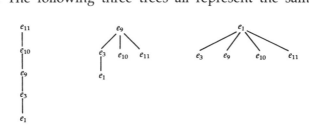

Each has its own performance characteristic with respect to **Which-set:** the last of the three obviously has the best performance (the while loop will be executed at most once) while the first one has the worst. In general, we wish to minimize the average cost of **Which-set** over all members. Before we try any such optimization, the basic **Set-union** algorithm should be detailed:

```
Procedure Set-union (s1, s2: Element-id):
  (* Form a new set as the union of two
     disjoint sets identified by s1 and s2 *)
  begin
    Set-parent (s1,s2)  (* make s1 the parent of s2 *)
  end;
```

(the set-parent procedure for the static representation in array **S** is simply

s[s1].parent: = s2)

Hence, **Set-union** of

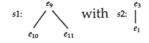

gives

The cost of **Which-set** for each of the members of the original set s remains the same now that they are members of a larger set. However, the cost for each member of set s2 has increased by one iteration of the loop: the overall cost of **Which-set** when used with each member of each set in turn has thus increased by two loop executions. If **Set-union** had been called with (s2, s1) then the representation

would have resulted. In this case the aggregated cost of **Which-set** increases by three loop executions: the representation is poorer. In fact, we can see that the extra cost is proportional to the number of elements in the second set, so to obtain the best tree with the algorithm we should execute **Set-union** with the larger set in the role of s1. This suggests that a size field should be incorporated in each root element, initially set to 1 when each element is in a different set. Let this field be accessed by **size** and set by **set-size**. We are led to an implementation of **Set-union** which follows. It makes use of a procedure, **Union**, to perform the actual union operation.

```
Procedure Union (s1, s2:Element-id);
  begin
    Set-parent (s1,s2);
    Set-size (s1, Size (s1) + Size (s2))
  end;
Procedure Set-union (s1, s2:Element-id);
  begin
    if Size (s1) > Size (s2)
      then Union (s1, s2)
      else Union (s2, s1)
  end;
```

To return to function **Which-set**, the changes above have no implications at all. The original version will still work. However, a version of **FIND** which reduces the heights of trees can be implemented. Consider **FIND(e_1)** in the example above.

When executing **FIND(e_1)**, a path is traversed to the root, e_9. By virtue of the semantics of sets, all trees which contain only elements e_1, e_3, e_9, e_{10} and e_{11} represent the same set. Therefore the element on this path can all be adjusted to give them the parent e_9. This will take as long to achieve as the basic algorithm itself, but may be worth while.

Alternatively, and particularly if accesses to a given node are grouped, we may opt for a gentler reconfiguring of the tree: we may simply wish to set the parent of e_1 to e_9 in this case. The former option is left as an exercise, the latter appears below:

```
Function Which-set (e:Element-id):Element-id;
   (* Return the identifier for the set containing e.
      Transform the tree to shorten future accesses *)
   var
        anc:Element-id;              (* ancestor of e *)
   begin
     anc:=e;
     while Parent (anc) <> null do  (* find the root *)
        anc:=Parent (anc);
     Set-parent (anc, e);           (* transform the tree *)
     Which-set:=anc                 (* return root as set-id *)
   end;
```

9.2 USING SETS

Equivalence classes are disjoint sets for which the above operations are fundamental. All members of a given set are equivalent. If a member from set $S1$ is then made equivalent to a member from a set $S2$ one of two things happens:

either $S1$ and $S2$ are the same set: the two elements are already known to be equivalent by virtue, possibly, of their defined equivalence to some third member;

or   by virtue of this new equivalence, every member of $S1$ is now equivalent to every member of $S2$ and vice versa, so a new equivalence class (a union of $S1$ and $S2$) must replace $S1$ and $S2$.

The two operations used in manipulating equivalence classes are

```
    Make equivalent:- (Element-id, Element-id)
```
and
```
    Equivalent       :- (Element-id, Element-id): Boolean.
```

These can be implemented as follows:

```
Procedure Make-equivalent (e1, e2:Element-id);
   var s1, s2: Element-id;      (* sets containing e1 and e2 *)
   begin
     s1:=Which-set (e1);
     s2:=Which-set (e2);
```

```
   if s1<>s2
      then Set-union (s1, s2)
   end;
Function Equivalent (e1, e2: Element-id):Boolean;
   begin
      Equivalent: = (Which-set (e1) = Which-set (e2))
   end;
```

Many applications of general sets appear in computer science. Frequently, it is natural to express algorithms in set notation. Instead of then transforming these to work on trees, sequences or one of the other possible contenders, it is better to take a data-abstraction approach and simply define these other types as representations of sets. In this way we maintain the advantages of data independence: we separate the formal development and proof of algorithms from the realization of the data types implied. This we do with the graph algorithms in the next chapter.

10

Type graph

To review Section 7.2, a *graph* consists of a set of nodes, N, and a set of edges, E. An edge consists of a pair of nodes (n_1, n_2), which are unordered if the graph is *undirected* and ordered if the graph is *directed*. A *directed edge* (n_1, n_2) can be traversed from n_1 to n_2 but not from n_2 to n_1.

Type *graph* is therefore parametrized by node. Its domain can be introduced by

> Specification for *graph* (*node*)
> Domain
> $N,E:N = set$ (*node*)
> $E = set$ ({*node* ϵN, *node* ϵN})

The fact that we have expressed a graph in terms of sets suggests realizations based on sets as earlier presented. We concentrate on the edge set as it is this which is most frequently manipulated in those algorithms based on graphs.

10.1 REALIZATIONS

10.1.1 Adjacency matrix

Use a bit array::Nodes are represented by consecutive integers **1..n**. An **array [1..n, 1..n] of 0..1** is maintained.

$$\textbf{Bit[i, j]} \text{ is } \begin{cases} 1 & \text{if edge \{i, j\} is in the graph} \\ 0 & \text{otherwise} \end{cases}$$

An undirected graph will be symmetric, with **Bit[i, j] = Bit[j, i]**, so can be represented by a triangular array.

The bit array is called an *adjacency matrix* for obvious reasons. It is assumed that at most one edge directly connects any node n_1 to any other node n_2. As an example, we take the graph

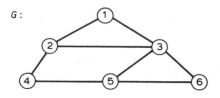

This undirected graph is represented by the matrix

	1	2	3	4	5	6
1	0	1	1	0	0	0
2	1	0	1	1	0	0
3	1	1	0	0	1	1
4	0	1	0	0	1	0
5	0	0	1	1	0	1
6	0	0	1	0	1	0

Note that the main diagonal values are all zero, and the matrix is symmetric about this diagonal. In fact we need only store the lower triangle in order to capture all the information in the matrix. For large graphs the adjacency matrix is likely to be sparse.

Sometimes an algorithm requires that each edge in a graph be given a label. If the graph represents a set of airports, with edges the flight paths between them (for simplicity assumed unique between any pair of cities), then the label could indicate a tariff, the distance or flight information depending on the environment. Such a graph would need to associate values with each 1-bit in the matrix. This is exactly one of the representations for sparse arrays discussed in Subsection 6.2.3.

Some algorithms are expressed naturally in terms of adjacency matrix operations. For example, we have shown an undirected graph in which every node is reachable from every other node: it is called a *connected* graph. A graph need not be connected. It may be of interest to know whether a graph, defined by an adjacency matrix, is or is not connected. Whether the graph is ordered or unordered, a more general requirement may be to produce the set of all node pairs $\{n_i, n_j\}$ such that a path exists from n_i to n_j in the graph (if such a path exists for all pairs, then the answer to our 'connected' query is 'yes').

Connectivity matrix

The set of all node pairs described above can be represented, once again, by a bit array. The question arises, can we generate this required bit array, which we call a connectivity matrix, starting from the adjacency matrix? Various algorithms have been devised which do exactly this. An

```
Procedure GenConnectivity(var c:Matrix);

(* Given an adjacency matrix c for a graph on n nodes,
   transform it into the connectivity matrix for c *)

   var
       i,j,k:Integer;
   begin
     for j:=1 to n do
       for i:=1 to n do
         if c[i,j]=1 then
           for k:=1 to n do
             if(c[i,k]=1)or(c[j,k]=1)
               then c[i,k]:=1
               else c[i,k]:=0
   end;
```

Listing 10.1 Roy–Warshall graph connectivity.

efficient version, known as the Roy–Warshall algorithm, after the two people who independently developed it, is implemented above as Listing 10.1.

This repeatedly checks for paths i to k, first via node 1, then via 1 or 2, etc., until possible paths via any nodes have been checked. The algorithm was developed by considering graphs in their adjacency matrix representation, the inverse of the approach taken earlier with sets. A different representation can shed new light on a problem, and suggest an alternative methodology for its solution.

10.1.2 **Adjacency lists**

Use Edge lists:: Nodes are represented by consecutive integers 1..**n**.
           An **array [1..n] of** *sequences* (lists) is maintained. **Sequence [i]** contains all nodes j for which $\{i, j\}$ is an edge. (Each sequence represents a set of edges out of the given node.)

The lists, called adjacency lists, may be represented in static or dynamic form: we assume dynamic. Taking the same example graph, we have Fig. 10.1. There is no necessity for the graph to be undirected: each arc is represented twice because of its bi-direction.

It is perhaps not surprising that this is yet another representation for a sparse array. A label for edge $\{i, j\}$ will be represented by an extra field in element j of list i, corresponding to the value of the $[i, j]$ element of a sparse matrix.

The adjacency list representation is useful for graph traversal algorithms, in which every node of a graph must be visited. Two

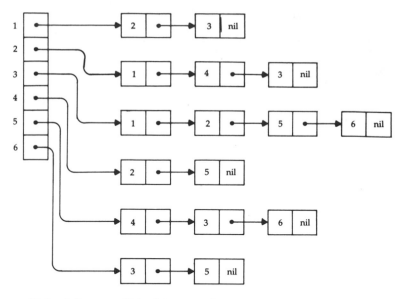

Figure 10.1 Adjacency lists for a graph.

important traversals for a graph are the Breadth First traversal and the Depth First traversal. Details of these algorithms can be found in Horowitz and Sahni (1978): they are based on the sequential processing of each adjacency list. This leads to a time complexity of $O(n+e)$, for a graph of n nodes and e edges. The equivalent algorithms using an adjacency matrix representation are $O(n^2)$ timewise. We study another problem with an efficient solution on graphs represented with adjacency lists.

Shortest route

Let each edge in a graph G be labelled with a value we will call its weight. Given a node in G designated as the *origin*, find the minimum cost of travelling from the *origin* to each other node in G. The cost of a path from the *origin* to a node is the sum of the weights of the edges involved.

E. W. Dijkstra suggested an efficient algorithm for solving this problem. A version of this algorithm follows.

> Given
>> A weighted graph $G=\{N,\ E\}$ with all weights positive and *origin* $\in N$
> Construct

A cost function
  cost:—(node, node): weight–value
which satisfies, for all $i, j \in N$,

$$cost(i, j) = \begin{cases} 0 & \text{if } i=j \\ weight(\{i, j\}) & \text{if } \{i, j\} \in E \\ \infty & \text{otherwise} \end{cases}$$

Sets $\begin{cases} T=N, \text{ each node having an associated distance attribute} \\ S=\{\} \end{cases}$

Perform
  For each $v \in T$ do
    distance $(v) := cost(origin, v)$;
  $T := T - \{origin\}$; $S := S + \{origin\}$;
  while size $(T) > 1$ **do**
    begin
      choose $u \in T$: *distance* $(u) = \min_{v \in T} (distance(v))$;
      $T := T - \{u\}$; $S := S + \{u\}$;
      for each $v \in T$ do
        distance$(v) := \min(distance(v), distance(u) + cost(u, v))$
    end

The resulting (*node, distance*) pairs in S form the set of minimum distances from the origin to the given nodes. To implement this algorithm we need to consider how to represent S and T, and how to efficiently implement *cost*. First consider S and T.

Initially $T=N$, $S=\{\}$. On each iteration of the algorithm we perform

  $T := T - \{u\}$; $S := S + \{u\}$

in effect moving a node from T to S. We therefore have the loop invariants

  $T \cup S = N$
  $T \cap S = \{\}$

In other words, T and S partition N. If they are stored together in a vector, say T in elements $1..size(T)$ and S in elements $size(T)+1..size(N)$, then we have an efficient representation. When a node is moved from T to S, we place it at position $size(T)$ (swapping with the element there) and decrement $size(T)$.

  type
    Nodeelt = record
              node : Nodevalue;

```
            edgeset:ˆ Edge;
            distance:Weightvalue
        end;
    Nodeset = array[1..max] of Nodeelt;
var
    tsize:1..max;   (* size of set T *)
    st:Nodeset;     (* sets S and T *)
```

The **edgeset** associated with each node is the adjacency list for that node. **Nodeset** therefore represents the graph G using adjacency lists, with extra attributes for each node in the form of its value (no longer implicit in its position in the array: nodes are going to be moved around) and its distance from the *origin* (or an approximation to it, in the case of T).

Recalling that we wish to remove from T the node with lowest distance on each iteration, it may be advisable to store the nodes in **st** as a heap. Operation *choose*(u) then combines with operation $T := T - \{u\}$ and $S := S + \{u\}$ in the code

```
Swap (st [1], st [tsize]);
u:=tsize;
tsize:=tsize-1;
Sift (tsize, 1)
```

Finally, we need an implementation for the *cost* function. It is used only in the context of an iteration over each node in the graph, so some contraction (optimization) is possible. Consider the first use:

for each $v \epsilon T$ do

$distance(v) := cost(origin, \ v);$

This translates into:

- Let the distance to all nodes be ∞
- except to the *origin*, whose distance is 0
- and to adjacent nodes, whose distance is the respective edge weight.

In setting all distances to ∞ we can use the iteration over all nodes to set up I initially, thus optimizing further. The adjacent nodes can be processed by following the edge list, in which each edge is represented as a

```
record
    to:Nodevalue;
    weight:Weightvalue;
    next:ˆ Edge
end;
```

```
(* Part i *)

  for v:=1 to nsize do               (* set up t *)
    with st[v] do
      begin
        node:=v;
        edgeset:=n[v].edgeset;
        distance:=infinity           (* with all distances infinity *)
      end;
  tsize:=nsize;
  with st[origin] do
    begin
      distance:=0;                   (* except the origin *)
      es:=edgeset;
      while es<>nil do
        with es^ do
          begin
            st[to].distance:=weight;   (* and adjacent nodes *)
            es:=next
          end
    end;


(* Part ii *)

  with st[u] do
    begin
      e:=edgeset;                    (* adjacency list, e *)
      distu:=distance                (* distu:=Distance(u) *)
    end;
  while e<>nil do                    (* for each v in t (adjacent to u) *)
    with e^ do
      begin
        distv:=st[to].distance;
        newdist:=distu+weight;   (* distu+Cost(u,v) *)
        if newdist<distv
          then st[to].distance:=newdist;
        (* st[to].distance is now min(distv,distu+Cost(u,v)) *)
        e:=e^.next
      end
```

Listing 10.2 Dijkstra's shortest route algorithm.

We arrive at the code segment shown in Listing 10.2. The final use of
cost is in:

> for each $v \in T$ do
> $distance(v) := \min(distance(v), \ distance(u) + cost(u, v))$

We note that:

- u is not a member of T so $cost(u,u)$ is not required.
- If $cost(u, v) = \infty$ then $distance(v)$ is to remain unchanged.
- This leaves only

$v:\{u,v\}$ is an edge

to be investigated.

Once again we make use of an adjacency list, this time for u (see Listing 10.2). We now have an efficient implementation for Dijkstra's algorithm, operating on an adjacency list representation of a graph.

10.1.3 Triples

Triples:: Assume that nodes are still represented by consecutive integers, $1 \ldots nsize$. Labelled edges are represented by ordered triples $\{i,j,l\}$ where $\{i,j\}$ is an edge with label l.

This is the third representation shared by sparse arrays. The list of triples may be ordered or unordered, depending on the application. Let us label graph G with weights, as we require for the shortest route algorithm:

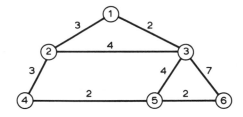

Its representation in triples is of the form

$\{1, 2, 3\}$
$\{1, 3, 2\}$
$\{2, 3, 4\}$
$\{2, 4, 3\}$
    etc.

An algorithm which processes edges in a non-random manner will find this representation compact and efficient. One such algorithm is now described.

Minimum spanning tree of a connected, undirected graph G.

Definition

Any tree comprising all nodes of G and only edges from G is called a *spanning tree* of G.

Spanning trees for our example graph include

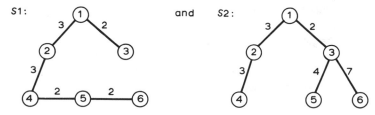

The first of these may look unlike a tree, but check it against the original definition. These trees are, in fact, not rooted trees.

Definition

The *cost* of a spanning tree is the sum of the weights of the edges in the spanning tree.

The cost of $S1$ is thus 12, and the cost of $S2$ is 19.

Definition

A spanning tree of a graph G is called a *minimum cost spanning tree* (or minimum spanning tree) if its cost is minimum over all spanning trees of G.

In fact, $S1$ can be shown to be the only minimum spanning tree for G as defined. $S1$ therefore shows how to keep G connected with the smallest associated cost.

The following algorithm will deliver a minimum cost spanning tree for a graph G. It works by building a set of unrooted trees of minimum cost: each arc is considered, in weight order. If an edge is from a node in one tree to a node in a different one, then the edge is accepted and the two trees become one. If the edge is between two nodes in the same tree, then it must be rejected: if accepted it would form a cycle and we would no longer have a tree. The algorithm terminates when $nsize-1$ edges have been accepted (for a graph with $nsize$ nodes): all spanning trees for G will have $nsize-1$ edges.

```
count := 0;
for each n ∈ N do
    initialize a tree containing only n;
while count < nsize − 1 do
    begin
        choose an arc {u,v} in E with minimum weight;
        Delete this arc from E;
        if u and v belong to the same tree
            then
```

                    discard the edge
            else
                begin
                    combine the tree containing u with that containing v;
                    accept $\{u, v\}$ as an edge in the spanning tree;
                    count : = count + 1
                end
        end;

The trees, in fact, can be represented as disjoint sets of nodes, and the minimum spanning tree as a list of edges (node pairs). With this in mind, consider the operations on trees:

> Do u and v belong to the same (disjoint) set?
> combine two disjoint sets to form one

These are exactly the operations involved in our efficient set implementation involving trees in parent notation: the trees are represented by sets of nodes which are represented by trees in parent notation. These parent-notation trees have nothing to do with the actual trees being represented except inasmuch as they comprise the same nodes: the representation of trees as other trees is a coincidence brought about by efficiency considerations.

   The graph itself (in particular the edge set for the graph) must be able to deliver edges in order of their weight. The most efficient representation is to store them in an array as triples:

```
Edge = record
         from,  to: Nodevalue;
         weight: Weightvalue
       end;
```

The array of edges can be organized as a heap, and minimum weight nodes extracted accordingly. On extraction, the edge from the 'bottom' of the heap replaces the 'root edge' and a sift is performed. The size of the heap reduces by one each time.

11
Type list

A linear list is a recursive, parametrized type. Such a list comprises an *atom* together with a linear list. It is usually specified as in Fig. 11.1. If we read *push* for *cons, pop* for *tail* and *top* for *head* then the semantics are exactly those for type *stack(atom)*. We are therefore more interested here in general *lists*. A general list, if it is not empty, consists of an *element* and a *list*. An element, in turn, is either an *atom* or a *list* (Fig. 11.2). *Atomic* will return true if the element is an *atom* and false if it is a *list*.

Specification for *linear__list* (*atom*)

Domain
   (*atom, linear__list*) ∪ {*null*}

Operations
   Newlist :–( ): *linear__list*
   head   :–(*linear__list*):*atom*
   tail   :–(*linear__list*): *linear__list*
   cons   :–(*atom, linear__list*): *linear__list*
   isnull :–(*linear__list*): *boolean*

Figure 11.1 Specifying type **LINEAR LIST**.

Specification for *List (Atom)*

Domain
   (*element, list*) ∪ {*null*}
     where *element* = *atom* ∪ *list*

Operations

   (* Operations are as above, substituting
      list for *linear__list*
   and *element* for *atom*
   together with one new operation...*)
    atomic:–(*element*): *boolean*

Figure 11.2 Specifying a general list.

It is an important property of a general *list* that many data structures can be represented by them. For example, a 2-ary *tree* can be represented by a *list* of (*node, leftsubtree, rightsubtree*) which, for the tree

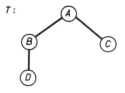

would be constructed in the form

$\quad$ T: (A, (B, (D)), (C))

(*T* is a list of three elements: the first is an atom, the other two are themselves lists. The notation fully parenthesizes each list, i.e. each non-atomic element.)

We would find that

$\quad$ *atomic*(*head*(*T*)) is true
$\quad$ *atomic* (*head*(*tail*(*T*))) is false

This is because *head*(*T*) is the atom *A*, while *head*(*tail*(*T*)) is the *list*: (*B*,(*D*)). Lists which represent trees in this way (including the degenerate case of linear list) are termed *pure lists.*

The *list* is the only data type available in the language LISP, so its generality is clearly of great importance there.

11.1 DYNAMIC REALIZATION

A list can be very efficiently represented as a linked structure. The elements must, of course, allow either lists or atoms to be represented. We use the Pascal variant record to construct such elements:

```
type Element = record
              case Atomic: Boolean of
                 true: (value: Atom);
                 false: (sublist: List)
          end;
```

The *list* itself is represented as

```
Type List    = ˆ ListElt;
     ListElt  = record
                    elt: Element;
                    tail : List
               end;
```

In fact, the rigid type structure of Pascal actually makes the use of lists, defined in this way, a little awkward. For example, operation *cons* must take an *element* as a first argument. We cannot, for example, write

cons('A', list2)

in one place (where *atom* is of type *char*) and

cons(list 1, list2)

in another: we need to create an element containing either 'A' or *list* 1 first. For example, we could write functions to allow

CONS (CREATEATOM ('A'), LIST2)

and

CONS (CREATELIST (LIST1), LIST2).

Rather than labour the implementation details, we note that the definitions given allow us to represent general *lists* adequately.

11.2 SHARED SUBLISTS

Consider the following lists

list1: (x, y, z)
list2: (list1, list 1)
list3: (list1, v, w, list2)

Figure 11.3 shows how these would be represented internally, according to the definitions of Section 11.1. We have lists with shared sublists: *list* 2

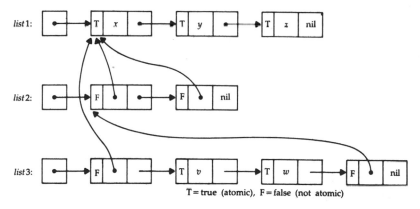

Figure 11.3 Lists with shared sublists.

and *list* 3 share *list* 1 as a sublist. Such lists are termed *re-entrant* provided that no list contains itself.

Suppose we wish to remove *x* from *list* 1 leaving (y, z). We would do this either by:

(i) Removing the element and making all references pointing to *list* 1 now point to element *y* rather than element *x*.

(ii) Copying element *y* over element *x*.

Method (ii) is clearly faster, in fact method (i) as outlined would be unreasonable for a system with a large number of lists. The problem is that it only works when the tail of the list is not null. This cannot be guaranteed in general. Hence, in many implementations we find the use of *list heads*. These are dummy first elements in lists, which are never deleted. Once a list exists it will always contain at least its head element. Hence, *list* 1 would be represented as

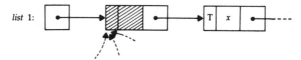

As can be seen, all references to *list* 1 actually identify its list head which never changes. The problem of method (i) disappears.

11.3 GARBAGE COLLECTION

If a system allows lists to be re-entrant, it will be very costly to check whether a list can be disposed of (i.e. returned the heap). Before doing so, a process would have to make sure that the list was not a sublist of any remaining lists in the system. This would take significantly more code and time than the algorithm would require, if bookkeeping of this kind were catered for and performed automatically. Recall that blocks of memory are allocated from the heap to store list elements. If any block becomes inaccessible from the process running, it can be collected, i.e. automatically *disposed* of. The automatic process which performs this task is called a *garbage collector*, and is an essential feature of a general-purpose list system.

All blocks which are used and cannot be collected must ultimately be accessible via defined variables, which will appear on the program run-time stack. Consider the program skeleton

```
program list_system
    var l1,l2:List;
    procedure proc;
        var l3:List;
```

```
    begin
      *2
    end;
  begin
    *1
    proc;
    *3
  end.
```

At *1, only **I1** and **I2** are on the program stack: no other variables have been declared. At this point, only blocks pertaining to elements accessible via operations on **I1** and **I2** are in use. Any others can be collected as garbage. At *2, we have **I1, I2** and **I3** on the program stack, so blocks associated with **I3** are also 'used'. On exit from proc, **I3** is removed from the program stack. We cannot immediately collect all the blocks associated with **I3** because some (or all) may also be associated with **I1** and/or **I2**: at *3 the garbage collector may be re-invoked to check this.

There are various algorithms which have been designed for the garbage collection role. We will look (not in detail) at a small, representative sample.

11.3.1 Reference counts

Let each list element (or each header element, if headers are used for all sublists which are shared) contain a count field. The value of the count field gives the number of references to that element in the system. Hence, the count field for element x in 11.2 is 4; for y it is 1 and for the head of *list*2 it is 2. Whenever a pointer is set to identify an element, the element's count field is incremented; the element which this pointer used to identify has its count field decremented. In this way the count field can be easily and efficiently maintained.

When the count field of an element reaches 0, that element can be collected as it is no longer in use: it is not accessible via any pointer in the system. The element is returned to the heap and any pointers it contains are followed, and the appropriate element counts decremented. In this way, for example, a whole tree of elements may be collected once the root node has a count of 0.

Reference counting cannot free all inaccessible structures in a system which allows cyclic lists (lists which contain themselves, either directly or indirectly). A simple example is given by the two lists

list 1 : (*list* 2)
list 2 : (*list* 1)

depicted as

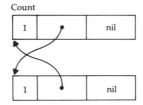

Each has a count field of 1, but neither is accessible from elsewhere: they should both be collected as garbage. Provided the lists are not cyclic this problem does not occur. If cycles do exist, then they will not be collected when they become detached: some other method would be required to trace these awkward situations.

The only remaining problem associated with this method is the space demand made by the *count* fields themselves. This overhead may not be great if headers are in use in any case, but it cannot be ignored.

In real-time situations garbage collection can become troublesome. If a very large tree structure is suddenly freed, then it may take some time before normal processing is returned: the whole structure is being collected. To alleviate this problem such structures may be freed in stages. When a reference count becomes zero, the element is returned to the free list but its own pointers are not followed: no further releases take place. The release of its sublists is delayed until the element is once again allocated: at this time its pointers are traced and the appropriate count fields decremented. Any which become zero result in more elements on the free list. In this way each element can be allocated and collected in constant time.

11.3.2 Marking

In this method, a *mark* bit is associated with each block allocated from the heap. When the heap becomes empty, a garbage collection algorithm traces all accessible elements by performing a traversal algorithm, and sets the *mark* bits to 1. Initially all mark bits are set to 0, so after the traversal all elements with a mark of 0 are inaccessible and so are collectable.

The basic algorithm uses a stack to store pointers to lists which have yet to be traversed. Elements which are *atomic* have only the *tail* to be traversed: for those which are not we need to traverse the designated sublist which is the *head* (Listing 11.1).

Having performed this algorithm, all blocks with a zero mark bit can be collected and returned to the heap. This can be done during a sequential sweep of memory.

```
procedure Mark(var s: Stack);

   (* Mark all elements accessible via the list pointers which
      are on the stack s when Mark is called ( this will be the
      value of all pointers from the program stack )          *)

   var
        p: ^ListElt;                    (* identifies next to be marked *)
   begin
     repeat
       p:=Top(s); Pop(s);               (* try next sublist *)
       if not Isnull(p) then            (* not empty and...   *)
         if Mark(p)=0 then              (* not yet traversed? *)
           begin
             Setmark(p,1);              (* set element marker to 1 *)
             if not Atomic(p)           (* and stack associated sublists *)
               then Push(s,Head(p));
             Push(s,Tail(p))
           end
     until Empty(s)
   end;
```

Listing 11.1 Marking free elements using a stack.

The major problem with this marking algorithm is that it requires stack space just when, presumably, the free space on the heap is exhausted. With this in mind, other variations of the marking algorithm have been devised. These use a link inversion technique similar to that presented earlier, in the context of trees.

Marking methods do not suffer from the problem associated with reference counts. If cyclic lists are being used, then marking can effectively remove inaccessible structures. This may be done either routinely or when the count method can free no more blocks.

PART THREE

An associative data structure:
table

12
Type table

The data structures so far discussed have the property that items stored within them are identified by their positions, whether absolute or relative, within the structure. The items themselves are treated as raw data: their values play no part in their retrieval. Type *table* is different: selection on type *table* is based on the value of the items stored there. The value of an item is therefore in two parts, the second of which may be null. The first part is called a *key* for the data item and the second is called its associated information. Information cannot be stored without an associated key, and information is retrieved by providing the associated key. For this reason *table* is referred to as an *associative data structure*. In fact, a table is a set of ordered pairs which can be specified in the manner of Fig. 12.1. We can depict a table as the set of pairs $\{(k_1, v_1), (k_2, v_2), \ldots, (k_n, v_n)\}$ where the k_i must all be defined and unique. Frequently, the tables constructed will be accessed randomly, that is, the probability that the next key to be selected will be k_i is constant for all i.

Specification for *table* (*key, value*)

Domain
  (*key, value*)*
Operations
  insert   : − (*table, key, value*) : *table*
  delete   : − (*table, key*) : *table*
  newtable : − () : *table*
  select   : − (*table, key*) : (*value, boolean*)
  isempty : − (*table*): *boolean*

  (*select* returns two results: the second reports whether or not the key is in the table)

Figure 12.1 Specifying the **table** data structure.

This is not always the case. In some algorithms the probabilities of access may be unequal for the k_i, or may depend on the preceding selection pattern. Also, the k_i may be selected in some sequence: for example, in lexicographic order. Realizations for *table* are therefore as varied as their selection patterns.

On execution of *select*, the key provided may be either a key which is in the table or a key which is not. The former will result in a *successful search*, the latter in an *unsuccessful search* of the table. Once again, prior knowledge of the proportion of successful searches to unsuccessful searches can affect the choice of a realization.

12.1 STATIC REPRESENTATION

A table with n keys can be represented in an array. Each element of the array will store one (*key, value*) pair:

```
Type Entry = record
                  key : Keyvalue;
                  value : Datavalue
             end;
     Table = record
                  n : 0 .. top;
                  entries : array [1 .. topplus1] of Entry
             end
```

(We have used **topplus1** instead of **top** so that we may use a sentinel technique for searching, described below.)

This representation allows several implementations of the various operations, each with different performance characteristics. We look at several of these possibilities, split between the main categories of ordered and unordered keys.

12.1.1 Unordered table

If the entries in the array are not made in order of key values then we have an unordered table. If we select a key, say k, then a sequential scan of the elements of the table must be made. Procedure select is implemented in Listing 12.1. The sentinel is used in order to simplify the test in the while loop: there is no need to test for passing the end of the table as we are guaranteed to find k. If it is found at position $n+1$ then it did not exist earlier, so we return the value false in **found**.

If all the keys in the table are selected with equal probability, then the average number of iterations for the while loop, representing the

```
procedure Select(var t:Table;k:Keyvalue;var v:Datavalue;var found:Boolean);

(* Input parameters:  Table t and key k;
   Output parameters: if k is in t then return its associated value in v
                                                    and true in found
                               else return false in found *)
   var
       i:Integer;
   begin
     with t do
       begin
         entries[n+1].key:=k;                  (* set sentinel *)
         i:=1;
         while entries[i].key<>k do i:=i+1;    (* search for k *)
         if i<=n                               (* k found? *)
           then                                (* yes: return (value,true) *)
             begin
               v:=entries[i].value;
               found:=true
             end
           else                                (* no:  return false *)
             found:=false
       end
   end;
```

Listing 12.1 Selection in an unordered table.

average number of key comparisons, is

$$\frac{n+1}{2}$$

An unsuccessful **select** requires $n+1$ comparisons.

If the keys are in the order $k_1, k_2, \ldots, k_n$ and key k_i has an associated selection probability of p_i then the average number of key comparisons is

$$\sum_{i=1}^{n} iP_i \quad (=(n+1)/2 \text{ if } P_i=1/n \text{ for } i \in 1..n)$$

This is minimized when the entries are placed in the array in non-increasing order of probability. These probabilities may not be known initially, and indeed they may vary with time. It is a well-known phenomenon for selections of a given key or group of keys to be grouped.

In such circumstances the array can be forced to self-organize by moving a selected item closer to the 'front' of the array. This may be done in one operation (an expensive operation with the array representation because intermediate entries must all be moved down the array) or more gradually, for example by swapping the entry with one l entries earlier in the array ($l = 1$ for the slowest migration). This latter method reorganizes the array much more slowly, so is not of use in tables used for few accesses or for which selection patterns vary with time.

12.1.2 Ordered table

If we suppose that entries in the table are in key order (a state which we can achieve by using one of the sorting methods of Chapter 13), then searching can be much faster. Consider the table

$$\{(k_1, v_1), (k_2, v_2), \ldots, (k_{mid}, v_{mid}), \ldots, (k_n, v_n)\}$$

(where $mid = (n \ \text{div} \ 2)$). Suppose we are selecting on key k. By virtue of the ordering of keys in the table we can assert the following:

To find k, if it exists, between k_{low} and k_{high}

if $k \leq k_{mid}$ then, if it is in the table, it is between k_{low} and k_{mid}
if $k > k_{mid}$ then, if k is in the table, it is between k_{mid+1} and k_{high}

We can repeat the process, if necessary, searching the appropriate slice of the array. This gives rise to the implementation of procedure **Select** given in Listing 12.2. The embedded procedure **FIND**, which embodies the algorithm above, is referred to as *binary search*.

Procedure **FIND** uses only tail recursion, so it is not difficult to convert it into its iterative equivalent. To do this, we replace the body of procedure **Find** by the following:

```
while low < high do
  begin
    mid: = (low + high) Div 2;
    if k < = t. entries[mid]. key
      then high: = mid
      else low: = mid + 1
  end;
Find: = high
```

The search range for **Find** is halved on each iteration. Its time complexity is $O(\log n)$.

For search on general ordered tables based solely on key comparisons, binary search is optimal. If, however, the keys are uniformly distributed over their domain, an algorithm with better asymptotic behaviour has been devised. This algorithm, known as *interpolation search*, calculates the expected position of the key given the

```
procedure Select(var t:Table;k:Keyvalue;var v:Datavalue;var found:Boolean);

(* Input parameters:  Table t and key k;
   Output parameters: if k is in t then return its associated value in v
                                         and true in found
                               else return false in found *)
   var
       i:Integer;

function Find(low,high:Index):Index;

(* Input parameters:  low,high - the limits of a search in t for k.
    On termination:    Find will return the index of k in t, if it exists *)

   var
        mid:Index;                       (* between low and high *)
   begin
     if low<high
       then
         begin
           mid:=(low+high) div 2;
           if k<=t.entries[mid].key
              then Find:=Find(low,mid)
              else Find:=Find(mid+1,high)
         end
       else Find:=high
   end;
begin
  i:=Find(1,t.n);
  with t.entries[i] do
     if k=key
       then
         begin
           v:=value;
           found:=true
         end
       else
         found:=false
end;
```

Listing 12.2 Selection in an ordered table.

values of k_{low} and k_{high}. If, say, k is mid-way between k_{low} and k_{high} then, given the uniform distribution of the keys, we can expect k to be in (or near) $k_{(low+high) div 2}$. In general we probe position

$$\text{int } ((k - k_{low})/(k_{high} - k_{low}) \times (high - low)) + low$$

rather than position *mid*.

The asymptotic behaviour of *find* based on this probe is $O(\log \log n)$, but its behaviour is very dependent on the uniform distribution property. Even with this property, the cost of the probe is more expensive than in binary search. We can therefore expect that binary search will in practice outperform interpolation search for n relatively small (how small will depend on each specific implementation).

The problem with ordered searching is, of course, that the table must be kept ordered. Whereas *insert* is $O(1)$ for an unordered table, it is $O(n)$ for an ordered one. This is acceptable only if insertions are relatively infrequent. If this is not the case then one of the alternative realizations (Chapter 14) must be considered. In fact, as we shall see, the performance of *select* can be improved even further by the use of a technique known as *hashing*. The advantage still retained by ordered searching is that of identifying a range of key values, for example in retrieving all values associated with keys in a specified range *minreqd... maxreqd*. A variant of binary search is extremely efficient for such requests, which cannot be efficiently answered using hashing (see Section 14.3).

12.2 DYNAMIC REPRESENTATION

Initially, let us concentrate on operation *select* and its associated search procedure *find*. Binary search works efficiently because it repeatedly halves the number of entries which need to be searched, until only one candidate remains. In the sequential case, the 'midkey' entry can be found each time by a simple calculation: a typical property of these representations. The parallel property for dynamic representations is that these critical entries are identified explicitly. Hence a projected representation would have the following properties:

A table is a set of (*key*, *entry*) pairs.
The entry which has key with median value is identified as *mid*.
The other entries are partitioned into two tables:
　　one contains all entries with keys less than *mid*;
　　one contains all entries with keys greater than *mid*.

If we read 'binary tree' for 'table' and 'root' for 'mid' then an obvious representation for an ordered table is

　　bintree(*entry*)

for which we already have a good dynamic representation. This leads to the following representation of a table in Pascal:

```
Type Table = ^Node;
     Node = record
                key: Keyvalue;
                value: Datavalue;
                left, right: Table
            end;
```

A non-null table can be depicted as

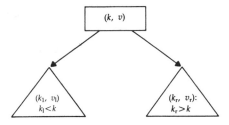

In fact, k does not have to be the median value for the tree to be used for search: only the ordering property is necessary.

Definition

A binary tree is a *binary search tree* if an ordering is defined for all items in the tree and the following properties hold:

- All items in the left subtree of the tree precede the root item in the defined ordering.
- All items in the right subtree of the tree succeed the root item in the defined ordering.
- Each subtree is itself a binary search tree.

If the root is the median item in the ordering, and this is true for all subtrees, then the tree will be complete and the associated *find* routine (see below) will be $O(\log n)$. If the tree becomes unbalanced then the performance will deteriorate: in the worst case the tree will degenerate into a linear list, in which case searches will take time $O(n)$. Algorithms for keeping a search tree balanced are discussed in Section 14.1.

Procedure **FIND**, written to be local to a **SELECT** procedure with parameters as defined earlier, takes the form of Listing 12.3 Procedure **SELECT** consists of the single Pascal statement **FIND(T)**. When inserting a new (*key*, *value*) pair we undertake a similar *find*, but expect to arrive at a null tree where a tree with key k would otherwise have been expected. A new node must be created at this point in the tree (Listing 12.4).

An in-order traversal of a binary search tree will visit the nodes in lexicographic order. This can be used to advantage in visiting all nodes in a given range (*lowkey...highkey*). This is embodied in procedure **SELECT RANGE**, in Listing 12.5. Of course, if the search tree is stored as a threaded tree then the procedure becomes even simpler: the first key not

```
procedure Select(t:Table;k:Keyvalue;var v:Datavalue;var found:Boolean);

  procedure Find(t:Table);
    begin
      if t<>nil                      (* tree not empty? *)
        then                         (* more checking to do *)
          if k=t^.key
            then                     (* found: report (value,true) *)
              begin
                v:=t^.value;
                found:=true
              end
            else                     (* not yet found: check a subtree *)
              if k<t^.key
                then Find(t^.left)
                else Find(t^.right)
        else                         (* key not present *)
          found:=false
    end;
begin(* Select *)
  Find(t)
end;
```

Listing 12.3   Selection in a binary search tree.

```
procedure Insert(var t:Table;k:Keyvalue;v:Datavalue);

(* Insert (k,v) into table t, a binary search tree.
   Exception: duplicatekey; key k already exists in t *)

  begin
    if t<>nil
      then                          (* find insertion point *)
        if k=t^.key                  (* key already inserted? *)
          then Report(duplicatekey)
          else                       (* not yet found: continue *)
            if k<t^.key
              then Insert(t^.left,k,v)
              else Insert(t^.right,k,v)
      else                          (* insertion point found *)
        begin
          new(t);
          with t^ do
            begin
              key:=k;    value:=v;
              left:=nil; right:=nil
            end
        end
  end;
```

Listing 12.4   Insertion in a binary search tree.

less than *lowkey* is identified, and **SUCC** is repeatedly used until a key value larger than *highkey* is returned.

We consider alternative representations suitable for random selections and insertions in Chapter 14. Before that, we turn our attention to algorithms which process all table entries in some defined order. These can be performed efficiently if the table is similarly ordered, so we briefly consider ordering, or sorting, procedures.

```
procedure SelectRange(t:Table;lowkey,highkey:Keyvalue);

(* Accept all entries in t with key values between lowkey and highkey *)

begin
  if t<>nil
    then with t^ do
      begin
        if lowkey<key
          then                            (* visit subset in left subtree *)
            SelectRange(left,lowkey,highkey);
        if (lowkey<=key)and(key<=highkey)
          then Accept(value);             (* visit root *)
        if key<highkey
          then                            (* visit subset in right subtree *)
            SelectRange(right,lowkey,highkey)
      end
end;
```

Listing 12.5   Selecting a range of keys in a binary search tree.

13

Sorting techniques

The object of a sorting algorithm is to take an unordered table as input and produce an ordered table as output. This table must be a permutation of the entries in the original table. If the algorithm uses only a small number of auxiliary variables and delivers the result in the same memory space as the original unordered table, then the sort is said to be performed *in situ*.

Tables may be sorted on their key, their value field or any function on, or subset of these. In particular, the value field may itself be compound and the sort may be on a subfield or subfields of it. We therefore distinguish between the key of an entry and the field or fields in an entry used for ordering the table. We call these sort fields the *sort key*. In general, therefore, we cannot assert that a set of sort keys will be distinct.

Sorting algorithms exhibit different behaviours with respect to certain important criteria. We define two of these below.

Definition

A sorting algorithm is said to be *stable* if entries which have the same sort key are left in the same relative order as before the sort.

Stable sorting algorithms are useful when sorting an ordered file on a different sort key: the resulting file will be sorted on the second sort key but the original sort key will define the ordering within entries having a common second sort key. As an example, consider a table of bank transactions sorted in chronological order (i.e. their first sort key is time). If this table is now sorted on account number, using a stable sort algorithm, then the resulting file will have entries for a given account number grouped together, and sorted within the group on time of transaction.

Definition

A sort algorithm is said to exhibit *natural behaviour* if its performance is improved by input tables which are already nearly ordered.

For some applications the input will be in good order, with few entries out of place. In others the input may be totally random. In the former situation, algorithms exhibiting natural behaviour are obviously desirable.

For algorithms which require entries to be frequently copied, moving them repeatedly about memory until they appear correctly placed in the output table, the size of an entry may have significant impact on performance. Under such conditions it may be best to change the representation of a table to one which uses *detached keys*. In this case, we represent a table by a set of

(*sortkey, item-identifier*)

pairs, with the non-sort-key fields of each entry stored in records identified by the second of each pair. This indirection allows us to manipulate these (much smaller) pairs with the sort algorithm chosen. Once sorted, the true output table can be constructed by a single pass over the pairs. For large entries with relatively small sort keys, this change in representation can result in significantly increased efficiency.

13.1 STATIC REPRESENTATION

When entries are stored in an array, all entries are equally accessible and algorithms are unconstrained. Two basic classes of algorithm exist under these circumstances. The first is based solely on comparing keys and moving elements on the basis of the result of each comparison. The second is based on address calculation: it uses a technique similar to that used in interpolation search to identify the general area of the array in which the entry should be stored. Basic key comparison may refine this first 'probe'. We consider key comparison methods. Those interested in the interpolation methods are referred to the Bibliography (Gonnet, 1984).

13.1.1 Key comparison methods

For n distinct sort keys there are $n!$ possible permutations of entries representing $n!$ representations of the same table: one of these is sorted (ordered). Theoretically we must make enough (binary) comparisons to distinguish between this number of different tables. Information theory tells us, therefore, that we need

$$\log_2 n!$$

comparisons. By Stirling's approximation we can rewrite this approximately as

$$\log_2 \sqrt{(2\pi n)} + n\log_2 n - n\log_2 e \Rightarrow n\log_2 n \quad \text{(as } n \to \infty)$$

The best asymptotic behaviour that we can expect from a key-comparison class algorithm therefore has time complexity

$$O(n\log n)$$

It should be kept in mind, however, that even if we do achieve an algorithm exhibiting this characteristic, it may, for a given data set, perform worse than a simpler algorithm which has complexity $O(n^2)$. This is because n may not be large enough for the algorithm to demonstrate its advantages: the lower order ('overhead') terms sometimes dominate for small n. The actual value of n at which the $n\log n$ behaviour becomes significant is highly dependent on the computer system being used, so any suggestions must be considered either speculative or particular to a given machine under given conditions, such as entry size.

Three basic approaches to achieving a sort are considered in this section. The first method repeatedly selects and removes the entry from the input table with lowest sort key, placing it immediately after the previous one selected. Such an algorithm is referred to as a *selection sort*. An *insertion sort* accepts the next entry irrespective of its key, and inserts it in its correct position with respect to those already in the output table. In an *exchange sort*, pairs of entries have their sort keys compared: the entries exchange positions in the table if they are out of relative order.

(a) Selection sort

The basic *in situ* selection-sort algorithm scans the entries sequentially to find the one with the smallest key. On iteration i, the smallest entry is swapped with the entry in position i of the array (Listing 13.1).

This procedure has two virtues as far as sorting is concerned: it is simple (there are few time-consuming house-keeping operations) and each complete entry is moved only a constant number of times (each is involved in two swaps and so is copied exactly four times). The number of comparisons made is $n/2 \times (n-1)$, and the algorithm is $O(n^2)$. This poor asymptotic behaviour is counterbalanced by the advantages given for small n and particularly for large entries, though detached keys become a significant alternative in this latter case. The usual 'rule of thumb' suggests using basic selection sort for $n < 10$ (with all the provisos made earlier).

The reason that selection sort behaves poorly for large n is that many of the comparisons are 'wasted': they result in no structural change and

```
procedure SelectionSort(var e:EntryArray;low,high:Index);

(* Sort the entries in e between low and high into key order.
   Functions/procedures used: Swap(entry,entry) *)

    var
        i,j,min:Index;
        emin:Entry;
        key:Integer;
    begin
      for i:=low to high-1 do              (* select the i-th smallest *)
        begin
          min:=i;                          (* min key so far is in e[min] *)
          key:=e[min].key;
          for j:=i+1 to high do            (* check for a smaller key *)
            if(e[j].key<key)               (* e[j] precedes e[min] ? *)
              then
                begin
                  min:=j;
                  key:=e[min].key
                end;
          Swap(e[min],e[i])
        end                                (* e[l] to e[i] is now ordered *)
    end;
```

Listing 13.1 Basic selection sorting.

the input entries remain random. We have discussed the issue of selecting the smallest from a set of entries when we introduced the tree heap. If we organize the input table as a heap, then the select operation itself becomes very simple. After each selection, the table must be resifted. Each sift is of $O(\log n)$, so n selections can result in a sort of the table in time $O(n \log n)$: its asymptotic behaviour is optimal for key comparison methods. The resulting procedure is called *heapsort*. In fact, heapsort requires one minor modification from the above if we are to sort *in situ*: the heap must always be in positions $1 \ldots i$, for some i, so the output table must be built 'backwards' from position n. This means that the heap must be organized to deliver the entry with the largest key each time: the change is minimal.

Heapsort now behaves as follows (see Fig. 13.1). On iteration

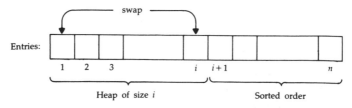

Figure 13.1 Heapsort in operation.

$(n-i+1)$ we swap **Entries[1]** (which is the largest remaining entry) with **Entries [i]**. The sorted section of **Entries** is now from positions i through n and the heap has been reduced in size to $i-1$. The entry now in **Entries[1]** must be sifted to its correct position in the heap. After $n-1$ iterations the sort will be complete. The skeleton of heapsort is

```
Formheap (* with maximum at root *);
for i:=n downto 2 do
    begin
        Swap (Entries[1], Entries[i]);
        Sift (1, i-1)
    end
```

Heapsort is not stable and does not exhibit natural behaviour. Its performance, however, is consistently good. We come across it again when considering tables which are too large to fit into main memory: such tables can be partially sorted using the array representations before other algorithms are used (Section 13.2).

(b) Insertion sort

Insertion sort, in its basic form, scans the partially constructed output table for the correct insertion point of the next entry. Entries which

```
procedure InsertionSort(var e:EntryArray;n:Index);

(* Sort the n entries in e into key order.
   Assumes e[0] is available for a sentinel *)

var
     i,j,min:Index;
     current:Entry;
     key:Keyvalue;
begin
   e[0].key:=smallestkey;              (* a sentinel *)
   for i:=2 to n do
     begin
       current:=e[i];
       key:=current.key;
       j:=i-1;                         (*extent of sorted output section *)
       while e[j].key>key do           (* move entries *)
         begin
           e[j+1]:=e[j];
           j:=j-1
         end;
       e[j+1]:=current                 (* j+1 is correct insertion point *)
     end
end;
```

Listing 13.2 Basic insertion sorting.

follow the new entry in the ordered table must all be moved to make room for the insertion. For an *in situ* sort, the output table is constructed in positions $1 \ldots i-1$, with the next entry to be considered being at position i (Listing 13.2).

Insertion sort is stable and exhibits natural behaviour, but its time complexity is $O(n^2)$ so it is useful only for small n. A marginal improvement can be made by recognizing that insertions are made into a sorted array slice, so the number of comparisons to find the insertion point can be reduced by using binary search. This improvement does not reduce element copying, so the overall performance is only marginally improved and its asymptotic behaviour is still $O(n^2)$.

The weakness of insertion sort is the slow way in which entries in the output table migrate to their correct (final) position: they move only one position at a time (in the 'move entries' loop). In a variation of insertion sort called *Shellsort* (named after D. L. Shell who first reported it), this weakness is overcome. Repeated insertion sorts are performed on subsets of the input table, with a final insertion sort of the whole table to guarantee a correct sort. The algorithm relies on the natural behaviour of insertion sort: the early passes over the data move entries quickly to positions close to their eventual 'home', and the final insertion sort therefore works on a fairly well-ordered table. Shellsort works as follows (see Fig. 13.2).

First of all an ordered set of k-values is devised, where the set must be strictly decreasing with the final k-value a 1. For each k-value, k_i, subsets of table entries are sorted by insertion sort. A subset will consist of all entries distance k_i apart. Two examples are shown, the first consisting of *entries*[1], *entries*[k_i+1], *entries*[$2k_i+1$], etc. There will be k_i such sets. When the table has been k_i sorted (by sorting all k_i subsets) it is then k_i+1 sorted. It will eventually be 1-sorted (i.e. simple insertion sorted). The insertion sorts cause entries to move k_i positions on each copy, thus speeding up their migration.

No sequence of k-values has been shown to be optimal for the algorithm, but some sequences have been shown to be very effective.

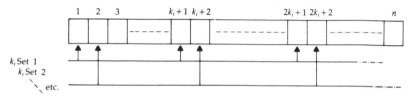

Figure 13.2 Shellsort in operation.

These include sequences in which

$$k_{i-1} = d k_i + 1$$

for d with value 2, 3 or 5. For example, with $d = 2$ we have the sequence

$$\ldots, \ 31, \ 15, \ 7, \ 3, \ 1$$

The asymptotic behaviour of Shellsort is approximately $O(n^{1.2})$, but its algorithm is simple and the overheads small so its behaviour experimentally is good even for $n \approx 10^4$. Above this value the $O(n\log n)$ algorithm heapsort may well outperform it.

Shellsort is not stable but does exhibit natural behaviour.

(c) Exchange sorting

This method is based on key comparisons. In its basic form, no sorted subtable emerges, but the whole table is gradually put into order. Entries migrate according to the result of comparisons. If two entries are found to be out of order they are immediately swapped ('exchanged'). In the simplest exchange sort, called *bubblesort,* only adjacent elements are compared. Bubblesort therefore suffers from the same problem as insertion sort and in fact has complexity $O(n^2)$. (The name 'bubble' sort comes from the fact that on each pass of the algorithm the entry with the smallest remaining key 'bubbles' to the top of the input entries, to join the output set.)

Quicksort is an exchange sort which overcomes the limitation of bubblesort by moving entries over much larger distances. It is a *divide and conquer* algorithm, in which the original table is partitioned into two smaller tables each of which can be independently sorted. This process is repeated recursively. Consider the diagram in Fig. 13.3. Indices i and j are swept progressively towards each other, i starting at low and j starting at *high*. Suppose the median key value in the table is *kmid*. First, i is repeatedly incremented until a value greater than *kmid* is found. Secondly, j is decremented until a value less than *kmid* is found. If j and i have not crossed then k_i and k_j are in the wrong halves of the array and can be swapped. After i and j have met, all keys to the left of *kmid* will be smaller than it, and all those to the right will be larger: the table is said to be partitioned about *kmid*. The same process can now be

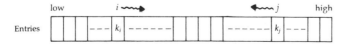

Figure 13.3 Partitioning entries in an array.

carried out on each half of the table, using the appropriate value of *kmid* in each case.

Stated in this way, the algorithm has a complexity of $O(n \log n)$ and, as its name suggests, has been found to be very efficient indeed in practice. There is one major flaw in the idea: *kmid* will not be known and cannot be computed cheaply. This means that the algorithm actually estimates *kmid* by choosing a random entry and partitioning about it. Various possibilities exist. *Entry*[1] may be chosen, but would result in the algorithm exhibiting unnatural behaviour. *Entry*[(*low* + *high*) div 2] could be chosen to overcome this, and is most often used. Whatever is chosen, there is always the possibility that a particular ordering of the input could result in the algorithm behaving according to its worst-case rather than average-case analysis. In the worst case the algorithm may take time $O(n^2)$. Because of its remarkable average-case performance, and the fact that the pathological worst cases can be made arbitrarily improbable by a suitable choice of partitioning value, Quicksort is a very popular choice for efficient sorting. Various versions of Quicksort do exist, some recursive and some iterative. We choose to show a recursive version (Listing 13.3) which uses selection sort to sort slices of the table smaller than some critical size (10 was suggested earlier). Note that the version

```
procedure QuickSort(var e:EntryArray;low,high:Index);
   var
       i,j:Index;
       midkey:Integer;
   begin
     if high-low>=critical              (* worth using Quicksort? *)
        then                            (* yes: perform Quicksort *)
          begin
            i:=low; j:=high;
            midkey:=e[(i+j)div 2].key;
            while i<=j do               (* partition about midkey *)
              begin
                while e[i].key<midkey do i:=i+1;
                while e[j].key>midkey do j:=j-1;
                if i<=j then            (* e[i] and e[j] on wrong sides *)
                  begin
                    if i<>j then Swap(e[i],e[j]);
                    i:=i+1; j:=j-1
                  end
              end;                      (* midkey is now in its correct place *)
            QuickSort(e,low,j);
            QuickSort(e,i,high)
          end
        else                            (* not worth using Quicksort *)
          SelectionSort(e,low,high)
   end;
```

Listing 13.3   Recursive Quicksort with selection sort for small intervals.

of Quicksort used defines the interval to be sorted, rather than assuming a sort from 1 to n.

The only further problem with Quicksort is that it requires a stack for controlling the recursion. This stack can give the algorithm a space overhead of $O(n)$ in the worst case, but a small variation in the calling sequence can reduce this to $O(\log n)$. When the two (recursive) calls on Quicksort are made, the smaller interval should be processed first: the current order of calls should be maintained only when $(j - low) < (high - i)$.

13.2 DYNAMIC REPRESENTATION

Suppose that a table cannot be randomly accessed, but instead is represented by a sequence. This is the situation when very large tables are represented as Pascal files and stored on external media such as disc or tape. The key comparison methods so far discussed are inapplicable to this situation, and new algorithms must be defined which are based only on the available sequence operations. It is perhaps surprising that, in spite of this limited access, algorithms have been developed with asymptotic behaviour $O(n \log n)$. Because of the limited access capabilities, these algorithms usually require extra storage space: the more independent media available the better the performance.

It is a characteristic of external media that algorithms are limited mainly by the number of transfers to and from main memory, rather than the number of instructions executed to achieve the sort. It is therefore the aim of these algorithms to minimize data transfers. The algorithms we look at are all based on the operation of *merging* two sorted files to form one. We refer to files rather than to tables to keep the representation in mind.

13.2.1 File merging

The input to a *file merge* algorithm consists of two sorted files which we will refer to as *in* 1 and *in* 2. The output is a single file, *out*, which is itself sorted and which consists of all entries from *in* 1 and *in* 2. If the first entry from *in* 1 precedes the first entry from *in* 2 in the defined ordering, then the *in* 1 entry is written to *out* and the next entry from *in* 1 takes its place; a similar operation occurs on *in* 2 whenever its current entry precedes that of *in* 1. When either *in* 1 or *in* 2 is empty, the other can be 'flushed' (all its remaining entries copied) to the *out* file. The full algorithm is given as Listing 13.4.

Procedure **Merge** uses only two input tapes, but in fact any number can be used. If N input tapes are in use the algorithm is called N-way

```
procedure Output(var i,o:Table);
  begin
    o^:=i^;
    Put(o);
    Get(i)
  end;

procedure Merge(var in1,in2,out:Table);

(* Input parameters:  sorted files in1 and in2.
   Output parameters: sorted file out of in1 merged with in2 *)

  begin
    while not(eof(in1) or eof(in2)) do        (* merge in1 and in2 *)
      if in1^.key<=in2^.key
        then Output(in1,out)
        else Output(in2,out);
    while not(eof(in1)) do                    (* flush in1 *)
      Output(in1,out);
    while not(eof(in2)) do                    (* flush in2 *)
      Output(in2,out)
  end;
```

Listing 13.4 Merging sorted Pascal files.

merge. We then have the problem of selecting the smallest key of N entries but, as N is likely to be small, a simpler linear search is adequate. Processing costs can be ignored, in any event, because it is **PUT** and **GET** which dominate, timewise. The algorithm uses an 'array of table' as its input parameter, and must continue merging until only one file is active. This can be done by keeping the indices of active files in an auxiliary array and processing until only one file is active, at which time that file can be flushed. The details are left as an exercise.

13.2.2 Basic merge-sort

N-way merge can be used as the basis of a sort algorithm, the time complexity for which is $O(n \log n)$. Let the n entries be distributed evenly across N files in random order. Each file contains a random subsequence of the original entries which we say contains n/N sorted subsequences of length 1. To talk of a sorted subsequence of length 1 is perhaps a tautology, but all iterations have to start somewhere. On each iteration we increase the length of the sorted subsequences to double their previous size. Eventually we achieve one single sorted sequence of length n.

Each time we completely copy all n entries we say we have made a *pass* over the data. On each iteration of basic merge we make two passes, one called the *split* and the second the *merge* pass. The merge pass does not merge complete files as in **MERGE**, but treats each subsequence as a complete file. On the first merge pass the algorithm treats each file as if it

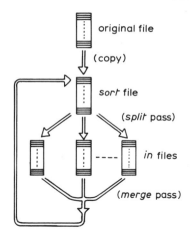

Figure 13.4 Merge-sorting a file.

had only one entry and signalled eof following it: when the output of the
resulting subsequence of length N is complete, a new merge begins
which operates on the next entry from each file. After this pass, the
output file contains a set of sorted subsequences of length N.

```
procedure Output(var i,o:Table;var count:Integer);

(* copy an entry from table i to table o and increment count *)

  begin
    o^:=i^;
    Put(o);
    Get(i);
    count:=count+1
  end;

procedure Copy(var i,o:Table;var n:Integer);

(* Copy table i to table o. Count entries and return in n *)

  begin
    n:=0;
    while not eof(i) do
      Output(i,o,n)
  end;

procedure FlushRun(var i,o:Table;count,runsize:Integer);

(* Copy entries from i to o until count has reached runsize or
   no more entries remain *)

  begin
    while not(eof(i) or (count>=runsize)) do
      Output(i,o,count)
  end;
```
Listing 13.5 Merge-sorting Pascal files.

```
procedure Split(var i,o1,o2:Table;runsize:Integer);

(* Split i by copying runs of length runsize alternately to o1 and o2.
   The final run may be of any size up to runsize *)

  begin
    while not eof(i) do
      begin                            (* copy runs alternately to o1 and o2 *)
        Flushrun(i,o1,0,runsize);
        Flushrun(i,o2,0,runsize)
      end
  end;

procedure MergeRun(var in1,in2,out:Table;runsize:Integer);

(* Merge one run from in1 and one run from in2 to out.
   The runs will be of size no greater than runsize *)

  var
      count1,count2:Integer;

  begin
    count1:=0; count2:=0;
    while not((count1>=runsize) or eof(in1) or
              (count2>=runsize) or eof(in2)) do   (* merge in1 and in2 *)
      if in1^.key<=in2^.key
        then Output(in1,out,count1)
        else Output(in2,out,count2);
    FlushRun(in1,out,count1,runsize);
    FlushRun(in2,out,count2,runsize);
    writeln
  end;

procedure MergeSort(var source,result:Table);

(* Produce a sorted version of source in result *)

  var
      in1,in2:Table;                   (* for the split/merge *)
      n:Integer;                       (* number of entries in source *)
      runsize:Integer;                 (* current size of a run *)
  begin
    Reset(source);
    Rewrite(result);
    Copy(source,result,n);             (* do not destroy source! *)
    Close(result,lock);
    runsize:=1;                        (* initial runs of length 1 *)
    while runsize<n do
      begin
        Reset(result);Rewrite(in1);Rewrite(in2);
        Split(result,in1,in2,runsize);
        Reset(in1);Reset(in2);Rewrite(result);
        while not(eof(in1) and eof(in2)) do
          MergeRun(in1,in2,result,runsize);
        runsize:=runsize+runsize
      end
  end;
```

If we make the original input tape the output tape for the merge, the process can be repeated until the file is sorted. This process is demonstrated in Fig. 13.4. A sorted subsequence is called a *run*. The algorithm must keep track of the current size of a run (this is done in **runsize**) and how much of each run has been read from each file (this is done in the count variables). Some useful procedures are developed before presenting the full merge-sort (Listing 13.5).

13.2.3 **Pre-sorting**

The initial run lengths for merge-sort as given are assumed to be 1: the initial file is assumed to be unsorted. We can significantly improve the performance of merge-sort by using main memory sorts to produce initial runs which are much larger: remember that it is the cost of **PUT** and **GET** which we are attempting to minimize, and hence the number of passes over the data. If we have a main memory capable of storing M entries (as well as an appropriate sort program) then we can certainly produce runs of this length initially on file **Result**, though it would be even better to combine this pre-sorting phase with the initial split and put the runs directly onto the input tapes for the merge phase. Instead of a straight copy of **Source** to **Result** we would read M entries at a time into an array, sort them, and output the runs produced alternately to **In1** and **In2** (and **In3**... if more files are being used). The runsize would initially be set to M, and the very first **Split** would not be carried out.

We can, in fact, do even better than this. If we use one of the selection sorts (as we are dealing with large files, heapsort will be best) we can replace selected entries (which can be written out directly) by incoming entries, provided the key of the incoming entry does not precede the key of the outgoing entry: if it does then it cannot belong to the current run and must be stored at the end of the array. When the array is full of such rejected entries, a new run is started. Using this procedure, the runsizes can be significantly lengthened.

In the case of heapsort, we have, in general the situation shown in Fig. 13.5

If the incoming key, k_s, is after k in the order, then it can join the current heap: put it in *heap*[1] and *sift* (see the top arrow). If it cannot join the current heap, then replace *heap*[1] by the last entry in the current heap (standard heapsort procedure), replace the last entry in the current heap by the incoming entry and decrease the size of the current heap. The new entry must find its correct place in the heap under construction: it will be sifted (but remember that it is in position l, so it will be compared with *entries*[$2l$] and *entries*[$2l+1$] initially). It has been shown (see Knuth) that, on average, the resulting runs are of length $2 \times M$.

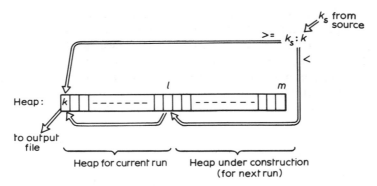

Figure 13.5   Using heapsort to optimize a pre-sort.

When we incorporate such pre-sorting into our merge-sort algorithm another change must be made: runs will average a length of $2 \times M$ but could in practice be anything from length M upwards. We can no longer rely on counting to signal the end of a run: a run must terminate only when an incoming key is less than the previous key from that file. A merge-sort which identifies the end of a run in this way is called a *natural merge-sort*. Such a sort will exhibit natural behaviour (as defined earlier).

13.2.4 Polyphase sorting

A merge-sort using F input files and one result file will operate in time $o(cn \log_F n)$. The larger we can make F, the fewer will be the passes to be made over the data. One fault with merge-sort is that it requires a split phase, during which no sorting work is performed: this doubles the number of passes actually made over the data. One possibility is to split the total files available into two sets: one set for input and one for output. As with the pre-sort we can perform the split as we merge, thus cancelling its cost. After each pass, the roles of the input and output tapes are reversed. This is called a *balanced merge-sort*. Of course, the new algorithm will operate in time dominated by

$$\log_{(F+1)/2} n$$

rather than

$$2 \log_F n$$

Polyphase merge-sort avoids this effective reduction in power while at the same time eliminating the separate split pass. It works as follows.

Consider the situation where $F = 2$. Under normal conditions we can expect to merge two input files to one output file, and also expect both input files to become empty simultaneously. Suppose, instead, we organized the runs so that, during the whole merge, only one input file ever became empty (had no runs left). As soon as one becomes empty, we can reverse the role of the current output tape and the (now empty) input tape. The other input tape will only be part way through, so it carries on as if nothing has happened. Eventually it will become empty, and roles are reversed again. This continues until each input tape has only one run left: the final merge produces a fully sorted file. The number of passes through the data is governed by the number of runs, not directly by their length, so in depicting polyphase merge-sort we show only the number of runs in each file at each stage (Table 13.1).

The initial distribution of runs is critical; it must be governed by a Fibonacci sequence. The basic Fibonacci sequence is defined as follows:

- The first two members of the sequence are 0, 1
- Each subsequent member is the sum of its two preceding members

The sequence therefore begins

$$0, 1, 1, 2, 3, 5, 8, \ldots$$

In the case of three tapes, two consecutive Fibonacci numbers are required. As we assumed thirty-four total runs from the pre-sort, this was achievable. Suppose instead the pre-sort delivered twenty-six: what would happen then?

In fact after one of the phases this would have resulted in two empty tapes simultaneously emerging, and the split phase would have had to be performed to recover the situation. To overcome this we always make up the number of runs with dummy runs, which cause a file to 'mark time' before declaring that it is empty. A little merge-power is occasionally lost (while files are delivering their dummy runs) but the overall performance is guaranteed to be good.

Table 13.1 Distribution of runs during a polyphase merge-sort.

Phase	Runs			Comment
	F_1	F_2	F_3	
Pre-sort	21	13	0	F_3 initial output tape
Merge 1	8	0	13	Thirteen runs merged from F_1 and F_2 Switch roles of F_2 and F_3
2	0	8	5	Switch roles of F_1 and F_3 etc.
3	5	3	0	
4	2	0	3	
5	0	2	1	
6	1	1	0	
7	0	0	1	

The number of files available for a sort is governed by system parameters. If the files are held on tape then we may be restricted by the number of tape drives, for example. If more than three files are to be used, the distribution of the initial runs is governed by higher-order Fibonacci sequences. The same basic principles still apply.

Other improvements have been made on polyphase merge-sort. For example, if the files are in fact tape files, then switching the roles of an input tape and an output tape is probably costly: both would have to be rewound on some systems, before the sort can continue. On tape drives which can read backwards as well as forwards, a modification to the algorithm can eliminate the need to rewind. In this modification, ordered and reverse-ordered runs must be processed: an ordered run being read on rewind will appear to be reverse-ordered. The algorithm must organize the runs so that each merge receives runs which are in the same relative ordering. The resulting algorithm is called *oscillating merge-sort*. Details of these algorithms can be found in books referenced in the Bibliography.

14

Further realizations

We have considered simple representations for type table based on array, tree and file. In the last chapter we emphasized the use of tables for processing entries in some specified order. We return to the more general situation of representations designed to facilitate random selections, insertions and deletions.

14.1 BINARY SEARCH TREES

The definition of this class of tree appears in Section 12.2 together with Pascal implementations for the select and insert operations. We first complete the realization by implementing operation *delete* and then look more closely at its performance.

14.1.1 Deletion

The tree of Fig. 14.1 depicts a table with *keyvalue* = **Char**. There are only three distinct cases which need to be distinguished in deletion; these are characterized by the number of children which the node containing the specified entry has.

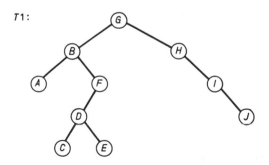

Figure 14.1 A binary search tree with *keyvalue* = **Char**.

Case 1

Node is a leaf.

This is the simplest of the three. To remove the entry with key C, for example, we need only set that subtree to the null tree. There are no repercussions elsewhere in the tree.

Case 2

Node has one child.

In this case we simply promote the single subtree, which takes the place of the tree originally rooted at the deleted entry. For example, if we delete F then the entry with key D becomes the new root of that tree. The subtree at B now becomes

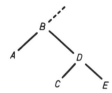

Case 3

Node has two children.

The deletion of node B is a case in point. The node is acting as a 'decision' node: on selection we use the key to decide whether to move left or right. The node cannot, therefore, simply be deleted: it must be replaced by a node which can similarly act as a decision node. We do not want major reorganization of the tree as this will be too costly.

The answer is to replace the node by a lexicographically adjacent one (i.e. one which is its immediate predecessor or immediate successor in the defined ordering). How is this found? The immediate successor can be defined as having the smallest key larger than the given key; but all entries with larger keys are in the right subtree of the tree, so this further translates into the smallest key in the right subtree. The smallest key is found by repeatedly moving left: it will be in the root of a tree with a null left subtree. Similar statements may be made about the predecessor of a node.

Our deletion algorithm will therefore overwrite the entry which contains the defined key by the entry of its immediate successor. This successor will be easy to delete: it is a Case 2 deletion. The full procedure, with its supporting procedures, appears as Listing 14.1. (Note that in this algorithm Case 1 deletion is achieved as a special form of Case 2.)

```
procedure Delete(var t:Table;k:Keyvalue);

(* Delete the entry with key k from t. If no such entry exists, do nothing *)

  procedure CopyEntry(t,s:Table);

  (* Copy the entry from node s to node t. Return node s to the heap *)

    begin
      t^.key:=s^.key;
      t^.value:=s^.value;
      Dispose(s)
    end;

  Function DeletedNeighbour(var t:Table):Table;

  (* Find and delete the leftmost node in t. Return its identifier *)

    begin
      if t^.left=nil
        then
          begin
            DeletedNeighbour:=t;        (* return identifier *)
            t:=t^.right                 (* delete node *)
          end
        else DeletedNeighbour:=DeletedNeighbour(t^.left)
    end;

begin (* Delete *)
  if t<>nil
    then                               (* find key k *)
      if k<t^.key                      (* k in left subtree? *)
        then Delete(t^.left,k) else
      if k>t^.key                      (* k in right subtree? *)
        then Delete(t^.right,k)
      else                             (* k has been found *)
        if t^.left=nil
          then                         (* no left: promote right subtree *)
            t:=t^.right
          else if t^.right=nil
            then                       (* no right: promote left subtree *)
              t:=t^.left
            else                       (* t has 2 children: swap with succ. *)
              CopyEntry(t,DeletedNeighbour(t^.right))
end;
```

Listing 14.1 Deletion in a binary search tree.

14.1.2 Characteristics

To determine the performance of a table realization we need to look at its average performance over all operation calls in its given environment. As we have not decided for what purpose the tree is to be used, no statistics of this nature are available to us. Let us suppose, however, that selection is the 'critical' operation, and we wish therefore to minimize the average expected time for a selection. Two distinct scenarios can be examined, each with its own area of applicability. In the first, all entries are equally likely to be accessed: the selections are truly random. In the second, a specific pattern of access for defined keys is known: a probability of access can be attached to each key in the table. The first situation, for example, is typical of tables used in data bases and other situations in which the key set is continually changing. The second scenario is applicable to dictionary look-up in a fixed dictionary. We consider each case separately.

(a) Equal probability of access

The cost of accessing a given node increases with its level in the tree and is reflected by the depth of recursion/number of iterations which the selection procedure requires. For simplicity, then, we will let the cost of an access be the level of a node in the tree. Using Fig. 14.1 we can deduce that the cost of selecting entry G is 1, that for B is 2 and that for C is 5. The cost of accessing each node in the tree once is said to be the cost of the tree. It can be represented as

$$C_T = \sum_{n \text{ in } T} \text{level } (N)$$

and so the average cost is C_T/n. For our example tree, we can calculate C_{T1} to be (with terms showing the cost of all nodes at a given level, starting from level 1)

$$1 + 4 + 9 + 8 + 10 = 32$$

so the average cost per access is

$$32/10 = 3.2$$

Unsuccessful searches require a similar approach, but it is useful to extend the tree in order to demonstrate their cost. An unsuccessful search will attempt to find the required key in the (non-existent) left or right subtree of a leaf node. If we augment the tree with special nodes, external to the tree in question, which represent the sets of keys which will result in a 'not found' condition on reaching that point, then we have an *extended binary search tree*. An extended version of Fig. 14.1 is given as Fig. 14.2. The stars represent the *external nodes*. The original nodes are now all *internal nodes*.

The cost of 'accessing' an external node, that is the cost of an unsuccessful search which terminates at that point, is defined as the cost of accessing its parent: it is therefore one less than its level in the tree. (It can be argued that its actual level is more representative: if this measure is chosen, the following comparisons must be adjusted accordingly. An

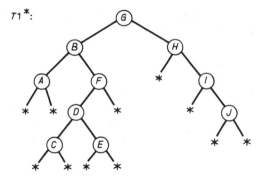

Figure 14.2 An extended binary search tree.

external node does not exist in the representation, so termination of iteration when we reach the parent is the cost measure chosen.)

The original cost, for successful termination, is now the sum of the levels of internal nodes in the extended tree. It is referred to as the *internal path length* of the tree and denoted I. The total cost of accessing each external node once is

$$\sum_{N \text{ in } L} (\text{level }(N) - 1) \quad \text{where } L \text{ is the set of leaf nodes in } T^* \text{ (i.e. the set of external nodes)}$$

This is denoted E_{T^*}. A calculation of E_{T1^*} ($T1^*$ as in Fig. 14.2) delivers the value

$$2 + 12 + 8 + 20 = 42$$

The average cost of an unsuccessful search is

$$E_{T^*}/(n+1)$$

which for the tree $T1^*$ is

$$42/11 \approx 3.8$$

The values of I_{T^*} *and* E_{T^*} are related in the following simple way:

$$E_{T^*} = I_{T^*} + n$$

This can be proved by induction, inserting nodes into an initially empty tree.

In summary then, the average cost of accessing a node in a binary search tree can be calculated as

$$C_T/n \qquad \text{(successful search)}$$
$$(C_T + n)/(n+1) \qquad \text{(unsuccessful search)}$$

where $C_T = \sum_{N \text{ in } T} \text{level }(N)$.

The cost of the equivalent extended tree C_{T*} (i.e. the cost including unsuccessful searches) is $2 \times C_T + n$.

(b) Given probability of access

Suppose each node N in a binary search tree is given a probability of access $S(N)$ (where $0 \leqslant S(N) \leqslant 1$). Suppose, initially, that all expected accesses will be successful: the time for unsuccessful accesses can be ignored. In this case we know that $\Sigma_{N \epsilon T} S(N) = 1$ and the cost of the tree is

$$C_T = \sum_{N \, in \, T} \text{level } (N) \times S(N)$$

If we now make unsuccessful searches significant, we must give probabilities to each of the '*' nodes in the extended tree. As before, let the set of external nodes be denoted L. We define a probability for each node N in L which we call $U(N)$ – the probability of an unsuccessful search terminating at that point in the tree. The total cost contribution of unsuccessful searches to the cost of the tree is

$$\sum_{N \, in \, L} (\text{level } (N) - 1) \times U(N)$$

Let B be the set of internal nodes for the extended tree. Then the probabilities conform to the following

$$0 \leqslant S(N) \leqslant 1 \quad \forall N \epsilon L$$
$$0 \leqslant U(N) \leqslant 1 \quad \forall N \epsilon L$$
$$\sum_{N \, in \, B} S(N) + \sum_{N \, in \, L} U(N) = 1$$

The total cost of a tree, for both successful and unsuccessful searches, is

$$C_{T*} = \sum_{N \, in \, B} \text{level } (N) \times S(N) + \sum_{N \, in \, L} (\text{level } (N) - 1) \times U(N)$$

14.1.3 Efficient binary search trees

A given table can be represented by many different binary search trees. As an example, an equivalent binary search tree to $T1$ is given as $T2$ in

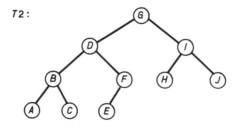

Figure 14.3   An equivalent binary search tree to $T1$.

Fig. 14.3. The total cost of this tree (equal probability of access to each node) is

$$C_{T2} = 1 + 4 + 12 + 12 = 29$$

so the average cost of a successful access, at 2.9, is lower than for $T1$. Similarly, the average cost of an unsuccessful access is down to 3.6. It is therefore advantageous if we use a representation which minimizes the cost of C_T, if only successful searches are of concern, or of C_{T*}, if unsuccessful searches are also of interest. A tree T which does this is called an *optimal binary search tree*.

(a) Equal probability of access: balanced binary search trees

If a binary search tree T is complete, then it is optimal. It is not hard to convince oneself of the truth of this statement: the proof uses reductio ad absurdum, hypothesizing a tree which is not complete but which has cost less than T. The tree of Fig. 14.3 is complete, and hence is optimal: an average access cost of 2.9 cannot be bettered for the given key set.

Unfortunately, when inserts are made into a complete tree it is a costly operation to keep it complete. In practice, therefore, we look to a weaker constraint on the shape of the trees. Balanced binary search trees guarantee good, though not optimal, performance: they are also fairly cheap to maintain in the presence of insertions and deletions. For these reasons they are preferred to complete trees as efficient representations of tables.

Balanced binary search trees

Balanced trees must have a difference in height of no more than 1 between their subtrees, which themselves must be balanced. Insertion into such a tree may disturb the balance: insertion will be at a leaf and may increase the height of a subtree. Fortunately, when this does happen, there are simple tree transformation operations available which will rebalance a subtree. Only four different transformations are necessary to enable us to keep trees balanced, and only one of the transformations need be used on any insertion. Any transformation must deliver a tree which has the same in-order traversal as the original tree (i.e. it must still be a search tree). Two *single rotation* transformations can in fact be presented by a simple equivalence: the mapping can be made in either direction.

Single rotation transformations

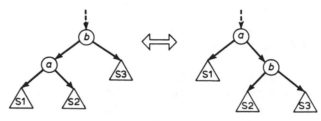

Note that the in-order traversal has been maintained: if the original was a search tree then so will be its transform. If we transform the left tree into the right, then it is called a right rotation about its root. The other transformation is termed a left rotation. The subtree ends up with a new root, so the pointer from its parent must be modified (dynamic tree representation).

Double rotation transformations

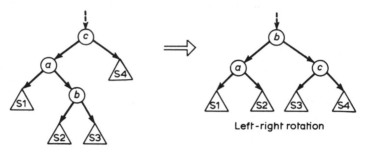

Left-right rotation

This transformation consists of a left rotation about *a* followed by a right rotation about *c*. Once again the root changes.

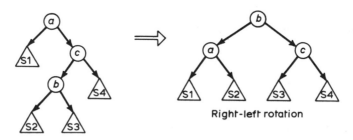

Right-left rotation

This is achieved by a right rotation about *c* followed by a left rotation about *a*. The root changes.

The procedures to achieve the basic rotations are shown in Listing 14.2. The double rotations can be achieved by appropriate calls on these.

```
procedure RightRotate(var root: Bintree);
  var
       t: Bintree;
  begin
    t:=root;
    root:=root^.left;
    t^.left:=root^.right;
    root^.right:=t
  end;

procedure LeftRotate(var root: Bintree);
  var
       t: Bintree;
  begin
    t:=root;
    root:=root^.right;
    t^.right:=root^.left;
    root^.left:=t
  end;
```

Listing 14.2 Single rotations in a search tree.

The residual question, then, concerns when and where to apply these rotations.

Applying rotations

All insertions are at leaves. On insertion the algorithm finds the eventual parent of the new node: it must obviously either have one child or be a leaf itself. If it has one child, then the insertion will form its other child and no imbalance can ensue:

The parent node must now be balanced. Transformation, therefore, is only necessary when inserting below a node which is currently a leaf and therefore evenly balanced (by default). Let us represent nodes with the following convention:

- Node is balanced
- Left subtree is higher
- Right subtree is higher

When inserting at a leaf, the nearest ancestor which is unbalanced is the potential pivot for any transformation: its current balance will determine whether or not the tree rooted at that point needs to be transformed.

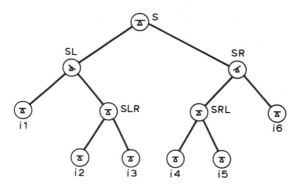

Figure 14.4 A balanced binary search tree.

Consider the tree in Fig. 14.4. There are six distinct insertion points in the tree, representing the six possibilities which arise in practice through inserting under a (current) leaf.

i1: Nearest unbalance ancestor: SL, ↘.
  Insertion: left of SL.
  Action: no transformation needed.
i2: Nearest unbalanced ancestor: SL, ↘.
  Insertion: right of SL; left of SLR.
  Action: right rotate about SLR; left rotate about SL.
i3: Nearest unbalanced ancestor: SL, ↘.
  Insertion: right of SL; right of SLR.
  Action: left rotate about SL.
i4: Nearest unbalanced ancestor: SR, ↙.
  Insertion: left of SR; left of SRL.
  Action: right rotate about SR.
i5: Nearest unbalanced ancestor: SR, ↙.
  Insertion: left of SR; right of SRL.
  Action: left rotate about SRL; right rotate about SR.
i6: Nearest unbalanced ancestor: SR, ↙.
  Insertion: right of SR.
  Action: no transformation needed.

The nodes of importance is deciding which transformations to make, if any, are therefore:

(i) The nearest unbalanced ancestor of the leaf under which the new insertion is to be made (the 'pivot').
(ii) Its child on the path to the insertion point (the 'child').

In general, insertion below a leaf on the same side that a subtree is unbalanced will necessitate a transformation.

Adjusting balances

When a node is added below a leaf node, *l*, the balance of *l* changes: if the insertion is on the left then it becomes left-heavy, and if on the right it becomes right-heavy. This is similarly true for the parent of *l*, if it was originally evenly balanced, and so on up to the (potential) pivot node.

For the diagrams in Figs 14.5 and 14.6, we represent the relative heights of subtrees by triangle depth. A node which is completely unbalanced (has a difference of 2 in the height of its subtrees prior to transformation) we mark with a '*'. This node is the 'pivot' node mentioned above. The node marked $\overline{\Delta}^x$ is the newly added node: whether as a left or right subtree of the $\triangle$ above it is irrelevant.

In the case of both single left rotation and single right rotation the pivot and child end up with even balances. In the case of double (right/left) rotation, we can deduce Listing 14.3, a fragment of the algorithm for adjusting balances.

A symmetric section of code can be developed for left/right double rotation.

Insertion in a balanced tree

The complete algorithm for insertion breaks up neatly into phases.

Phase 1

Search and insert.

Trace a path through the tree to the node below which the new node is to be inserted. On the way down, set *pivot* to any node which is at the root of an unbalanced subtree. At termination of this phase *pivot* will be

```
case newroot^.balance of
   leftheavy:  begin                        (* case (i) *)
                  pivot^.balance:=even;
                  child^.balance:=rightheavy
               end;
   rightheavy: begin                        (* case (ii) *)
                  pivot^.balance:=leftheavy;
                  child^.balance:=even
               end;
   even:       begin                        (* case (iii) *)
                  pivot^.balance:=even;
                  child^.balance:=even
               end
end;(* case *)
newroot^.balance:=even
```

Listing 14.3 Code to adjust balances after a double (right/left) rotation.

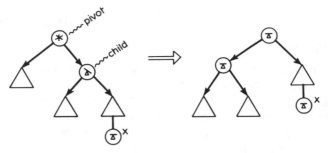

Figure 14.5   Left rotation about a pivot.

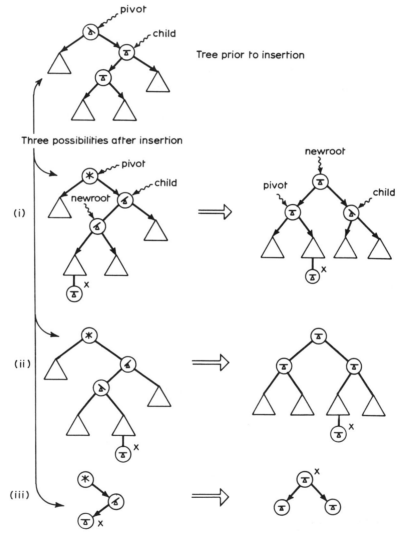

Tree prior to insertion

Three possibilities after insertion

(i)

newroot

(ii)

(iii)

Figure 14.6   Double rotation: right about child then left about pivot.

the nearest unbalanced ancestor to the insertion point (or the root node if all ancestors are balanced) and *curr* will identify the insertion point.

Phase 2

Identify child and set balances.

Identify the child of *pivot* on the path to *curr*. Trace the path to *curr* setting the balance of each node (previously even) to *leftheavy* or *rightheavy*, depending on the new node being in the left or right subtrees, respectively.

Phase 3

Check pivot balance and transform tree if necessary.

Let us say that the insertion is *leftheavy* if it is to the left of the pivot and *rightheavy* if it is to the right. We will call this value the *potential-imbalance* of the new tree. Three cases must be considered.

Case 1: The *pivot* is evenly balanced,
      – set it to the same value as *potential-imbalance*.

Case 2: The *pivot* has the opposite balance to the *potential-imbalance*,
      – its new balance is even.

Case 3: The *pivot* has the same balance as the *potential-imbalance*,
      – transform the tree,
      – adjust balances,
      – reattach the subtree, which now has a new root, to its correct
        place in the parent tree.

The last stage of Case 3 acknowledges that the pivot node was the node used to identify this subtree in the full binary search tree. The subtree must now be identified by *newnode*. We must therefore execute the following program steps:

```
if parent_of_pivot = nil
   then (* pivot was the root of the whole search tree *)
   search_tree: = newroot
   else
      if pivot = parent_of_pivot^. left          (* pivot a left child?*)
         then parent_of_pivot^. left: = newroot
         else parent_of_pivot^. right: = newroot
```

This completes the insertion algorithm.

Although the insertion of a node in a balanced binary tree precipitates at most one rotation, the same is not true of deletion. Up to log*n*

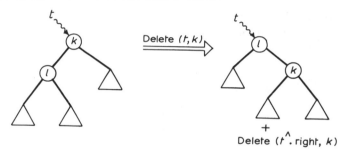

Figure 14.7 Deletion may precipitate up to $\log n$ rotations.

rotations may be necessary, the algorithm being best written recursively to achieve the desired rebalancing. An example of the recursive nature of the process is given in Fig. 14.7.

(b) Given probability of access: optimal binary search trees

All binary search trees for the same set of keys have the same in-order traversal: the sorted order of those keys. To simplify our notation, let the internal nodes in the extended tree be indexed according to this order, so that the smallest key has index 1 and the largest has index n. We can now refer to these nodes as $N_i (i \in 1 \ldots n)$ and their probabilities of access as Si $(i \in 1 \ldots n)$. Let us further suggest that each external node, if it existed in the actual search tree, would immediately follow an internal node in the in-order traversal: all, that is, except the leftmost external node. We therefore refer to $U_i (i \in 0 \ldots n)$ where U_0 is the probability of an (unsuccessful) access for a key smaller than any in the tree. For all i $(i \in 1 \ldots n-1)$ we define U_i to be the probability of an unsuccessful access for a key larger than N_i but smaller than N_{i+1}; we define U_n to be the probability of an access for a key larger than any in the tree. These facts are represented in Fig. 14.8.

To build the tree we need to identify the root node: let this be N. Once identified, we can create the tree by specifying N_m to be the root and repeating the process for $N_1 \ldots N_{m-1}$ (the left subtree) and $N_{m+1} \ldots N_n$ (the right subtree). There are various algorithms for computing the root, most of them suboptimal. An algorithm for constructing truly optimal binary

Nodes (in order)	N_1	N_2	N_3	N_4		...	N_{n-1}		N_n
Successful	S_1	S_2	S_3	S_4		...	S_{n-1}		S_n
Unsuccessful	U_0	U_1	U_2	U_3	U_4	...		U_{n-1}	U_n

Figure 14.8 Notation for given probabilities.

trees (Knuth, 1973) uses a dynamic programming technique. Its time-complexity and storage-complexity are both $O(n^2)$. The algorithms producing suboptimal search trees can reduce this to $O(n \log n)$ time and $O(n)$ space. The fact that these 'heuristics' produce suboptimal trees is perhaps not too significant: the probabilities are almost certainly inexact and the resultant trees perform well; they are sometimes referred to as *nearly optimal binary search trees*. We describe one heuristic, and leave a second for the exercises.

Suboptimal binary search trees

Choose N_m such that the probability of an access to the left subtree is as close as possible to that in the right subtree. We thus choose m to minimize

$$\left| \left(U_0 + \sum_{i-1}^{m-1} (S_i + U_i) \right) - \left(U_m + \sum_{i=m+1}^{n} (S_i + U_i) \right) \right|$$

(We call m the median node.) Let

$$P_{kj} = U_k + \sum_{i=k+1}^{i} (S_i + U_i)$$

(in other words P_{kj} stands for the probability of searching the subtree containing nodes N_{k+1} to N_j). Then for the first step we wish to choose m to minimize

$$|P_{0,m-1} - P_{m,n}|$$

This process is demonstrated in Fig. 14.9, where n is taken to be 9. Having done this we perform a similar task on the left subtree (nodes 1 to $m-1$) and the right subtree (nodes $m+1$ to n).

The skeleton of the algorithm for building such a tree, which we call

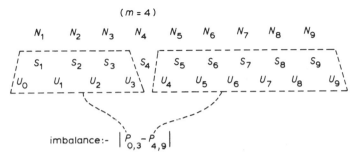

Figure 14.9 Heuristic: choose m to minimize the imbalance.

```
Procedure CreateTree(var t:Bintree;size:Index;n:Nodevector;s,u:Probvector);

(* Create a nearly-optimal search tree in t using the median heuristic.
   Nodes are in n, associated probabilities of accessing nodes in s.
   Probabilities for unsuccessful searches are in u.
   n is already sorted on its key attribute. *)

   Function Build(i,j:Index;p:Probability):Bintree;

   (* Build a search tree with nodes n[i+1] to n[j].
      p is the probability that a search will be conducted in this subtree *)

       var
           pl,pr:Probability;          (* left and right subtrees about median *)
           imbal:Probability;          (* |pl-pr| *)
           m:Index;                    (* median node *)
           pl1,pr1:Probability;        (* as pl and pr but about (median+1) *)
           imbal1:Probability;         (* |pl1-pr1| *)
           finished:Boolean;
       begin
         if i<j
           then                        (* Internal node: build a tree *)
             begin
               m:=i+1;                  (* try first node as median *)
               pl:=u[i];
               pr:=p-pl-s[m];
               imbal:=abs(pl-pr);
               finished:=(m=j);
               while not finished do
                 begin                  (* try (median+1) *)
                   pl1:=pl+s[m]+u[m];
                   Pr1:=pr-s[m+1]-u[m];
                   imbal1:=abs(pl1-pr1);
                   if imbal1<imbal
                     then               (* (median+1) is a better estimate *)
                       begin
                         m:=m+1;pl:=pl1;pr:=pr1;
                         imbal:=imbal1;
                         finished:=(m=j)
                       end
                     else               (* median is confirmed: terminate loop *)
                       finished:=true
                 end;
               Build:=Compose(Build(i,m-1,pl),n[m],Build(m,j,pr))
             end
           else                        (* external node: null tree *)
             Build:=NewTree
     end;
   begin (* CreateTree *)
     t:=Build(0,size,1.0)
   end;
```

Listing 14.4 Building a near-optimal binary search tree.

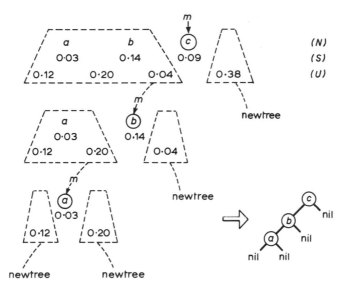

Figure 14.10 Behaviour of function **Build**.

Build, is thus:

```
Build (i,j)::if i<j
            then (* Internal node: build a tree *)
            begin
              Find (median);
              Build:=Compose (Build (i,m−1), N[m], Build (m, j))
            end
            else (* External node: null tree *)
              Build:=Newtree;
```

In practice we add a further argument to the **Build** function, for efficiency reasons. This argument is the subtree probability, P_{ij}. The full procedure for creating a nearly optimal binary subtree using the median heuristic is shown as Listing 14.4.

To demonstrate the behaviour of the algorithm we choose a small node set: cardinality 3. The tree keys are a, b and c and the associated S and U probabilities are (0.03, 0.14, 0.09) and (0.12, 0.20, 0.04, 0.38), respectively. The behaviour of function **Build** is demonstrated in Fig. 14.10. The tree built has a total cost (C_{T^*}) of 1.88. This is not optimal: the tree

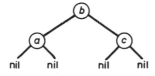

has a cost of only 1.86 and is, in fact, optimal for the given details. The generated tree is the second best of the five possible binary search trees.

14.2 B-TREES

In a binary search tree which is complete, the maximum cost of accessing a node is

$$\lfloor \log_2 n \rfloor + 1$$

For an N-ary tree it would be

$$\lfloor \log_N n \rfloor + 1$$

so an obvious way of reducing the cost of a tree (as measured by C_{T^*}) is to increase its degree. This, of course, is not the whole story. Although we are reducing the average number of nodes accessed per selection, the cost of deciding which of the N subtrees to search at each stage must be counted also. In general, then, N-ary trees show little advantage for tables stored in main memory. When the table is to be stored externally, on a random access device such as a disc, the cost of processing a node can be ignored (a point we made earlier). The reduction in the number of nodes accessed is then an overriding advantage. For the following, let M be $N-1$.

As with binary search trees, performance deteriorates if the trees become too unbalanced. The *B-tree* data structure will guarantee that:

 (i) No node will have an out-degree of less than $(M/2+1)$, except possibly the root node.
(ii) All leaf nodes will be at the same level.

The performance of these trees is good when random insertions, deletions and selections are to be made.

B-trees have the unusual behaviour (for trees in computer science) of growing from the root. The tree can only increase in height when the root node is caused to 'split', necessitating a new root node to be inserted above the two siblings created. All nodes in the tree (except the root) must contain between $M/2$ and M keys. The out-degree of a node will be one greater than the number of keys (as with binary trees):

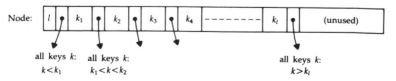

all keys k: all keys k: all keys k:
$k < k_1$ $k_1 < k < k_2$ $k > k_l$

The properties associated with a B-tree must be maintained by the

```
(* Representation of Btree *)

type
     Btree=^Node;
     Node=record
              s:0..mm;
              key:array[1..mm] of Keyvalue;
              val:array[1..mm] of Valptr;
              t:array[0..mm] of Btree
          end;

(* end of representation of Btree *)
```

Listing 14.5 Representing a B-tree ($mm \equiv 2*m$: M in the text)

Insert and Delete procedures. Insert will cause a leaf node to split into two if it already has M keys in it; Delete will cause a reorganization if the key is in a node with only $M/2$ keys. In our discussion of B-trees we will take the maximum number of keys in a node (M) to be $2 \times m$ for some m. In the examples we choose $m = 1$, resulting in a B-tree often referred to as a 2–3 tree (2 refers to the maximum number of keys per node, and 3 to the maximum degree of a node). A representation for B-trees is given in Listing 14.5, and discussed below.

14.2.1 Selection in a B-tree

To find a key k, we start at the root node. The keys in the node are ordered on increasing key value. They are searched (binary search if m is large) to find the largest key not greater than k. If no such key exists then 0 is returned, otherwise the index of the appropriate key is returned. Let the value returned be i. If k was not found then $t[i]$ must be searched. The algorithm is Listing 14.6.

The values associated with the keys may be stored in the tree, but fewer keys could then be stored in each node. To keep the branching factor high, we have stored pointers to values, rather than the values themselves. We could have gone one step further by only storing these pointers at the leaves: the **val** array becomes a variant alternative (Pascal records) of array **t**. Such B-trees are referred to as *Index B-trees*. These B-trees store only keys in branch nodes, for decision making. All key values will appear in the leaves, so a key value may be duplicated in the tree.

14.2.2 Insertion in a B-tree

As with binary search trees, insertion will always be made at a leaf. The algorithm for insertion has phases not unrelated to those for insertion in

```
procedure Select(b:Btree;k:Keyvalue;var v:Datavalue;var found:Boolean);
  var
        i:0..mm;                        (* index in Node *)
  begin
    found:=false;
    while (not found) and (b<>nil) do
      begin
        i:=PosnInNode(k,b,found);
        if not found
          then b:=b^.t[i]
      end;
    if found
      then v:=b^.val[i]^
  end;
```

Listing 14.6 Key retrieval using B-trees.

a balanced binary tree. During phase 1 the insertion point is found, using a search similar to the one used in select (Listing 14.6). On insertion, the node may be found to be full. This will result in a node 'split': the keys are evenly distributed between the original node and a newly created node. The middle key (there must have been $M + 1$ keys altogether and m will have been placed in each leaf node) becomes the 'decision' key: all nodes with lower keys are in the original leaf node, those with higher keys are in the new leaf node. It must therefore be inserted in the parent node – which may itself split. Phase 2 is therefore similar to balancing phase 3, but $\log_N n$ splits may result altogether. If the root node splits then the height of the tree increases by 1; a new root node will contain the single decision key for the next level.

(a) An example

Consider a tree in which m is 1: a 2–3 tree. We will insert the following keys into the tree, in the order given:

25, 58, 12, 17, 14, 80, 3, 70

For simplicity, we will not represent the value field in the diagrams. Initially, 25 and 58 will be inserted into a root node:

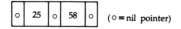

An insertion of key 12 necessitates a split: we are attempting to put [12, 25, 58] into a single node, so 12 must be placed in the current node: 58 into a new sibling node and 25 must be placed in the parent together with a pointer to the new node. As there is no parent, one must be created: the tree has 'grown' a new root:

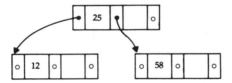

Key 17 will now be inserted alongside key 12. Key 14 belongs in the same node: the node must split again. This time 14 is the median key, so 12 remains; 17 is placed in a new sibling node and 14 must be placed in the parent (the root) along with a pointer to the new node:

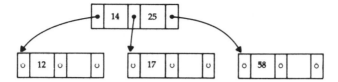

Insertions of 80 and 3 can proceed without any splits, giving the tree

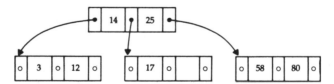

Finally, we add key 70. Initially, the node containing 58 and 80 is selected: if it were not full then 70 would belong there. As it is, we see that 70 is the median of the three contenders, and the node must be split with 70 as the decision key:

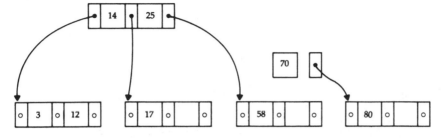

The median key, 70, must now be inserted into the parent node: the root. This is full, so a further split is necessary. This time, 25 is the

median so a new sibling node is created for key 70. Key 25 must be inserted into the parent node, but as it does not exist we must create a new root: the tree has grown from the root again:

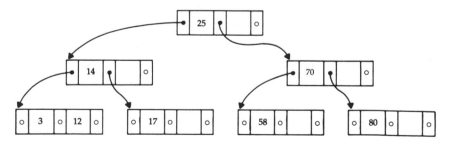

The fact that new nodes are only ever created as siblings, except when a new root is required, guarantees that all leaf nodes are at the same level. The fact that a split only occurs when $(2m+1)$ keys wish to share the same node guarantees that a node will never have less than m keys (except the root node): the split will be m to the original node, m to the new sibling and one to be inserted in the parent. This method of controlling insertion therefore guarantees the B-tree properties.

(b) The algorithm

In the insertion algorithm we use recursion to move down the tree on a path to the proper insertion point (a leaf node). On the way back up the tree (as the insertion unwinds) we see whether a new key is to be inserted at the current level, that is, whether a split occurred in the level below. If a key is to be inserted, and if there is no room in this node, then a split is performed and the median key, together with a pointer to the sibling node newly created, is handed back to the next level of the tree (which must then insert it, and so on recursively). If no split is necessary, then this is signalled and the recursion unwinds back up the tree without making any further transformations. As a special case,

```
procedure Insert(var b:Btree;k:Keyvalue;v:Datavalue);

(* Exception: DuplicateKey; k is already in b *)

var
        split:Boolean;              (* split at child level? *)
        insertKey:Keyvalue;         (* median key of split- to be inserted *)
        insertval:Valptr;
        sibling:Btree;              (* new node of a split *)
        newroot:Btree;              (* in case tree grows *)
```

Listing 14.7 Insertion of a key in a B-tree.

s = ActiveKeys
mm = NoKey
b = Tree
k = NewKey
v = NewInfo

```
procedure InsertInTree(b:Btree);
  var
      i:Integer;
      found:Boolean;
  begin
    if b<>nil
      then with b^do
        begin                              (* insert k in appropriate subtree *)
          i:=PosnInNode(k,b,found);
          if not found                     (* should not be there already *)
            then                           (* not yet found: continue *)
              begin                        (* k belongs in t[i] *)
                InsertInTree(t[i]);
                if split
                  then     ↙ NoKey         (* caused a split: insert median key *)
                    if s<mm
                      then                 (* room for key insertion *)
                        begin
                          PutInNode(b,insertKey,insertval,sibling);
                          split:=false
                        end
                      else                 (* further split caused *)
                        SplitNode(b,sibling,insertKey,insertval)
              end
            else                            (* k found: error *)
              begin
                Report(DuplicateKey);—  Duplicate := true
                split:=false
              end
        end
      else                                  (* bottom of tree: simulate a split *)
        begin
          insertKey:=k;
          New(insertval); insertval^:=v;
          sibling:=nil;
          split:=true
        end
  end;(* InsertInTree*)

  begin (* Insert *) ← Duplicate := False
    InsertInTree(b);
    if Split
      then                                   (* new root needed *)
        begin
          New(newroot);
          with newroot^do
            begin
              t[0]:=b;
              Key[1]:=insertKey;
              val[1]:=insertval;
              t[1]:=sibling;
              s:=1
            end;
          b:=newroot
        end
  end;
```

when we reach the bottom of the tree we indicate that a split has occurred below the leaf: then the same code can deal with insertion in the leaf as is there to deal with insertion in parent nodes (caused by actual splits). The special case is effected when B is nil on entry, and this is reflected in the algorithm which is fully presented in Listing 14.7. This algorithm has one exception condition: if the key is found in the tree then insertion cannot take place (there must be no duplicates). In this case we report the exception 'Duplicate key' and terminate the search: **split** is set to false to indicate no further action on backing up the tree.

14.2.3 Deletion from a B-tree

As with binary search trees, deletion in a B-tree cannot be directly from a branch. If a key from a branch node is to be deleted, it must first be replaced by its nearest neighbour (in this case we will use its immediate successor). If it has been replaced by its nearest neighbour, then it is the original copy of the nearest neighbour (it must be on a leaf in this structure) which is now to be deleted. Once again the procedure is recursive: we go down the tree looking for the key and note its position if we find it. On reaching the bottom, we overwrite the key with its successor, if this is required, and delete the appropriate leaf entry. If this leaves the node with fewer than m keys then we must perform the following.

> **If** a sibling node has greater than m keys
>> **then** redistribute the keys between the nodes, changing the decision key value in the parent
>> **else** the nodes between them have $2m - 1$ keys. Form one node with $2m$ keys by combining the two nodes together with the decision key from the parent

If a join is performed, then a deletion must be made from the parent node: as the recursion unwinds each parent is transformed if necessary. The **JOINED** flag signals a join at the child level. It is set to true initially on reaching the bottom of the tree, to initiate the whole process.

(a) An example

Let us take the final B-tree developed in Subsection 14.2.2(a) through repeated insertions. We delete the keys in the order

> 12, 17, 25, ...

Delete 12: 12 is on a leaf node. Its deletion leaves the node viable, so no transformation is required. The resulting tree is

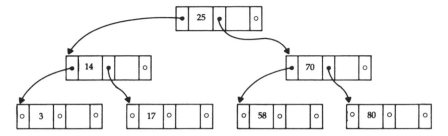

Delete 17: 17 is on a leaf node. Its deletion does leave the node non-viable, so a transformation must be made. We cannot distribute keys from its sibling, as it is only just viable itself. The two must therefore be combined, removing the decision key 14 from the parent node:

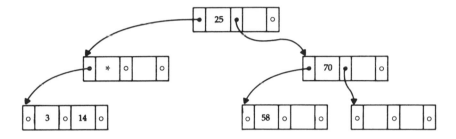

The removal of key 14 from the parent node precipitates a further transformation: the parent node itself is non-viable. Again, its sibling is only just viable so redistribution cannot help. A combining operation is again called for. In this case the decision key is extracted from the root node: it becomes non-viable itself, so is deleted. The tree has decreased in height:

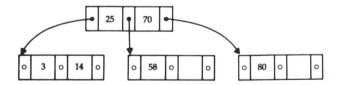

Delete 25: 25 is not on a leaf node. It must be overwritten by its successor (which can be found by following **t[i]** then **t[0]** repeatedly until we reach a leaf: the successor is **key [1]**). The copy of the successor

in the leaf node must then be deleted:

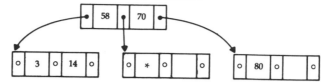

The deletion of 58 from the leaf makes the node non-viable, but this time its sibling has keys to spare: the keys are evenly distributed with the median key (14) becoming the new decision key:

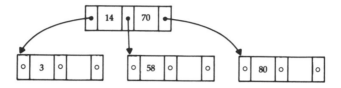

(b) The algorithm

The only complication which arises in the algorithm for deletion occurs when deletion is from a leftmost subtree. Except in this situation, the sibling is always a predecessor node of the node being searched. This special case is signalled by the test 'if i = 0' in procedure **Delete-from-tree**, and by the test 'if k < kmid' where it appears in procedures **Combine-nodes** and **Distribute-nodes**. Procedure **Take-from-node** removes **key[i]** and **t[i]** from a node disposing of **t[i]** and moving all succeeding entries forward one position. Note that argument **Decisionkey** must be designated **var** in procedure **Distribute-nodes**, because its value will change.

A full implementation of procedure **Delete** is given in Listing 14.8. The major routine is procedure **DeletfromTree**, which can be studied in isolation from the support procedures.

```
procedure Delete(var b:Btree;k:Keyvalue);
    var
        joined:Boolean;                    (* children combined? *)
        homenode:Btree;                    (* node where k found *)
        homeposn:Integer;                  (* posn of k in home node *)
    (* dummy variables... *)
        temp,sib:Btree;
        v:Valptr;

    procedure TakeFromNode(var b:Btree;i:Integer);
        var
            j:Integer;
        begin with b^do begin
            if i=0 then i:=1;              (* special case: leftmost *)
            (* dispose(t[i]) *)            (* subtree redundant: already combined *)
```

Listing 14.8 Deletion from a B-tree

```
        s:=s-1;
      for j:= i to s do
        begin
          key[j]:=key[j+1];
          val[j]:=val[j+1];
          t[j]:=t[j+1]
        end
  end end;

procedure CombineNodes(b:Btree;kmid:Keyvalue;vmid:Valptr;sib:Btree;
                                special:Boolean);
    var
        i:Integer;
        l,r:Btree;                    (* left and right of kmid *)
    begin
      if special                      (* special case of no left neighbour? *)
        then begin l:=b; r:=sib end
        else begin l:=sib; r:=b end;
      with l^do
        begin
          s:=s+1;
          key[s]:=kmid;               (* move mid accross *)
          val[s]:=vmid;
          t[s]:=r^.t[0];              (* ... with leftmost of r *)
          for i := 1 to r^.s do
            begin                     (* move key,ptr pairs accross *)
              s:=s+1;
              key[s]:=r^.key[i];
              val[s]:=r^.val[i];
              t[s]:=r^.t[i]
            end
    end end;

procedure DistributeNodes(b:Btree;var kmid:Keyvalue;var vmid:Valptr;sib:Btree;
                                  normal:Boolean);
    var
        i,j,squota,bquota:Integer;
    begin
      squota:=(sib^.s+m) div 2;
      bquota:=(sib^.s+(m-1))-squota;
      if normal                         (* normal case? *)
        then with b^do                  (* sib is to left of b *)
          begin                         (* copy from end of sib to start of b *)
            j:=bquota;
            for i:= m-1 downto 1 do      (* make room for new keys *)
              begin
                t[j]:=t[i];
                key[j]:=key[i];
                val[j]:=val[i];
                j:=j-1
              end;
            t[j]:=t[0];
            key[j]:=kmid;                (* move decision key accross *)
            val[j]:=vmid;
            i:=sib^.s;
            for j:= j-1 downto 1 do       (* move keys from sib accross *)
```

```
          begin
            key[j]:=sib^.key[i];
            val[j]:=sib^.val[i];
            t[j]:=sib^.t[i];
            i:=i-1
          end;
        t[0]:=sib^.t[i];
        kmid:=sib^.key[i];                (* set new decision key in parent *)
        vmid:=sib^.val[i]
      end
    else with sib^do                      (* sib is to right of b *)
      begin                               (* copy from start of sib to end of b *)
        b^.key[m]:=kmid;                  (* move decision key accross *)
        b^.val[m]:=vmid;
        i:=1;                             (* start of sib *)
        for j:= m+1 to bquota do          (* move keys from sib accross *)
          begin
            b^.key[j]:=key[i];
            b^.val[j]:=val[i];
            b^.t[j]:=t[i];
            i:=i+1
          end;
        kmid:=key[i];                     (* set new decision key in parent *)
        vmid:=val[i];
        t[0]:=t[i];                       (* compact sib *)
        for j:=1 to i do
          begin
            key[j]:=key[j+1];
            val[j]:=val[j+1];
            t[j]:=t[j+1]
          end
      end;
  sib^.s:=squota;
  b^.s:=bquota
end;

procedure DeleteFromTree(b:Btree;var midkey:Keyvalue;var midval:Valptr;
                         var sibling:Btree;special:Boolean);
  const
      sibtoleft=false;                    (* not special *)
      sibtoright=true;                    (* special case *)
  var
      i:Integer;
      found:Boolean;
  begin
    if b<>nil
      then with b^do
        begin                             (* delete k from appropriate subtree *)
          i:=PosnInNode(k,b,found);
          if found
            then
              begin
                homenode:=b;
                homeposn:=i
              end;
          if i=0                          (* special case: no left neighbour? *)
```

```
      then
         begin
            i:=i+1;
            DeleteFromTree(t[0],key[1],val[1],t[1],sibtoright)
         end
      else DeleteFromTree(t[i],key[i],val[i],t[i-1],sibtoleft);
   if joined                         (* child has taken midkey? *)
      then                           (* yes: delete it from this node *)
         begin
            TakeFromNode(b,i);
            if (s<m)and(sibling<>nil)
               then                   (* non-viable and not the root *)
                  if sibling^.s=m
                     then            (* join nodes: cannot borrow *)
                        begin
                           CombineNodes(b,midkey,midval,sibling,special);
                           joined:=true
                        end
                     else            (* borrow from sibling *)
                        begin
                           DistributeNodes(b,midkey,midval,sibling,not special);
                           joined:=false
                        end
               else                  (* node is viable *)
                  joined:=false
         end (* of deletion at this level *)
   end

         else                        (* bottom of tree *)
            if homenode<>nil         (* key in tree ? *)
               then                  (* yes: trigger its deletion *)
                  begin
                     if midkey<>k    (* k not a leaf ? *)
                        then         (* overwrite k with its succ, midkey *)
                           with homenode^ do
                              begin
                                 key[homeposn]:=midkey;
                                 val[homeposn]:=midval
                              end;
                     joined:=true
                  end
               else                  (* key not in tree: ignore *)
                  joined:=false
   end; (* of DeleteFromTree *)
begin  (* Delete *)
   sib:=nil;
   homenode:=nil;
   DeleteFromTree(b,k,v,sib,false);
   if b^.s=0
      then                           (* root no longer required *)
         begin
            temp:=b;
            b:=b^.t[0];
            (* Dispose(temp) *)
         end
end;
```

14.2.4 **Variations**

We have already mentioned Index B-trees in which all (*key, value*) pairs are stored in leaf nodes, and branch nodes contain only key values. This significantly increases feasible branching: when used on direct access devices other than main memory, information is transferred in blocks of a fixed size, and the B-tree is implemented in such a way as to utilize one block per node. The (*key, value*) pairs themselves can be stored in any way we wish: they may be in a sequential file, for example. B-trees can therefore be used for fast random access via a specified key, even when the original file is designed for sequential processing. A structure which gives fast access to individual records of an ordered file, according to a key value, is called an index; hence the name of this variation. More than one such index can be built for the same file, if more than one key exists for a record. For example, we may wish to have fast access to *person* records by both *name* and *National Insurance number*. An Index B-tree can be built on each of these keys. A study of these issues is more pertinent to a data-base-techniques course and is not pursued here.

A variation on the insertion algorithm leads to a modified behaviour whereby the average number of keys stored per node is increased. A B-tree with this behaviour is sometimes called a *B*-tree*. In a B*-tree, when an insertion is to be made into a full node, it does not automatically split. Instead, the algorithm is modified to parallel the behaviour on deletion: if a sibling exists which has space, then the keys are distributed evenly between the two. This automatically leads to better utilization figures. As an example, consider the insertion of key 70 in Subsection 14.2.2(a). With the standard B-tree approach a node splits, eventually causing the tree to grow a new root. In B*-trees, the following would happen instead:

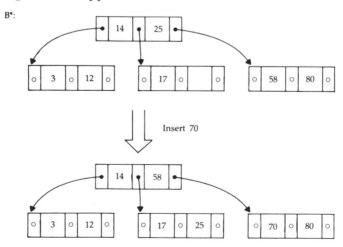

14.2.5 **Non-unique keys**

We have tacitly assumed that the keys used in B-tree creation are unique: not two table entries have the same value. It can be useful to relax this constraint in the case of Index B-trees. Consider a table of (*key*, *value*) pairs where:

key   is a National Insurance number;
value   is a record with attributes
        (*name, employment, ...*).

If the table is to be used not simply for key retrieval but also, say, for random retrieval on name or employment, then a modified Index B-tree can be built for each of these. The difference is that duplicates must be allowed. To enable this, we replace the value field in a leaf node by a pointer to a *ring* identifying all entries with a given value in the (search) key field. We therefore have a structure of the form shown in Fig. 14.11. These flexible structures are the basis of several data-base systems.

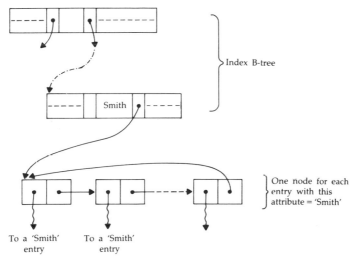

Figure 14.11   Index B-tree with Rings

14.2.6 **Summary**

A B-tree is an *N*-ary tree which has special properties designed to keep the tree reasonably balanced. The trees will never be less than half full and will average about 70% utilization under random insertions and deletions. This figure can be improved by using the B* discipline.
    Because the height of a B-tree can be kept much lower than an

equivalent binary search tree, B-trees are ideally suited to random access devices such as discs, for which the cost of retrieving a node is dominant. B-trees are good, not only for single key retrieval but also for the retrieval of values associated with ranges of key values. Index B-trees facilitate retrieval on several different keys, with one Index B-tree for each key, irrespective of how the (*key, value*) pairs are stored. The pairs are frequently stored as a sequential file.

14.3 HASH TABLES

We return to the static representation of a table: an array of entries. We could build an Index B-tree which delivers an array index rather than a value pointer in its leaf nodes, and which therefore gives efficient key retrieval: this is, in a sense, a parallel of access vectors for multi-dimensional arrays. If we accept this analogy then we could reasonably ask whether there is an analogue of mapping functions. Such an analogue would be a function which, given a key rather than a sequence of indices, would deliver the address of the desired entry. What would the properties of such a function be?

Take a table on n keys, and let them be $k_1, k_2, \ldots, k_n$. Let these keys be from a domain *keyvalue* which has a cardinality much greater than n. (If this were not so, we would say that we have *thick keys* and we could set aside one element for each possible key, and use *keyvalue* as an index type to the array.) We would like a function h such that:

(i) $0 \leqslant h(x) < n$ for all x in $\{k_1, \ldots, k_n\}$.
(ii) $h(x_1) = h(x_2) \Rightarrow x_1 = x_2$ for x_1, x_2 in $\{k_1, \ldots, k_n\}$.

In other words

(i) The function must always deliver an index within the table.
(ii) No two different keys will be mapped to the same index.

There are two major problems with finding such a function. In the first place $\{k_1, \ldots, k_n\}$ (known as the *active domain*) is unlikely to be fixed: keys will in general be inserted and deleted at random. Secondly, any function which exhibits property (ii), even for a fixed set of random keys, is likely to be extremely convoluted and inefficient. We must relax the constraints.

Relax (i) to $0 \leqslant h(x) < m$ for all x in $\{k_1, \ldots, k_n\}$, $m > n$.
Relax (ii) to allow 'collisions': different keys may be mapped to the same entry position.

A function which performs under these relaxed conditions is called a *hashing function*. A table in which insertions and searches are performed with the use of a hashing function is called a *hashing table*. Algorithms for searching and placement in a hashing table must have the following properties:

- They must use a good hashing function, which will cause few collisions (keys will be placed 'randomly' in the table).
- They must handle collisions efficiently, having a placement policy for keys which are hashed to a full location.

Unlike trees, for which search times depend on the number of keys in the tree, the performance of hashing tables depends only on table load. The *loading* of a table, α, is the ratio n/m. For good performance this should not be allowed to grow much above 90%.

14.3.1 A hashing function

We require a Pascal function which is of the form

Function h (k: Keyvalue): Index

where **Index** is defined to be $0\ldots(m-1)$. Initially let us assume that **Keyvalue** is type **Integer**. We want a randomizing function to convert one integer into another integer, but in the range $0\ldots(m-1)$. The **Mod** function meets the need well, so we can define h to be

k Mod m

Unfortunately keys are not always integers. Consider a key domain

packed array[1..20] of Char

This is not untypical and will serve our purpose as an example of situations in which more complex functions are needed. There are two problems:

(i) **Mod** is not defined on characters.
(ii) Even if it were, we really want the whole key to play a part in the result of h. Failure to do this may lead to a non-random distribution.

Point (ii) is exemplified by the choice of the first or last characters for hashing: it is not uncommon for keys to have common prefixes or common suffixes. For the sake of discussion let us suppose that two characters can be packed into a single computer word. Let us further assume that no type-checking is enforced: any computer word can be used in any logical or arithmetical operation (as is the case in assembly language programming). The technique we use to achieve a suitable hash function is called *folding*: we 'fold' pairs of characters over each other until only two are left. A suitable fold operation is the *exclusive-or*:

we take successive pairs of characters (each pair in a single world) and exclusive-or them with the first two characters in the key. We repeat, until we have a word representing the result of this set of exclusive-or operations. This word now gives us, if interpreted as an integer, the k value to use in our hashing function.

Needless to say, folding techniques are not well suited to Pascal with its strong type enforcement. We can still develop folding techniques within Pascal by using the **Ord** function, which converts from character to integer for us. Folding can be performed on a character-by-character basis, using addition and/or multiplication (but we should be wary of possible arithmetic overflow). For now, we will assume **Integer** keys and the simple (non-folding) function.

One last point to make about the hashing function is that m should, in general, be a prime number: this will give a better randomizing effect.

14.3.2 Collision handling

In the event of a collision we need to inspect the table locations in a deterministic manner until we find a free location or the desired key.

On insertion, finding the desired key implies an error; on selection, finding a free location implies an unsuccessful search. There are two basic techniques for collision handling, each with many variations. In the first, called *chaining*, entries which hash to the same location are chained together in a sequence. In the second, a succession of locations in the table is tried: each check of a location is called a *probe*, and the sequence of locations probed is called a *probe sequence*. The technique is referred to as *open addressing*. The first probe is of the location defined by the hash function itself.

(a) Open addressing

With an open-addressing technique we step through the table in a reproducible manner. The various techniques are characterized by the stepping functions used: we will look at three.

Linear Probing

A function linear in the number of probes

$$probe_i = h(k) + i \qquad (probe_0 \text{ is the initial probe})$$

This function is obviously cheap to compute: $probe_{i+1} = probe + 1$. It suffers from a problem known as primary clustering. Clustering is a phenomenon whereby the random nature of places in the table is disturbed: the entries tend to 'cluster' in the table, reducing its effectiveness. Consider the following table of keys in which 'used' locations are shaded. X, Y and Z are all free locations:

We can make several observations about insertion into this particular table. Location Z will only be used next if a key hashes directly to it. Location Y will be used if a key hashes directly to it or to its immediate predecessor. Location X will be used if the key hashes initially to it or any of the three preceding locations. Therefore, X is twice as likely to be used next as Y which, in turn, is twice as likely to be used as Z: the clustering will be reinforced. Even though this is true, probability analysis suggests that clustering will not become a major problem until α becomes large: with α at 0.8 the expected number of probes for a successful search is only three. Unfortunately, the expected number of probes for an unsuccessful search at this loading is as high as thirteen (Amble and Knuth, 1974).

The algorithm for linear probing is uncomplicated. We assume that a function exists for testing whether a location is empty or not, and present the skeleton in Listing 14.9.

There are improvements which should be made to this basic search. Its first limitation is that it will not work for an unsuccessful search on a full table, something that may not be significant in practice as α should not be allowed to approach 1.00. It can be overcome by calculating the address of the nth probe: no key can have required more than n probes to place it as there could only have been $n-1$ collisions. The

```
Procedure Find(var t:Table;k:Keyvalue;var p:Index;var found:Boolean);

(* Linear probe. Assumes t is non-full *)

  begin with t do
    begin
      p:=H(k);
      while not((Empty(entries[p])or(entries[p].key=k)) do
        p:=(p+1) mod m;
      found:=entries[p].key=k
    end
  end;
```

Listing 14.9 Searching a hash table: linear probing (basic).

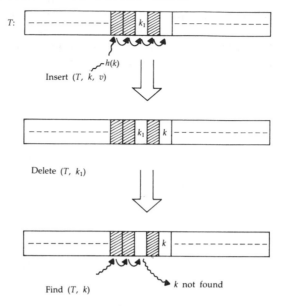

Figure 14.12   The problem of deletion.

absolute limit of probing during any given *find* should therefore be $(i + n - 1)$ mod m. Perhaps more significantly, we are not taking any account of possible deletions from the table. Consider the insertion and deletion represented on the table given in Fig. 14.12

If we delete an entry by making the location empty, then further *finds* may fail: the search for k in Fig. 14.12 terminates prematurely on finding the now empty location previously occupied by k_1. Let us introduce a tag on each entry, to give its status. Type flag can be defined as

type Flag = (used, empty, deleted)

with the table entries modified to include

tag: Flag

On search, we must treat **used** and **deleted** in the same way, so that the control loop uses.

while not ((entry [p]. tab = empty) or (entry [p]. key = k)) do

On insertion, given that the key is not duplicated, we can treat Empty and Deleted in the same way: either can be used as an insertion point.

Note that once a location in the table has been used, it can never again become empty. This means that unsuccessful searches will become longer, the table behaving as if a far higher value of α were current. When the ratio of (deleted + used) to m becomes high, the table needs to be transformed, removing the deleted entries. This is done by *in situ* rehashing, a technique discussed in (c) below. This is a general solution to the deletion problem, which can be used with any probing method. There is a simpler solution applicable only in the case of linear probing, and performed at the time of a deletion. Each location following the deletion point and up to the next empty location is possibly affected by the deletion, so each is checked in turn: if it is affected, then it can be moved into the location of the newly deleted entry and its original location treated in turn as a newly deleted entry.

Quadratic Probing

A function on the square of the number of probes, e.g.

$$probe_i = h(k) + i^2 + i$$

for which we have a sequence with $probe_{i+1} = probe_i + 2 \times i$. Again this can be cheaply calculated, repeatedly adding two to an increment variable. There are two problems with quadratic probing: it can be shown that only half the locations in a table will be searched; and it suffers from secondary clustering. The first is not a serious problem: failure to find a free location is unlikely to occur before α is unacceptably high. It can, however, be overcome by quadratic residue search, a search in which the probe sequence is

$$h(k); \ h(k) + i^2; \ h(k) - i^2; \dots$$

For certain values of m the table is guaranteed to be fully probed (Radke, 1970). *Secondary clustering* is a less troublesome form than primary clustering – if two different keys initially hash to the same location, they will continue along the same probe sequence. Quadratic probing gives a significant improvement in performance over linear probing: the expected number of probes is still less than three for successful searches in a table with loading 0.9, and unsuccessful searches have an expected probe length of less than six at a table loading of 0.8.

Double Hashing

Step size is a function of the key value.

$$probe_{i+1} = probe_i + f(k) \qquad (f \neq h)$$

This removes the problems of primary and secondary clustering. The step size, $f(k)$, must be relatively prime to m, but if m is a prime this is unrestrictive. In fact, the step size can be produced very cheaply on current machines. When integer division is performed, both the quotient and the remainder are delivered. We use the remainder for the hashing function h (the **mod** function in Pascal): we can use the quotient, Q, in computing $f(k)$:

$$\textbf{if } Q = 0 \textbf{ then } f := 1$$
$$\textbf{else } f := Q$$

The resulting performance is marginally better than for quadratic probing. The more significant advantage, however, is that the use of double hashing enables us to transform hashing tables in order to improve their performance: an entry can be safely moved without any knowledge of the history of its insertion. This facet is utilized in some of the transformation techniques of Subsection 14.3.2(c). Insert and Select, using double hashing, appear in Listing 14.10.

```
Procedure Find(var t:Table;k:Keyvalue;var p:Index;step:Integer;var found:Boolean);

(* Double hashing. Assumes t is non-full *)

    var
        finished:Boolean;
    begin with t do
        begin
            while not finished do with entries[p] do
                begin
                    if tag=used
                        then finished:=(key=k)
                        else finished:=(tag=empty);
                    if not finished
                        then p:=(p+step) Mod m
                end;
            found:=(entries[p].tag=used)
        end
    end;

Procedure Insert(var t:Table;k:Keyvalue;v:Datavalue);

(* Exception: duplicate; key already present *)

    var
        p,q:Index;
        step:Integer;
        finished,found:Boolean;
    begin
        p:=H(k); step:=F(k);
        with t do
            while not finished do with entries[p] do
                begin                           (* check each probed location *)
                    if(tag=used)
                        then finished:=(key=k) (* finish on finding k *)
                        else finished:=true;   (*    or a usable entry *)
```

Listing 14.10 Double hashing with deletion.

```
          if not finished
             then p:=(p+step) mod m
       end;
   q:=p;
   Find(t,k,q,step,found);      (* check for a duplicate *)
   if not found                 (* should not be *)
      then                      (* ok: insert entry *)
        with t.entries[p] do
          begin
            tag:=used;
            key:=k;
            value:=v;
            t.n:=t.n+1
          end
      else                      (* duplicate key: report *)
        Report(duplicate)
end;

Procedure Select(var t:Table;k:Keyvalue;var v:Datavalue;var found:Boolean);

(* Find the entry with key k. Return value in v and success status in found *)
   var
         p:Index;
   begin
     p:=H(k);
     Find(t,k,p,F(k),found);
     with t.entries[p] do
       if found
          then v:=t.entries[p].value
   end;
```

(b) Chaining

The advantage of open addressing is its lack of memory management: all entries are placed in the same, static table space. The use of chaining normally implies the use of dynamic memory allocation, though in one variant the sequence is maintained in the main table. The overhead of the implementation of the sequences (mainly in the form of extra space for pointer fields) is balanced by very good average performances from these structures.

Simple Chaining

Hash table contains pointers to chains.

Each chain is a sequence of entries with dynamic realization. The initial probe identifies the start of a sequence. If the hashing function is good then the sequence lengths will be small, and both successful and unsuccessful searches will be fast. Procedure select is shown in Listing 14.11.

```
Procedure Select(var t:Table;k:Keyvalue;var v:Datavalue;var found:Boolean);
  var
       p:Entryptr;
  begin
    p:=t.entries[H(k)];
    found:=false;
    while not(found or SeqEos(p)) do
      begin
        found:=(SeqSelect(p)^.key=k);
        if not found
          then SeqNext(p)
      end;
    if found
      then v:=SeqSelect(p)^.value
  end;
```

Listing 14.11 Selection with simple chaining.

The sequence operations are all prefixed by Seq- to distinguish them. Seq-select is assumed to return an entry identifier. Entries no longer need a tag field: deletions can be performed by a sequence delete operation.

The load factor, α, is not constrained to be less than 1.00 in simple chaining, so it is a useful data structure when eventual table size is unknown. The sequences can be stored either in main memory (with entries taken from the heap) or on direct access secondary storage, such as disc. In the latter case, the sequence elements will be disc addresses of blocks which may contain several entries each. Apart from this, the general concept is not different from the algorithm presented. What does differ is the memory management strategy required for efficient searching: the sequence elements (if more than one block is required) should be positioned on disc so that disc seek time and latency are kept to a minimum. For example, when an entry is added to a sequence which fully occupies one block (the 'home' block) it should be placed in a block (an *overflow block*) on the same track, or at least within the same cylinder. This will eliminate seek time whilst searching a specific chain.

Coalesced Chaining

Chaining within an array.

For this data structure an extra field is added to each table entry. This field contains item identifiers: in this case array indices. These allow sequences to be built within the table but, as the name suggests, these sequences sometimes coalesce. This is because locations may be claimed in either of two ways. In the first case, a location is allocated because a key hashes directly to it and it is empty (or deleted) at the time. In the second case, an insertion leads to a search of the sequence starting at the initial probe location. If the end of the sequence is reached without finding the key, a new key is inserted: a random, unused element from the array is allocated and added to the sequence. If, at some later stage, a further key hashes directly to this randomly allocated location, it will find it full and assume it is at the head of a sequence starting at that point. In fact, it will have made its initial probe into the tail of a longer sequence: the sequences will have coalesced. The element of the array to be allocated in the second case can be found by a simple linear scan of the array. The table representation together with procedure select are shown in Listing 14.12.

```
(* Representation of TABLE *)

      Entry=record
              tag:Flag;
              key:Keyvalue;
              value:Datavalue;
              succ:0..m
           end;
      Table=record
              n:Index;
              entries:array[Index] of Entry
           end;

(* end of representation of TABLE *)

(* Implementation of TABLE *)

Procedure Select(var t:Table;k:Keyvalue;var v:Datavalue;var found:Boolean);
  var
        p:Index;
        finished:Boolean;
  begin
    p:=H(k);
    repeat
      with t.entries[p] do
        begin
          finished:=(tag=empty)or(key=k)or(succ=null);
          if not finished
            then p:=succ
            else                    (* key found or not in table *)
              if key=k
                then
                  begin
                    v:=value;
                    found:=true
                  end
                else
                  found:=false
        end
      until finished
  end;
```

Listing 14.12 Selection with coalesced chaining.

(c) Increasing the efficiency for open addressing

There are three basic methods for increasing efficiency, which is inversely proportional to the expected number of probes by procedure select.

Method 1

Increase the information kept about a probe sequence, for use in later retrieval.

Method 2

Spend more time on insertion with a view to shortening probe sequences.

Method 3

Decrease α so that expected probe sequence lengths decrease.

We look at examples of each method in turn.

Pass-bits (Method 1)

A *pass-bit* is one extra bit added to each entry. It is initially set to zero for all entries, but is set to 1 whenever an insertion procedure probes a location and 'passes on'. A search may be terminated when a zero pass-bit is encountered. The pass-bit method shortens the expected search length for unsuccessful searches only.

Ordered hashing (Method 2)

Suppose we have a sequence of entries ordered on increasing key value. A search can be terminated as soon as an entry is found which has a key larger than the one for which we are looking. The average search length for unsuccessful searches will be halved. There is a parallel in hashing tables. Suppose we insert the keys in a hashing table in increasing order. Consider inserting a key k: all previous keys inserted must have key value less than k. The keys on the probe sequence used for any key k must therefore precede it, and a probe to a location with key larger than k must signify its absence. Unsuccessful searches can be terminated early.

Clearly the insertion of keys in their defined order is an unrealistic restriction for most situations. However, an insertion algorithm does exist which will guarantee that a table is maintained in the state in which it would be if its keys had been inserted in key order: time must be spent reorganizing the table on each insertion. Because keys are to be moved during an insertion, the double-hashing technique must be used in preference to quadratic probing.

The algorithm works on the basis of key displacements. If the insertion of a key, k, results in a probe to a location with key l then the following happens:

if $k > l$ then the probe sequence continues for k
if $k < l$ then k replaces l in the table and the probe sequence for l is resumed

It is the resumption of the probe sequence for l which necessitates the use of double hashing. This simple modification to Insert is all that is

```
Procedure Insert(var t:Table;k:Keyvalue;v:Datavalue);

(* Exception: duplicate; key already present *)

    var
        p:Index;
        step:Integer;
        finished:Boolean;
    begin
      p:=H(k); step:=F(k);
      repeat with t.entries[p] do
        begin
          finished:=(tag=empty);
          if not finished
            then                            (* calculate new probe *)
              begin
                if k<key
                  then                       (* displace the current entry *)
                    begin
                      Swapkey(k,key);
                      Swapvalue(v,value);
                      step:=F(k)             (* new step size *)
                    end;
                  p:=(p+step) Mod m
              end
            else                            (* insert pending (k,v) pair *)
              begin
                key:=k;
                value:=v;
                tag:=used;
                t.n:=t.n+1
              end
        end
      until finished
    end;
```

Listing 14.13 Insertion: ordered hashing.

required to allow termination of searches on the condition

entry[p].key > = k

resulting in better performance for unsuccessful searches. The insert algorithm, ignoring for the moment the questions of key deletion and duplicate keys, is given in Listing 14.13.

Binary tree hashing (Method 2)

This technique improves performance for successful searches and so is preferable to ordered hashing in situations in which successful searches predominate. It is made possible by the feasibility of displacing keys, so is once again dependent on the use of double hashing. The binary tree in the title is a tree of reorganization possibilities, and is not fully built in practice: it is conceptually traversed on a level-by-level basis. Consider a key k to be inserted. If location $h(k)$ is empty (let us ignore deletions for the moment) then k may be placed there immediately. If not, let the resident key be k_1. This is the root of a tree of possibilities: we may continue the probe sequence with either k (leaving k_1 where it was) or k_1 (displacing k_1 and inserting k in its place). If the first of these results in probing an empty location then it is taken as the best placement policy. If the second one alone leads to an empty location then it is taken as the best policy instead, and k is swapped with k_1. Alternatively, neither leads to a probe of an empty location and the four possibilities for $probe_2$ are checked in sequence. This process is demonstrated in Fig. 14.13 for

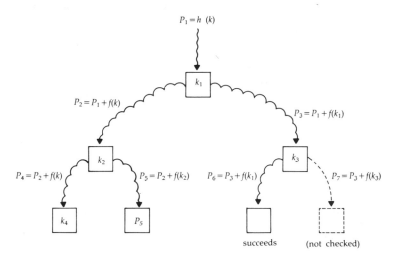

Figure 14.13 Binary tree hashing: tree of possibilities.

the situation in which an insertion succeeds on $probe_2$. The process actually carried out will be

$probe_0$:   find $p_1 = h(k)$
$probe_1$:   displace k_1, replace it by k
          find $p_3 = p_1 + f(k_1)$
$probe_2$:   find $p_6 = p_3 + f(k_1)$
          (empty): insert k

The algorithm for binary tree hashing must build the tree level by level until a free location is probed (see Fig. 14.13). The state of the traversal can best be represented by building the tree in positional notation, moving a pointer (i) through the representation array: the elements in positional notation are stored level by level. Each element in the array must contain the index of the location in the table probed at that point, and the stepsize in use at the time. The representation of the tree in Fig. 14.13 is shown in Fig. 14.14.

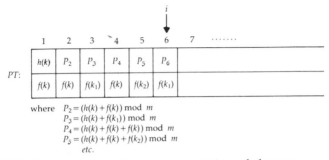

where $P_2 = (h(k) + f(k)) \bmod m$
        $P_3 = (h(k) + f(k_1)) \bmod m$
        $P_4 = (h(k) + f(k) + f(k)) \bmod m$
        $P_5 = (h(k) + f(k) + f(k_2)) \bmod m$
        etc.

Figure 14.14   Binary tree hashing: representation of the tree.

In our example, we succeed in finding an empty location when $i = 6$. Because we are using positional notation, we can trace back to the root to find which decisions were made. At each step moving down the tree· we must have either:

continued with the current value of k

or

displaced a key, and continued with it as the new k

In our representation, a left child implies 'continue' and a right child implies 'displace'. Note that in every case

go left $\rightarrow$ move to an *even* index
go right $\rightarrow$ move to an *odd* index

We know, therefore, that

$even(i) \rightarrow$ we continued with the same k at the previous level
$odd(i) \rightarrow$ we displaced at the previous level

Let us define a type

action = (continue, displace)

We can stack the decisions taken as we move back up the tree, using the logic

**if even(i) then Push(s,continue)
else Push(s,displace)**

and moving back to the next level with the statement

i: = i Div 2

```
Procedure Insert(var t:Table;k:Keyvalue;v:Datavalue);

(* Exception: duplicate; key already present *)

  var
        emptyloc:Boolean;              (* empty location found? *)
        i,current:1..max;             (* indexes in position tree *)
        pt:array[1..max] of
           record
              p:Index;                (* posn in table *)
              step:Integer            (* stepsize of probe sequence *)
           end;
        s:Stack;                      (* of decisions *)
        p:Index;                      (* probe position *)
        step:Integer;                 (* step size for probes *)

  Procedure Check(i,s:Integer;var emptyloc:Boolean);

  (* check whether a step of size s from the parent location
     probes an empty location. Return result in emptyloc *)

    var
        parent:Integer;
    begin
      parent:=i Div 2;                    (* parent address in pt at this index *)
      with pt[i] do
        begin
          p:=(pt[parent].p+s)Mod m;    (* probe from parent *)
          step:=s;
          emptyloc:=(t.entries[p].tag<>used)
        end
    end;

  begin (* Insert *)
    p:=H(k); step:=F(k);
    emptyloc:=(t.entries[p].tag<>used);
```

Listing 14.14 Insertion: binary tree hashing.

```
pt[1].p:=p;                        (* set root of decision tree *)
pt[1].step:=step;
i:=1;
current:=1;
while not emptyloc do with t do    (* build decision tree level by level *)
  begin                            (*   until empty loc found.          *)
    Check(2*i,pt[i].step,emptyloc);(* probe left child of i *)
    if emptyloc
      then current:=2*i            (* left child is nearest empty loc *)
      else                         (* check right child *)
        begin                      (* displacement: change stepsize *)
          Check(2*i+1,F(entries[pt[i].p].key),emptyloc);
          if emptyloc
            then current:=2*i+1    (* right child is empty *)
            else i:=i+1            (* expand next subtree *)
        end
  end;

(* current now represents the end of a path to be traced through
   the decision tree: replace this path, stacking the decisions made *)

Newstack(s);
while current>1 do
  begin                            (* stack decision for this level *)
    if Even(current)
      then Push(s,continue)
      else Push(s,displace);
    current:=current Div 2         (* move up to parent *)
  end;

(* s now contains the decisions to be taken: obey them *)

while not Stackempty(s) do
  with t.entries[p] do
    begin
      if Top(s)=displace
        then
          begin
            Swapkey(k,key);
            Swapvalue(v,value);
            step:=F(k)
          end;
      p:=(p+step) Mod m;
      Pop(s)
    end;

(* p now identifies the empty entry for the final insertion *)

with t.entries[p] do
  begin
    key:=k;
    value:=v;
    tag:=used
  end;
t.n:=t.n+1
end;
```

Once we reach the root, we can accomplish the changes represented on the stack: displace a key if $top(s) = displace$, continue with the current value of k otherwise (see ordered hashing insertion, Listing 14.13).

The full algorithm for insertion using binary tree hashing is shown as Listing 14.14. Selection from these tables is perfectly standard, and very efficient. The expected number of probes for a successful search is very close to two even when α becomes very close to 1.00. The overhead, of course, is in the insertion cost: this increases significantly as α approaches 1.00.

In situ rehashing (Method 3)

There are two ways of reducing the effective value of α for searching. In the first case, a preponderance of 'deleted' items may be making probe sequences unacceptably long: if we can 'purge' the table of deleted items we will succeed in shortening these sequences. In the second case we can actually decrease the value of α by increasing the table size, m. We will concentrate here on purging deleted entries: increasing m will be shown to be a minor extension.

If a new array is available for our purged table, then the purge becomes trivial. We scan the original table and hash 'used' entries into the new table. A more interesting, because more useful, algorithm is for a purge *in situ*. The skeleton of the algorithm is the same, but rehashed entries may collide with entries which have yet to be rehashed: this does not represent a true collision in the final (purged) table. Consider rehashing an entry currently residing in location i (entries in locations $1 \ldots (i-1)$ will have already been dealt with on previous iterations). Let it hash to location p. **entries[i].tag** must be set to *empty*. The status of **entries[p]** determines which action to take for the probe sequence initiated:

(i) **entries [p]** is **empty** or **deleted**: overwrite with the entry from location i and mark **entries [p]** as **rehashed**; the probe sequence terminates.
(ii) **entries [p]** is **rehashed**: this is a true collision in the transformed table; continue the probe sequence.
(iii) **entries [p]** is **used**: this is not a true collision; the entry from location i belongs in this position in the transformed table – displace **entries [p]** and put **entries [i]** in its place with **tag** value **rehashed**; initiate a new probe sequence, using the displaced entry.

Note that type **flag**, used for the **tag** field, must be extended to include

(empty, used, deleted, rehashed)

Once again we are using displacement in our algorithm, so double

```
Procedure Rehash(var t:Table);
   var
        displaced:Entry;
        p,i:Index;
        step:Integer;
   begin
     for i:=0 to m-1 do with t do
       begin
         displaced:=emptyentry;
         case entries[i].tag of
           deleted:entries[i]:=emptyentry;
           used:with displaced do                (* rehash entries[i] *)
               begin
                 Swapentries(entries[i],displaced);
                 repeat                           (* probe and displace where necessary *)
                   tag:=rehashed;
                   p:=H(Key);
                   step:=F(Key);
                   while entries[p].tag=rehashed do
                       p:=(p+step)Mod m;          (* new m if table extended *)
                   Swapentries(entries[p],displaced)
                 until(tag=empty)or(tag=deleted)
               end;
           empty,rehashed:(* nothing to do *)
         end (* case *)
       end;
     t.n:=0;
     for i:=0 to m1 do with t.entries[i] do
       if tag=rehashed
         then
           begin
             tag:=used;
             t.n:=t.n+1
           end
   end;
```

Listing **14.15** Rehash *in situ* to purge deleted entries (after Standish, 1980).

hashing must be used. On each of the *m* iterations, if a **used** entry is found then a probe sequence of the form above is undertaken.

Finally, the table must be scanned setting the **tag** fields of **rehashed** entries to **used** (all other entries will already have **tag** value **empty**). The *in situ* rehash is now complete and the table has been purged. The algorithm appears as Listing 14.15.

If the table is to be increased in size, then the probe sequences initiated are performed with the new value of *m*. This is the only change required to Listing 14.15.

14.3.3 **Summary**

Hashing tables use a static representation of a table for the random insertion of (*key, value*) pairs, and the random retrieval of an entry given a key. Unlike search trees, they do not allow the selection of a set of entries on a range of keys. They are therefore preferable only when single key retrieval is required. Selections are fast: the expected number of probes can be kept to as low as two, compared with log n for a search tree. Hashing algorithms may use either chaining or open addressing to resolve collisions. If open addressing is used then the performance of the data structure can be tuned according to its use: if unsuccessful searches predominate then ordered hashing may be considered; if successful searches predominate then binary-tree hashing should be considered. Deletions can become a problem: deleted entries cannot simply be removed as they may mark a probe path to another entry. When performance deteriorates because of the number of deleted entries in the table, a purge should be performed using *in situ* rehashing. If α is considered too high, then m may be increased at the same time as the purge is in progress.

15

Table *as a realization for other types*

15.1 SPARSE ARRAYS

In the 'triples' representation for sparse arrays, a two-dimensional array can be stored with each non-zero element taking the form

(*rowindex, columnindex, value*)

If we define the pair (*rowindex, columnindex*) to be the key, then we can realize a sparse array as a table. The best realization for the table depends on how the elements are to be accessed. If they are to be accessed in a known sequence, for example, whole rows at a time, then a tree representation is indicated. If accesses are totally random, then a hash table realization is to be preferred. If we decide on a hash table realization then we must decide which method is going to give the best response. Access to a zero-valued element in the array is the equivalent of an unsuccessful table selection: are these common, or are non-zero elements normally referenced? If accesses are truly random then unsuccessful searches will predominate, and we can deduce that ordered insertion hashing should be considered. The array operations themselves can be trivially implemented in terms of table operations.

15.2 SETS

The elements in a set can be identified by their key: this may be the whole element, or just a part of it. All of the Pascal set operations can be performed using a table realization. Consider, as an example, the operation of set difference. We wish to take two random sets of elements and perform the operation

$Set3 := Set1 - Set2$

To do this we can choose a table representation of *Set*3: in fact a table which is, in turn, realized as a hashing table would be ideal. *Set*3 is initially given the value of *Set* 1 (the table is loaded by repeated insertion of elements from *Set* 1). We may now perform the set difference operation as follows:

Difference :: for each element (k, v) in *Set* 2 do
   begin
      Select (Set3, k, value, found);
      if found
         then Delete (Set3, k)
   end

Similar implementations can be formed for the other set operations.

Appendix A
Exercises

Chapter 1

1.1 Specify type boolean. Suggest a realization.

1.2 Consider the specification of type real. What are the problems?

1.3 Give your own definition of each of the technical terms listed at the end of Section 1.2.

1.4 What is the associative equivalent to the following Pascal fragment?

```
begin
   i: = 1;
   j: = 3 − i;
   Write (j)
end;
```

Chapter 3

3.1 Specify type alarm-clock. What is a suitable realization? Display the model for your type.

3.2 Suggest efficient implementations for the Pascal set operations.

3.3 A program accepts single-letter instructions such as

> E: Exit the program
> U: Up
> D: Down
> L: Left
> R: Right

Use sets to implement an efficient 'command' module which will accept characters and respond with

> '!' followed by the character input, if it is a command
> '?' followed by the character, otherwise.

3.4 Modify 3.3 so that all legal commands are written to a Pascal file. On receiving the command 'E', the file must be printed in full.

3.5 A memory of 40×20 characters is to be used for storing VDU images. Initially all characters are set to (space). Implement a module which allows a trace of '*' characters to be drawn in the memory starting from the 'bottom left', using the commands of Exercise 3.3 to position further '*'s. Command E should cause the finished picture to be printed on the screen.

3.6 Read two integers, storing them in the heap. Print their sum.

Chapter 4

4.1 Implement queue in a static representation using a **STATE** variable to allow the array to be fully utilized.

4.2 Investigate the realization of a queue (static representation) if the convention is changed so that **FRONT** actually indexes the front item on the queue.

4.3 We could make the convention that an empty queue (dynamic representation) still has one element – a header. Develop this realization.

4.4 Complete the insertion algorithms of Subsection 4.4.2(a), catering for insertion into an empty sequence.

4.5 Implement a concatenate operation which will combine two singly linked circular lists into one.

4.6 Specify type sequence in such a way that it is useful for realizing single sentences in a text processing system. Fully realize the sequence, using a doubly linked dynamic representation. Be sure to cater for empty sequences.

Chapter 5

5.1 Implement type stack for the modified dynamic representation.

5.2 Investigate a modified dynamic representation for each of the following:

  (i) type queue;

  (ii) type sequence.

  If (ii) were used for storing English text, what would you consider to be a suitable blocksize?

5.3 Prove the correctness of your implementatiom of a stack in Exercise 5.1. A stack can be denoted by

$$S: [t, P: [A, T]]$$

where A is a vector of items and T is a list of such vectors.

5.4   For each of the following program fragments, and assuming n to be a power of 2, derive:
(i) How many '*'s will be printed, as a function of n.
(ii) The order of complexity of the code.

(a)
```
for i:=1 to n do
    for j:=i to n do
    Write ('*');
```

(b)
```
j:=1;
for i:=1 to n Div 2 do
  begin
    s:=0;
    while s<n do
      begin
        s:=s+j;
        Write ('*')
      end;
    j:=j*2
  end;
```

(c)
```
for i:=1 to n Div 2 do
  begin
    s:=1;
    j:=1;
    while s<n do
      begin
        s:=s+j;
        j:=j*2;
        Write ('*')
      end
  end;
```

5.5   Develop a program which uses type queue. The program is to accept commands of the form

J⟨char⟩: Join ⟨char⟩ to the queue
L :   Remove a character from the queue (leave)
F :   Identify the current front of the queue (print it)
A :   Print all the characters on the queue, removing them as they are printed
E :   Exit from the program

Chapter 6

6.1   Derive a mapping function and access tables for the array **A** below:

```
type Item   = record
                  first,  last: Integer
              end;
        Matrix = array [ − 2..7,  3..15] of Item;
        var A: Matrix;   (* Base address 500 *)
```

6.2   Derive Iliffe access tables for the matrix A of Exercise 6.1. Given an array definition

        var B: array [o1..l1, o2..l2] of dataitem

develop a Pascal program which will generate the values to be stored in the appropriate Iliffe access tables.

6.3   Write an efficient purge routine for removing zero-valued elements from **V**, in the bit-map representation of Subsection 6.1.3 (a).

6.4   Could we use access tables for columns too, in the structure of Subsection 6.1.3 (b)?

Chapter 8

8.1   Write a program to print a binary tree 'sideways' on the screen. For example, the tree

should be printed as

$$E$$

$$A$$

$$D$$

$$B$$

$$C$$

(*Hint*: traverse the tree, supplying a 'level' parameter. This dictates the number of spaces to print at the start of a line.)

8.2   Write a recursive procedure which can navigate through a binary tree according to commands as follows:

   L: Move to the left subtree and print its root
   R: (Similarly for right subtree)
   P: Move to the parent node and print it
   E: Exit the program

8.3   What is the depth and degree of the following tree?

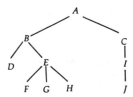

8.4   Test the procedures for building and processing a threaded tree to your own satisfaction. Develop an efficient pre-order traversal procedure.

8.5   Fully implement the file compression routines and decode procedure. Use the program to compress its own source file and decompress it again. Check how much space could be saved by storing it in compressed form.

8.6   Draw a tree which is balanced but not complete.

Chapter 9

9.1   Modify procedure Which-set(*e*) so that all elements on the path from *e* to the root are given the root as their immediate parent.

9.2   Sets are to be realized using a static representation of parent notation. Each element of the array is to be a record with two fields:

    parent

and

    value

Develop the realization and use to test the equivalence algorithm. The program should accept pairs of characters which you are declaring to be equivalent, and characters of which you want all equivalences. Choose some suitable way of terminating your program at the end of the tests. (*Hint*: use an array indexed on **Char**.)

Chapter 10

10.1   Complete the program for Dijkstra's shortest route algorithm, and run it on the graph of Subsection 10.1(c).

10.2   Develop realizations of the data structures necessary for efficient operation of the minimum spanning tree algorithm. Transform the algorithm into Pascal and run it on the given graph.

Chapter 12

12.1 Realize a binary search tree specified as

    bintree(*integer*)

Test your implementation thoroughly. Now modify it to allow the development of equivalence sets of integers. **Which-set** must look up an integer in the search tree. Each node of the tree must be a record with attributes

    parent

and

    value   (an integer)

What should the type of a parent be? Implement these equivalence sets fully, and test your implementation.

Chapter 13

13.1 Transform procedure Quicksort:

(a) To minimize the necessary stack size.
(b) To its iterative equivalent form, using an explicit stack.

Chapter 14

14.1 Develop the insertion algorithm for the balanced binary search trees. Use your answer to Exercise 8.1 or Exercise 8.2 to check the shape of the tree. During testing, construct the tree

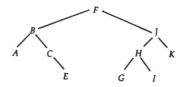

and insert D into the tree. (What should the resulting tree be?)

14.2 A suboptimal binary search tree, for known probabilities of access, can be constructed bottom-up (cf. Huffman encoding) using what is known as a 'Greedy' algorithm.

    Let the probabilities be stored in sequence, viz.

    $Q_0 \; P_1 \; Q_1 \; P_2 \; Q_2 \; \ldots \; P_n \; Q_n$

The algorithm treats each Q probability as a weight given to a tree initially containing one node, and each P value as the probability attached to a node storing the relevant key. The sequence is a sequence of such trees. At each stage the algorithm finds a subsequence

$$Q_{i-1} \; P_i \; Q_i$$

which has the lowest aggregate weight (weight(Q_{i-1})+ weight(P_i) + weight(Q_i)). A tree is constructed using the tree at Q_{i-1} (Q_i) as the left (right) subtree and with the appropriate key as the root. The weight attached to this new tree is the sum already calculated. The tree replaces Q_{i-1}, P_i and Q_i in the sequence. The process is repeated until only one tree exists in the sequence: this is the suboptimal binary search tree. Implement this heuristic.

Appendix B
Selected Bibliography

Initial reading

Goldschlager, L. and Lister, A. (1982) *Computer Science: A Modern Introduction.* Prentice-Hall, Englewood Cliffs, NJ.

Jensen, K. and Wirth, N. (1975) *Pascal User Manual and Report,* 2nd edn. Springer-Verlag, Berlin, New York.

Welsh, J. and Elder, J. (1982) *Introduction to Pascal.* Prentice-Hall, Englewood Cliffs, NJ.

General references

Gonnet, G. H. (1984) *Handbook of Algorithms and Data Structures.* Addison-Wesley, Reading, MA.

Horowitz, E., and Sahni, S. (1978) *Fundamentals of Computer Algorithms.* Pitman, London.

Knuth, D. (1973) *The Art of Computer Programming,* Vols. I, III. Addison-Wesley, Reading, MA.

Standish, T. A. (1980) *Data Structure Techniques.* Addison-Wesley, Reading, MA.

Wirth, N. (1975) *Algorithms + Data Structures = Programs.* Prentice-Hall, Englewood Cliffs, NJ.

Academic papers of interest

Backus, J. (1978) Can programming be liberated from the von Neuman style? A functional style and its algebra of programs. *Commun. ACM,* **21**, No. 8.

Floyd, R. W. (1979) The paradigms of programming. *Commun. ACM,* **22**, No. 8.

Guttag, J. V. (1977) Abstract data types and the development of data structures. *Commun. ACM,* **20**, No. 6.

Guttag, J. V., Horowitz, E. and Musser, D. R. (1978) Abstract data types and software validation. *Commun. ACM,* **21**, No. 12.

Languages catering for data abstraction

Ada

Barnes, J. G. P. (1982) *Programming in Ada*. Addison-Wesley, Reading, MA.

Clu

Liskov, B., Snyder, A., Atkinson, R. and Scheffer, C. (1977) Abstraction mechanisms in CLU. *Commun. ACM*, **20**, No. 8.

Pascal-Plus

Welsh, J. and Bustard, D. W. (1979) Pascal-Plus: another language for modular multi-programming. *Soft. Prac. Exp.*, **SE-9**, No. 11.

Sorting and searching

Amble, O. and Knuth, D. (1974) Ordered hash tables *Comput. J.*, **17**, No. 2.

Dijkstra, E. W. (1982) Smoothsort: an alternative for sorting *in situ*. *Sci. Comput. Program.*, **1**.

Knott, G. D. (1975) Hashing functions. *Comput. J.*, **18**, No. 3.

Lorin, H. (1975) *Sorting and Sort Systems*. Addison-Wesley, Reading, MA.

Martin, W. A. (1971) Sorting. *Comput. Surv.*, **3**, No. 4.

Maurer, W. D. and Lewis, T. G. (1975) Hash table methods. *Comput. Surv.* **7**, No. 1.

Radke, C. (1970) The use of the Quadratic Residue Search. *Commun. ACM*, **13**, No. 2.

Index